Foundational Pasts
The Holocaust as Historical Understanding

Alon Confino seeks to rethink dominant interpretations of the Holocaust by examining it as a problem in cultural history. As the main research interests of Holocaust scholars are frequently covered terrain – the anti-Semitic ideological campaign, the machinery of killing, the brutal massacres during the war – Confino's research goes in a new direction. He analyzes the culture and sensibilities that made it possible for the Nazis and other Germans to imagine the making of a world without Jews. Confino seeks these insights from the ways historians interpreted another short, violent, and foundational event in modern European history – the French Revolution. The comparison of the ways we understand the Holocaust with scholars' interpretations of the French Revolution allows Confino to question some of the basic assumptions of present-day historians concerning historical narration, explanation, and understanding.

Alon Confino is a professor of history at the University of Virginia, where he has taught since 1993. He has written extensively and influentially on historical memory, historical method, and German history. Among his books are *The Nation as a Local Metaphor: Württemberg, Imperial Germany, and National Memory, 1871–1918* (1997) and *Germany as a Culture of Remembrance: Promises and Limits of Writing History* (2006). As a visiting professor, Confino has taught at the Hebrew University, Tel Aviv University, and École des Hautes Études en Sciences Sociales in Paris, and was a visiting fellow at the European University Institute in Florence. He received a 2011 Guggenheim Fellowship for his new project on Nazi memories that made the Holocaust, as well as grants from the Fulbright, Humboldt, DAAD, and the Lady Davis Foundations; the Institute of Advanced Studies at the Hebrew University; the Social Science Research Council; the Israel Academy of Sciences; and the Center for Advanced Holocaust Studies at the United States Holocaust Memorial Museum in Washington, DC.

Foundational Pasts

The Holocaust as Historical Understanding

ALON CONFINO
University of Virginia

CAMBRIDGE
UNIVERSITY PRESS

CAMBRIDGE UNIVERSITY PRESS
Cambridge, New York, Melbourne, Madrid, Cape Town,
Singapore, São Paulo, Delhi, Tokyo, Mexico City

Cambridge University Press
32 Avenue of the Americas, New York, NY 10013-2473, USA

www.cambridge.org
Information on this title: www.cambridge.org/9780521736329

First published 2012
Printed in the United States of America

A catalog record for this publication is available from the British Library.

Library of Congress Cataloging in Publication Data
Confino, Alon.
Foundational pasts : The Holocaust as historical understanding / Alon Confino.
p.   cm.
Includes bibliographical references and index.
ISBN 978-0-521-51665-5 (hardback) – ISBN 978-0-521-73632-9 (paperback)
1. Holocaust, Jewish (1939–1945) – Causes.   2. Holocaust, Jewish (1939–1945) –
Historiography.   3. Germany – History – 1933–1945.   4. National socialism –
Moral and ethical aspects.   5. Antisemitism – Germany – History – 20th century.
6. Germany – Ethnic relations – History – 20th century.   7. Germany – Politics and
government – 1933–1945.   I. Title.
D804.3.C668   2011
940.53′18 – dc22   2011015054

ISBN 978-0-521-51665-5 Hardback
ISBN 978-0-521-73632-9 Paperback

To Paolo and Davidi,
foundational

Contents

Preface

Foundational Pasts works on two levels: one presents a specific interpretive argument about the Holocaust, whereas the other advances several claims about historical reconstruction. The two levels are connected, but each also makes arguments that stand independently. My intention is that readers will read this rather short text in one sitting and with minimal interruptions; I have therefore kept endnotes to a minimum. The aim is to be suggestive, not comprehensive. I hope that readers will take different things from this book depending on their interests and inclinations and, whether or not they agree with some of the arguments, will find it good to think with. I do not see the book as a package deal, a sort of hermetic argument that requires the reader either to accept or to reject it. It has several faces. Scholars of the Holocaust may read it somewhat differently than do other scholars. But it does invite each historian to probe his or her ways of reconstructing the past.

In different ways, this book has been on my mind for a long time. I first thought about the associations between the French Revolution and the Holocaust when I was a graduate student at the University of California at Berkeley. I then went on to write on other topics in German history, although the Holocaust was never far from my mind. Several years ago, when I began to have doubts about some of the tenets of Holocaust historiography, I wrote an essay on Nazi fantasies of Jews. From that starting point, the book simply wrote itself in an intense, short spell. I have since rewritten and revised it and, while doing so, incurred enormous debts to friends and colleagues who shared with me their wisdom, knowledge, and time.

With my friends Paul Betts (University of Sussex), Amos Goldberg (Hebrew University), Dirk Moses (European University Institute,
Florence), and Dan Stone (Royal Holloway, University of London), I
shared many thoughts about the topics discussed here; I benefited
immensely from their insight and erudition as well as from their splen-
did company. With Allan Megill (University of Virginia), I have had
many conversations over the years that pushed me to sharpen my ideas
about history. Maiken Umbach (University of Manchester) encouraged
me to keep on with the project and shared with me her excellent ideas.
Edward Ayers (University of Richmond), Doris Bergen (University of
Toronto), Jane Caplan, Nick Stargardt, and Lyndal Roper (all Oxford
University), and Mark Roseman (Indiana University) made good comments that improved the book along the way. Freddie Rokem (Tel Aviv
University) directed my attention to the theatrical relations between the
French Revolution and the Holocaust. Monica Black (University of Ten-
nessee) and Sophia Rosenfeld (University of Virginia) read an early draft
of the entire manuscript; I am grateful for their comments. At the University of Virginia, I benefited from the friendship and assistance of more
people than I can possibly mention. Its Jewish Studies Program has been
an excellent home in which to test and exchange ideas in an intellectually rewarding way; I am particularly grateful to Asher Biemann, Gabriel
Finder, Jennifer Geddes, Jeffrey Grossman, and James Loeffler. In the
History Department, I benefited from the good fellowship and scholarship of Lenard Berlanstein, Herbert Tico Braun, Charles McCurdy, Erik
Midelfort, Neeti Nair, and Brian Owensby.

I presented part of the book at the fantastic research group "Ethnogra-
phy and Experience: Theory, History, and Interdisciplinary Practice" at
the Institute of Advanced Studies at the Hebrew University. I am grateful
to my fellow members Galit Hasan Rokem and Carola Hilfrich (both at
the Hebrew University), Amy Shuman (Ohio State University), Arkady
Kovelman (Moscow State University), and especially to Ilana Pardes
(Hebrew University); they pushed me to think of history as method and
imagination. José Brunner, director of the Institute for German History
at Tel Aviv University, kindly invited me to give the 2006 Walter Grab
Memorial Lecture, in which I had the opportunity to present some of my
ideas. Thanks too to the invigorating environment of the research group
"Globalization of the Holocaust" at Van Leer Jerusalem Institute and
to Haim Hazan (Tel Aviv University) and Amos Goldberg, who invited
me to participate. My editor Eric Crahan enthusiastically supported me

in this project from the beginning and guided it with a wise and steady hand; he is a model for the profession. My heartfelt thanks to them all; they made clear to me what I meant to say, or thought I meant to say, before I could articulate it.

This book belongs also to Francesca, Paolo, and Davidi.

Introduction

Edges of the Past

History exists only in relation to the questions we pose to it.
Paul Veyne[1]

The recognition of the pastness of the Holocaust is a novelty in a culture where the presence of the event has been entrenched in the last generation. Recognition of its pastness is not the same as forgetting it, nor is it simply a result of the passing of more than three score years since 1945. Indeed, it is actually partly a result of the very intense public and professional preoccupation with the Holocaust, the cumulative effect of which has been to make the event not only an integral part of German, Jewish, and European history but also a signifying moral event in human history.[2]

Knowledge is a key to a new understanding. We know infinitely more about the Holocaust today than we did in 1970, 1980, or 1990. The shock of Holocaust representation – think for example of Claude Lanzmann's 1985 *Shoah*, Art Spiegelman's 1986 *Maus*, or David Grossman's 1986 *Momik* – has been absorbed and given way to somber reflection.[3] The startling revelations of historical studies have made their way into mainstream historiography.[4] The Holocaust shocked and startled because it was so much part of the present. It still shocks and is still part of the present, but it is also receding into the past. This sense of pastness opens up new ways for understanding and interpreting it.

After a period of moderate engagement with the Holocaust between 1945 and 1975, Holocaust consciousness from the mid-1970s to the present has been characterized by two simultaneous trends. The first trend, prominent in history, philosophy, the arts, and literature, has involved a strenuous attempt to acknowledge the Holocaust and to cope with the difficulty of representing it. This attempt has been distinguished by a high degree of self-conscious reflection, as is evident in such book titles as *Admitting the Holocaust* and *Probing the Limits of Representation*.[5] The second trend, which might appear to stand in opposition to the discussion of the limits of Holocaust representation, has been manifested in the massive cultural production of the Holocaust in history books, novels, films, plays, comics, and other media. But in fact, the two trends are complementary, not contradictory. Despite their theoretical trepidations about the limits of representing the Holocaust, historians have been at the forefront of this cultural production: a lasting contribution of historical studies has been the detailed recounting of the Holocaust in works that now add up to an immense specialized historiography. The result has been a vast new body of knowledge and a level of understanding and sensitivity that, I contend, anchor the Holocaust in the past in a way that was not previously possible.

This ending of a certain period in Holocaust consciousness comes into sharp focus when we consider Saul Friedländer's 1989 essay "The 'Final Solution': On the Unease in Historical Interpretation."[6] In his doubts about the possibility of producing any kind of historical representation of the Holocaust, Friedländer reflected the public and scholarly consciousness of his time. But precisely the development of Holocaust historiography in the last generation makes us see these doubts not as inherent to the event but as reflecting a specific perception bounded in time. As Dan Stone has observed, "[I]t is not that with Auschwitz one encounters special problems of representation but rather that Auschwitz makes especially clear *the* problem of representation: the fact that there always exists a lacuna between the representation and what is represented."[7] This view opens up new ways of understanding the Holocaust. It entails a shift in historical sensibility from conceiving of the Holocaust not only in terms of the limits of its representation to conceiving of it – because of generational, professional, interpretive, and cultural changes – also in terms of the possibilities and promises of historical representation.

In attempting to make sense of current Holocaust historiography, two difficulties that are well known to historians exist – one interpretive and connected to Holocaust historiography itself, and the second methodological and largely connected to broader historical understanding. I see these difficulties not as obstacles but as challenges providing interpretive opportunities.

The first difficulty is that the tremendously rich and complex historiography of the Holocaust has in the last decades been fragmented into varied fields of research, with varied methods, approaches, and languages. Nazism is the most written about historical subject. Separate topics (such as the decision for the Final Solution in 1941–1942) have been explored in meticulous detail and comprise in themselves developed and almost self-contained bodies of work. Consequently, no single interpretation and conceptual framework can encompass the history of the Holocaust. And yet, every historiographical body of work is part of and results from its surrounding culture and professional approaches and, as such, has often imperceptible interpretive common denominators across the various distinct topics and views. One aim of this book is to discern dominant conceptual categories that have informed, across interpretive differences, Holocaust historians' arguments and methods; such categories create boundaries of interpretive common sense. To think of possible new directions for research, it is imperative to know the often implicit assumptions that are embedded in current historical thinking about the Holocaust.

The second difficulty in making sense of current Holocaust historiography is the real or perceived limits of historical representation. For decades some scholars and laypersons alike have argued that the Holocaust faces fundamental problems of historical narration and explanation, if it can be narrated and explained at all. Many still share this view, which assumes the historical uniqueness of the Holocaust against all other events. In contrast, this book joins the work of other scholars who have considered the Holocaust to be an extreme event that remains at the limits of historical interpretation, but have assigned this view a different meaning: it sees the Holocaust not as an extreme event that faces inherent limits of historical explanation, but on the contrary as one that reveals, precisely because of its extremity, the overall limits and possibilities of historical interpretation. The difficulties of Holocaust interpretation should be seen not as intrinsic to the event; instead, as an extreme event, the Holocaust exposes difficulties of historical explanation that are fundamental to the discipline as a whole. Viewed from this perspective, interpretations of the Holocaust reveal more clearly basic elements of historical explanation, providing the potential to understand, via an analysis of Holocaust interpretations, some central components of historical reconstruction. Differently put, because the Holocaust was an extreme event that stretches the historical discipline to its limits, it makes particularly plain the problems of historical narration, explanation, and interpretation that are inherent to the historian's craft. This books seeks to follow the road to these edges of the past.

How are we to combine, then, a critique of current Holocaust interpretations with an investigation of the Holocaust as an extreme historical event that reveals basic elements of historical reconstruction?

I approach this question not only as a historian of Germany but also as a student of historical method and writing, interested in problems of historical evidence and narrative. To understand the Holocaust as an extreme event that uncovers general problems of historical interpretation, I have identified four such problems; they are bedrocks of historical reconstruction. My plan is to subject interpretations of the Holocaust to an investigation of these four problems:

The problem of beginnings and ends. In relation to the Holocaust, the question is how to place it, as a short, radical, and (perceived by contemporaries as) unprecedented event, within a narrative of origins and outcomes. How can we place the first experience of attempted total extermination within familiar narratives of the twentieth century? To have a perspective of origins and outcome means giving the Holocaust a chronological definition, to argue that it started at some point in time (with eternal anti-Semitism? Modern anti-Semitism? In 1933? 1941?). Problems of definition and periodization are important because they tell us about issues of causality, continuity, and rupture.

The problem of context. In relation to the Holocaust, the question is what role did the circumstances of World War II play in generating the violence of the Holocaust. There have been two debates here. One has discussed whether the extermination was a result of the circumstances of a brutalized war and Nazi policies or of long-term anti-Semitism that preceded 1933. The other has assessed the behavior of the Nazi perpetrators by asking what was the weight of motivations and agency, on the one hand, and of circumstances of the war, on the other, in the frenzy of the killing. It is important to articulate the problem of context precisely because context, which is fundamental to historical reconstruction, is often seen as self-explanatory. But what are the promises and the limits of historical context as an explanation? What can the context explain, and what can it not explain? And does the reconstruction of a historical context constitute, in itself, an explanation?

The problem of contingency. The challenge for the historian is to understand the Holocaust as neither a sheer accident nor an inevitable necessity. How can we reconstruct a narrative that, at any given time between 1933 and 1945, could not anticipate its future? Here the demand on the historian is to think of various possible outcomes of Nazi intentions and policies on the persecution and later the extermination of the Jews.

Finally, the problem of ideas, ideology, and culture in explaining human motivations. The notion of Nazi ideology – a more or less systematic set of ideas about racial superiority and anti-Semitism – has dominated understanding of the Holocaust. But is the concept of ideology sufficient to capture values, beliefs, and mentalities? Ideology is a part of culture, not culture itself: is it not too cerebral to embrace the elusive area of human affairs we call culture, which is neither as self-conscious as ideology nor as vague as beliefs?

These four interpretive problems make up every historical reconstruction, whether the historian is fully conscious of them or not, whether he or she discusses them explicitly or leaves them in the background. This book attempts to understand the historical reconstruction of the Holocaust via these four problems. This mode of proceeding is different from posing questions that seek an answer to a specific historical problem. Instead I ask how historians currently use the notions of beginnings and ends, context, contingency, and culture to understand the Holocaust. One advantage of this approach is that it goes against the recent fragmentation of Holocaust historiography. By reading the historiography against the grain of these four interpretive problems we are able to go beyond some of its highly specific and detailed debates and to uncover hidden assumptions that govern it.

Shortly after I began my work I came to see that I ran the danger of producing an interpretive vicious circle in which I read the historiography against itself. There was no good way to evaluate and control the importance of the arguments about historical method without an intermediary, without a body of work against which I could read the Holocaust and also think about my own methodological assumptions. Yet which body of work? An obvious choice would be to compare the Holocaust to other modern genocides, about which there is now a wide and sophisticated literature. As I read through this body of work, I realized a pitfall. In comparing the Holocaust with other genocides we compare events of a similar kind (extermination) but not of a similar degree of perceived historical significance. No other genocide constituted such a historical and epistemological break as the Holocaust. To understand the Holocaust via the four interpretive problems outlined earlier, I needed to think via another historical past that people have viewed as foundational.

But which one, and what does a foundational past mean? By "foundational past" I mean an event that represents an age because it embodies a historical novum that serves as a moral and historical yardstick, as a measure of things human. The foundational element is not an inherent quality of the event, but exists rather in people's subjectivity and is a historical construction. In the West, the Holocaust has become a, perhaps *the*, foundational past of our age. It appears to have taken on "the character of an icon of a now-past saeculum – something like the ultimate core event of 'our' time."[8] It is considered *the* rupture in contemporary historical time, morality, representation, and experience. The importance of the Holocaust is less pronounced in Africa, Asia, and Central and South America; it is bounded mostly to Europe, North America, Israel, and Oceania. And still, when in 2005 the United Nations agreed to observe annually on January 27 an International Day of Commemoration in Memory of the Victims of the Holocaust, it gave a seal of recognition to the universal meaning of the extermination of the Jews.[9]

Which other past in modern European history has been viewed as foundational? I turned to read the Nazis, to let them articulate against which past they measured themselves. In a radio broadcast on April 1, 1933, Joseph Goebbels, the Nazi Minister of Propaganda, proclaimed it clearly : with the Nazi revolution "the year 1789 has been expunged from the records of history." It was obvious to all why Goebbels compared 1933 to 1789: any contemporary, whether schooled in history or not, instinctively knew that the French Revolution was the measure of things in the modern world. "[W]e want to eradicate the ideology of liberalism and the freedom of the individual," stated Goebbels, "and replace it with a new sense of community" in which human equality and free will would give way to a racial order.[10]

Like the Holocaust, the French Revolution was a historical novum: the Declaration of the Rights of Man and the Citizen, and the Terror redefined politics and morality. The Revolution gave birth to ideas and practices that determined modern European and world history from 1789 onward: liberalism, socialism, feminism, human rights, *levée en masse* (mass conscription), and the idea of revolution itself. It was the first modern experience both of democracy and of state-orchestrated terror and as such was viewed as a new standard against which to measure modern history: for the British commentator Edmund Burke it was a model to be avoided at all costs, while for Lenin it was one to emulate. It was seen as a rupture in the consciousness of historical time and representation and as breaking all historical patterns. When Saint-Just declared that, with the Revolution "the eighteenth century should be placed in the Panthéon" ("le dix-huitième siècle doit être mis au Panthéon"), he demonstrated a historical awareness similar to that of Goebbels: an awareness of living through a rare turning point in human history.[11] (The comment evinces a tension between two meanings, and both place the Revolution as the grand event of the century: according to one the eighteenth century should live on forever in our memory, but there is also an implication of death, namely that the Revolution, by beginning a new historical period, ended the eighteenth century, which is over and done, but should not be forgotten.)

For contemporaries who lived in the 1930s and 1940s, measuring 1933 against 1789 was an obvious comparison, whether the new world created by Nazis as an alternative to the values of the French Revolution generated for them a sense of foreboding or of hope. Nazi scholars and ideologues predicted that January 30, 1933, the date when Hitler was appointed chancellor, would eclipse July 14, 1789, the fall of the Bastille, as a historical turning point.[12] The historical importance of 1789 was the idea of democracy, wrote Alfred Rosenberg, the self-designated ideologue of the Nazi Party, in a special issue of *School Letters* (*Der Schulungsbrief*) dedicated to the topic "From the French to the Ethnic Revolution": "Today we stand, however, in front of a similarly important historical fact . . . that millions and millions forsake the altar of democracy" and join the racial revolution.[13] Applauding the Nazi nationwide book burning of May 10, 1933, Ernst Bertram, professor of German at the University of Cologne, spoke "against the enemy of life – rationality, against destructive Enlightenment . . . against every kind of the 'ideas of 1789,' against all anti-German tendencies."[14] Hitler himself drew on the Revolution as a source of revulsion and admiration. Revulsion – because the Jew was the "midwife" of this Revolution, attaining equal rights in order to subjugate Aryans and others. But even Hitler could not remain indifferent to the pull of the event. The celebration of July 14, he said with a tinge of envy in 1929, "evokes the memory of historical passion." In spite of the Jews it was a "heroic" age that gave rise to Napoleon and his empire. Hitler the empire builder thus found a revolutionary legacy to embrace.[15]

Victor Klemperer made the association between the French Revolution and Nazism into a minor but recurring theme in his celebrated diary. As a scholar of modern French literature working on a major study on Voltaire and Rousseau, he was especially sensitive to the historical and linguistic affinities between the two periods. Studying Rousseau, he wrote that the Third Reich is "going through my mind. . . . Whole passages could be from Hitler's speeches. . . . [His] political model (no matter whether

the Führer has read it or not) is the *Contrat social.*"[16] He compared
the Nazi leaders to Robespierre, while ridiculing the Nazi attempt to
build a new society by giving German names to the months in contrast to
the revolutionaries' creation of a new calendar.[17]

During the Nazi period, historians outside Germany interpreted contemporary events as marking the passing from one historical era to the
next. A paper read at the December 1940 meeting of the American Historical Association by Beatrice Hyslop of Hunter College and published in
April 1942 in the *American Historical Review* begins with the following
paragraph:

A little over two years ago the one hundred and fiftieth anniversary of the beginning of the French Revolution was being celebrated. No one, even among skeptics
and detractors of that movement, could have predicted the events of the following twelve months. It is possible that the era dominated by the concepts initiated
by the French Revolution, embodied in the trinity of words, "Liberty, Equality,
Fraternity," has passed forever or that a different emphasis and meaning will be
given to each of the words.[18]

In 1948, Hyslop began an essay on the Revolution, published in the
Journal of Modern History, with a tone that not so much celebrated
the victory over Nazism as it recorded the terror, still felt several years
after 1945, occasioned by contemplating the possible consequences of
Nazism's triumph: "The greatest challenge to the 'principles of 1789'
since 1815 culminated in September 1939. . . . Had the Nazis and their
allies won the war, there is little doubt that the French Revolution and
its principles could have sunk into historical oblivion."[19]

Implicit and explicit analogies between the Revolution and Nazism
came up regularly in post-1945 art and history. When Peter Brook staged
Peter Weiss's *Marat/Sade* in 1964, Susan Sontag observed that "the heart
of the play is a running debate between Sade, in his chair, and Marat, in
his bath, on the meaning of the French Revolution, that is on the psychological and political premises of modern history, but seen through a
very modern sensibility, one equipped with the hindsight afforded by the
Nazi concentration camps."[20] In 1982 François Furet, one of the greatest
scholars of the Revolution in the twentieth century, chaired with Ray-
mond Aron a conference on the Holocaust at the École des Hautes Études
en Sciences Sociales (ÉHÉSS) in Paris; among the participants were Saul
Friedländer, Christopher Browning, Raul Hilberg, Amos Funkenstein,
and Pierre Vidal-Naquet.[21]

After 1945 the French Revolution regained its place as a compass of modern European history. The dominance of French historiography after the war kept debates over the Revolution important, even though key historians of the Annales school, the leading French historical approach originated by Lucien Febvre and Marc Bloch in the 1920s, studiously avoided writing about the Revolution in favor of such topics as total and social history and the history of mentalities, practiced by historians such as Fernand Braudel, Jacques Le Goff, and Febvre himself. The study of the Revolution was based almost entirely at the Sorbonne rather than at the ÉHÉSS (with the exception of Furet). There was some truth, even with its touch of French self-importance, in Furet's claim in 1980 that no historical argument "[is] so intense and so heated as the one which takes place in every generation about the French Revolution."[22] This claim reflected a shared idea that the French Revolution particularly mattered to modern politics, history, and morality.

It is precisely this idea that had changed. As the scope of the extermination of the Jews became acknowledged from the 1960s on, the Holocaust began taking the place of the Revolution as the event that generated fundamental questions and concerns in a world described as postmodern. It was perhaps fitting that Furet famously declared the French Revolution to be "over" in 1978, in the same period that witnessed the rise of the Holocaust into the status of a foundational past. Whereas once the Revolution was a crucial measure of things human, now it has become the Holocaust. Its global symbolic power has been such that its appropriation has been viewed as essential by groups who seek legitimacy for their suffering. Debates about the Revolution turn now for interpretive guidance to the Holocaust, which has become a field of study that sets disciplinary agendas. Recent discussion of the anti-revolutionary revolt in the 1790s in the Vendée, a region in western France on the Atlantic, and its brutal suppression has centered not on political loyalty and counterrevolution, but on whether it was a genocide like the Holocaust and with what historical and moral implications.[23] Proclaiming 1789 and its consequences as forerunners of Hitler became the ultimate weapon to tarnish the Revolution. What these studies lacked in historical value, they gained in public sensation.[24]

There has been a tradition since 1933, then, of thinking about the French Revolution and Nazism in tandem because doing so was a useful way of articulating meanings and values of modern history. In the relations between these two events I seek a tool to evaluate the current state of

Holocaust scholarship and consciousness. Scholars know how difficult it is to talk about the Holocaust while keeping a sense of historical perspective, that is, preserving the important historical aspects of the Holocaust while not making the event into a unique, central point of history.[25] One way of addressing this difficulty is to think of Holocaust consciousness and historiography in tandem with the consciousness and historiography of the French Revolution. When Furet published his essay "The French Revolution is Over" he knew well that in France this ur-event of modern history would on some level never be over. "The Revolution does not simply 'explain' our contemporary history; it *is* our contemporary history," he wrote. But that, he added, "is worth pondering over."[26] He called for a new interpretation that would go beyond the "revolutionary catechism" influenced by Marxism, beyond the right–left political divisions in France, and that would recognize that the passing of time, of memories, and of histories now enabled a new understanding of 1789.[27]

The Holocaust is over in a largely similar way. Of course, the Holocaust *is* still our contemporary history. Some survivors are still alive, and their nightmare will never be over as long as they live. The attempt to exterminate the Jews is and will remain a moral signifier of Judeo-Christian civilization. But now that the Holocaust is part and parcel of history, memory, and the wider culture, a stage in the process of internalizing it has come to an end. It is time for new ways of historically imagining the Holocaust. This is the starting point of this book.

In the introduction to his edited book published after the ÉHÉSS conference, Furet wrote that "by its very excess, Nazism remains, forty years after its fall, a sort of enigma for historical rationality. The 'Final Solution,' which is Nazism's culmination point, remains the horrifying embodiment of this mystery."[28] This statement reflected his view about the different historical challenges posed by the Revolution and Nazism. Furet could subject the Revolution to his historical principle that "une œuvre, c'est une question bien posée," or "a study is based on a well articulated problem," but Nazism seemed to him to defy historical method. It is interesting that Furet resigned himself to the "mystery" of the Holocaust, reflecting a popular perception of the extermination of the Jews, rather than attempting to challenge its mystification with the historical tools and skills that he had used to understand the Revolution. The Holocaust seemed not to fit his historical training and approach: writing in the tradition of the Annales school and of Bloch, Febvre, and Braudel, Furet shared with them a confidence, perhaps an overconfidence, in the ability of the historical discipline to explain and interpret. One almost hears Furet's sigh of relief when he returns to examine the actions and motivations of Danton, Marat, even Robespierre. But historical writing is unpredictable and takes unexpected turns, as when the historiography of the Revolution, not least in Furet's own work, becomes in this book an inspiration to pose questions about the Holocaust.

In this book, what mode of proceeding relates the Revolution to the Holocaust? The events are obviously completely different, different are the century, the country, the characters. The intangibles that made up the events' sensory experiences were dissimilar: the smells of industrial Germany were wholly foreign to agrarian France; the fire that lit the darkness for Louis XVI and his subjects was totally transformed by the bright, permanent light made available by electrification. Cruelty was transformed, as the swish of the guillotine's blade in Place de la Concorde gave way to secretive and anonymous deaths in the gas chambers. To a world of ideas shaped by Voltaire, Rousseau, and Montesquieu were added the revolutionary thoughts of Marx, Nietzsche, Freud, and Einstein. The list can go on. And yet the Revolution and the Holocaust shared an important quality: they were foundational events – brief, radical, violent, and self-avowedly transformative.

Being foundational, they uncover better than other events problems of historical narrative and explanation.[29] Reading them in tandem articulates new thinking about the Holocaust and about the ways historians reconstruct the past. Their extremity and short time span bring forcefully to the fore the interpretive problems raised earlier. Let me put the problems briefly in the form of questions: How can we place the exceptionality, brevity, and radicalness of the two events within a narrative of origins and outcomes? In the murderous behavior of the revolutionaries in the Terror and the Nazis in the Holocaust, what weight should be given to individual motivations and agency, on the one hand, and to the circumstances of the unfolding events, on the other? How can we understand the Revolution and the Holocaust as neither chance circumstances nor inevitable? How can we understand the role of culture in the making of such short but intense events?

My mode of proceeding is to use (parts of) the historiography of the French Revolution to help decode the historiography of the Holocaust. Historians are often wary of comparisons, and treating together events so different as the Holocaust and the French Revolution is sure to provoke opposition on various grounds. It is therefore important to outline the scope, aims, and methodological rationale of this approach. Let me begin by outlining what this approach does not do. I am neither writing a history of nor comparing the two events. They are, as we all know, utterly different. My aim is also not to provide a comprehensive account of the historiography of the events, a task that has already been done exemplarily by many scholars who were much more suitable for the task than I am.[30] I also do not focus on all the important historiographical debates, however significant they have been (such as the role of the revolutionary private and public spheres in generating female activism or the timing of the decision for the Final Solution in the critical months in late 1941 and early 1942).

Rather my aim is to read the four interpretive problems by going back and forth between the two historiographies. My interest is in the Holocaust; the French Revolution serves as an interpretive sounding board to raise new questions, make new connections, and tell us what we already know but from a different perspective. There is a give-and-take in this approach: we lose at times the rich texture of events on the ground, while we gain an insight into some of the hidden assumptions that give meaning to this texture. Both points of view are useful; each teaches us something different. By exploring these four interpretive questions, I hope to cut through agitated debates to the heart of how historians understand, often implicitly, the Holocaust. By considering another foundational event, the approach of this book has the advantage of providing a distance from and a sense of perspective on the Holocaust, an event that tends to elicit in scholars and laypersons self-imposed limits on imagination, methods, and interpretation. There are explicable moral reasons for these limits, but to understand the Holocaust historically there are also good reasons to go beyond them.

All historical understanding is based on a certain range of analogy, association, and comparison, even in studies that are not at all comparative. We cannot think historically without putting phenomena in comparative relation. Historians think in associations all the time: the question is how explicitly they discuss this in their analysis, if at all. My mode of proceeding is to think in association about the historiography of the French Revolution and the Holocaust via these four interpretive questions. Insight comes from the identification of similar and different problems of explanation and narrative. I pick and choose elements from both historiographies that are useful for my presentation. Because I am interested in ways that arrange differently our current histories of the Holocaust, I focus in the historiography of the Revolution on the moment of tremendous interpretive change in the 1970s and 1980s, when the Revolution came to be viewed as a cultural artifact by historians such as Furet, Lynn Hunt, Maurice Agulhon, Keith Baker, Mona Ozouf, and others. No doubt, there have been other important developments in the historiography of the Revolution since then, some of which are alluded to in the text, and the cultural approach has been revised and refined. But as the last fundamental interpretive turning point in the historiography of the French Revolution it remains a rich source on issues of method, theory, and narrative.

I take the liberty, then, of being strictly methodological while at the same time being somewhat anarchic. The understanding I seek comes from the framing of the four precise questions, and my investigation is bounded by them. They serve, in terms of the historical method, as the theoretical glue that holds the inquiry together. At the same time, the book's mode of proceeding – juggling the two events in relations of association – does stretch the historical discipline. Very well, let it be stretched. One aim of this book is precisely to inquire about thresholds and limits of historical reconstruction.

My main interest is to look for ways to capture what Johan Huizinga called historical sensation:

There is in all historical awareness a most momentous component that is most suitably characterized by the term historical sensation. One could also speak of historical contact. Historical imagination already says too much, and much the same is true of historical vision . . . this contact with the past, that is accompanied by the absolute conviction of complete authenticity and truth, can be provoked by a line from a chronicle, by an engraving, a few sounds of an old song. . . . Historical sensation does not present itself to us as a re-living, but as an understanding that is closely akin to the understanding of music, or, rather, of the world *by* music.[31]

I interpret the notion of historical sensation to mean two things. It is first, an essential element in the mental world of people in the past that the historian seeks to capture. Capturing it demands linking elements that seem unconnected, seeing things that are hidden, and finding meanings that contemporaries wished to obscure. But it is also a necessary awareness of the historian as he or she reconstructs and understands the past. It is an awareness not only of the specific context of the past but also of the element of total strangeness of the past – we may call it the mystery of the past. Historical sensation, which requires a certain intuition, commingles with historical method. Both are parts of historical reconstruction, which requires going beyond the logical sequence of events into the human elements of a period.

We know an enormous amount about the Holocaust – about the political, military, and administrative process of extermination, about the involvement of German society and ordinary Germans, about the system of camps, killings, and property exploitation, and about Nazi anti-Semitic public expressions, stated intentions, and ideological formulations. But detailed accounts of the Third Reich are not sufficient to capture the elements of strangeness of Nazi anti-Semitism. There is something too cerebral, too cautious, in current explanations of the Holocaust for a topic whose essence is fantasies about a nonexistent Jewish threat to destroy Germany.

The Holocaust is not strangely unique. Rather, all pasts are strange, and the historian's task is precisely to elucidate this strangeness, not to overcome it. Our task is not to master the past, but to find ways to account for the historical sensation of the period that shaped the event and the subjective experience of contemporaries. Doing so is one way to find narratives of the persecution and extermination of the Jews that will continue to challenge our perceptions.

PART ONE

THINKING THE HOLOCAUST

Between the French Revolution and the Holocaust

Events That Represent an Age

I begin with several points of departure that articulate opposed and related qualities that have dominated the understanding of the French Revolution and the Holocaust.[1] These qualities raise topics that frame the discussion of this book and form insights that outline an understanding of the Holocaust as a problem of culture.

Both the French Revolution and the Holocaust have provided, first of all, a moral-historical compass, although with different human inflections and political directions. While after 1789 the Revolution was both embraced and rejected, the Holocaust is now universally condemned as evil. This difference carries interpretive consequences. As a moral compass, the Revolution pointed to diametrically opposed directions. The revolutionaries, as well as successive Marxist and liberal historians, viewed it as an agent of progress and liberty that propelled premodern France, Europe, and the world into the modern era. This view was shared by historians as different as Alfred Cobban (1901–1968), the British liberal historian who launched a massive attack against the Marxist interpretation of the Revolution, and Albert Soboul (1914–1982), the French Marxist who held the prestigious chair of the History of the French Revolution at the Sorbonne. The Revolution was a source of political inspiration and imitation for generations of republicans, socialists, and communists, and even the Terror found defenders, particularly among Marxist historians such as Soboul and Albert Mathiez (1874–1932), who devoted most of his career to studying and championing Robespierre.

The Revolution was widely viewed as an event of human redemption. Alexander Herzen (1812–70), the Russian intellectual, stands for successive generations when he described his emotions on his journey from

Russia to Paris in 1847: "We were accustomed to associate the word 'Paris' with memories of the great events, the great masses, the great people of 1789–1793; with memories of the colossal struggle for thought, for rights, for human dignity. The name of Paris is closely linked with all the best hopes of contemporary man. I arrived here with my heart beating timidly, as once people arrived in Jerusalem and Rome." He finally entered the city: "And so I was really in Paris, not in a dream but in reality. In Paris, of that minute I had been dreaming since my childhood. If I might only see Hôtel de Ville, the Café Foy in the Palais Royal, where Camille Desmoulins picked a green leaf, stuck it on his hat for a cockade and shouted 'à la Bastille!'"[2]

But right from the beginning, a rich tradition developed among historians and nonhistorians alike that also viewed the Revolution as unnecessary and indeed morally wicked: One can think of Edmund Burke (1729–97), who as early as 1790 attacked the Revolution in *Reflections on the Revolution in France*, and of Hippolyte Taine (1828–93), a major thinker of the Revolution in the nineteenth century who, admiring the empirical thinking and gradual historical development of England, observed in his monumental study *The Origins of Contemporary France* that "the best qualified, most judicious and profoundest observer of the Revolution will find nothing to compare to it but the invasion [by the barbarians] of the Roman Empire in the fourth century."[3] Most recently, the Revolution has been attacked from both the right and the left. Opponents of the Revolution, such as Pierre Chaunu, have compared it to Nazism, and the war in the Vendée to genocide, while feminists and historians of gender have condemned the Revolution as bad for women's rights.[4]

For all these disagreements, however, the French Revolution has offered inspiration to many, and with good reason. Even if not all of its promises were fulfilled in the years after 1789, it was a revolution that opened up entire new ways of political discourse and action based on democracy, participation, liberty, and human and individual rights. It showed potential avenues of human emancipation unimaginable before 1789. And if this event continues to excite and disturb us after so many years it is precisely because it also showed a new kind of brutality, orchestrated in a bureaucratic fashion, that arose in the service of a doctrine of individual rights and liberty. Promise and brutality often go together in human history, but the dark side of the Revolution cannot obliterate the hope it aroused. Tolstoy captured this duality and the ultimate value of the Revolution in the opening pages of *War and Peace*: "'The Revolution was a grand fact,' asserted Pierre Bezukhov. 'Yes, the idea of plunder, murder, and regicide,' an ironical voice interjected again. 'Those were extremes, of course [answered Pierre]; but the whole meaning of the Revolution did not lie in them but in the rights of man, in emancipation from prejudice, in equality."[5]

The Holocaust has no such redeeming qualities. As a moral-historical compass, it is uniformly viewed as an ultimate evil. The idea of someone minimizing, justifying, or denying the Holocaust or parts thereof imposes enormous strain on public, historical, and political discourse. Such cases occur, but they provoke revulsion and are seen as a result of deep moral and human failure. They function as exceptions that prove the moral rule. Between the Revolution and the Holocaust there is an unbridgeable gulf of human intentions: in the Holocaust, intentions were all evil, while those underlying the Revolution were not. Unlike the French Revolution, the Holocaust can never inspire; it can make us reflect on the cruelty of human character, but "inspire" is just the wrong word to attach to the extermination of human beings. Herzen was eventually disappointed by the freedoms offered by France and England, but such infatuated rhetoric as his about the Revolution could obviously never be used to describe the Holocaust.

There have been attempts to represent (part of) the Holocaust as a story of heroism: In 1959 Israel created a national Remembrance Day for the Holocaust and its Heroism (*Yom Hashoah Vehagvura*), in which a Zionist historical narrative commingled an opprobrium of the diaspora Jews who went to their death "like sheep to slaughter" with admiration of Jewish partisans and ghetto fighters. In American and Israeli schools it is common to teach the story of Anne Frank as one of heroism.[6] But these are either politically motivated narratives or well-intentioned but deeply misleading clichés. The Holocaust included stories of personal heroism, but it is not a heroic story. There is nothing heroic in being an Auschwitz inmate or hiding in a tiny attic in Amsterdam.

The moral verdict on the Holocaust is clear cut, and it is precisely this feature that makes historical understanding more difficult, not easier. The principal problem posed by the Holocaust is how to explain evil, and it is more difficult to explain evil than to explain, as in the case of the French Revolution, the relations of good and evil. The good historian takes into account as many factors as possible – cultural, political, intellectual, and social, as well as diverse human reactions, sensibilities, motivations, and moral considerations. He or she juggles these factors, hoping to make illuminating connections in an attempt to decide which elements were more important than others at specific historical junctures. The Revolution is a classic case. Historians have at their disposal a whole gamut of different elements. The historical actors – the Jacobins and Girondins, nobles and sans-culottes, Louis XVI and Robespierre, Danton and Saint-Just – exhibited a range of historical combinations of intentions and results, propelled by good, bad, or just stupid motivations. For contemporaries and people ever since, the Revolution was a moral-historical drama with multifaceted inflections of good and evil.

The history of the Holocaust is also about good and evil: the goodness of those who helped Jews and confronted Nazi anti-Semitism, the evil of the perpetrators, and the ambiguous zone inhabited by bystanders.[7] As in every human activity, there existed in the Holocaust shades of human motivations, sentiments, and morality. Even in the concentration camps there existed what Primo Levi called "the gray zone": "The network of human relationships inside the Lagers was not simple: it could not be reduced to the two blocs of victims and persecutors... [we cannot] separate evil from good.... It remains true that in the Lager, and outside, there exist gray, ambiguous persons, ready to compromise... within the gray band, that zone of ambiguity which radiates out from regimes based on terror and obsequiousness."[8]

This is true, but we have to consider an additional aspect. The primary intentions and results of the perpetrators of the Holocaust do not lend themselves to the same complex political and moral gradations of good and bad as did those of the primary agents of the Revolution. We cannot find worthy motives among Adolf Hitler, Heinrich Himmler, or Reinhard Heydrich, the head of the SS Reich Security Main Office (Reichssicherheitsdiensthauptamt, or RSHA). Nor can we find redeeming qualities in the soldiers of Reserve Police Battalion 101 who, as middle-aged, lower middle-class residents of Hamburg, with no particular Nazi past or beliefs, shot 38,000 Polish Jews and deported to Treblinka an additional 45,200 between July 1942 and November 1943.[9]

The historian of the Holocaust cannot use "good" and "bad" in the same way as a historian of the Revolution. There are different explanatory elements to juggle. Political, social, and economic motivations, which have been at various times crucial to understanding the Revolution, are negligible factors in explaining the Holocaust because the murder of the Jews had no tangible political and utilitarian basis. Primo Levi articulated this in *The Drowned and the Saved*, the same book that includes his discussion of "the gray zone." I read his statement as a historical interpretive task: "What had happened... was irrevocable... it would prove that man, the human species – we, in short – had the potential to construct an infinite enormity of pain, and that pain is the only force created from nothing, without cost and without effort."[10] Interpreting the Holocaust, therefore, requires facing the problem of explaining the meaning of motivations, sentiments, and values. Although this explanatory task is also a problem of regime ideology, institutional dynamics, and context of war, it is essentially a problem of culture.

But which culture? German or European? Of age-old roots or of some recent alien influence from outside Germany? Thinking of the place of the Enlightenment and the Revolution in European history in relation to the place of Nazism in Europe will help us offer some answers to these questions: the Holocaust was not a direct result of long-standing Enlightenment ideas of social engineering, while at the same time Nazism was also not devoid of European traditions; the Third Reich was a variant of European civilization, an attempt to build a Nazi civilization that reconfigured old and new ideas into a novel way of life.

By the sheer power of their ideological and political traditions, the Enlightenment and the French Revolution set a model against which interpretations of Nazism came to be measured. For some conservatives, Nazism was a result of the Enlightenment. After the total bankruptcy of the German national state and idea, Friedrich Meinecke (1862–1954) and Gerhard Ritter (1889–1967), the leading German historians of the first half of the twentieth century, attempted to rehabilitate German national tradition and historical writing by opposing homegrown historicism to the European Enlightenment. Long before the Third Reich, an important school of conservative critique, historicism, viewed the Enlightenment as a period of political mobilization and ideational universalism. The German historicist tradition emphasized the uniqueness of historical events and personalities, the significance of specific cultural traits and motivation, and the power of the state as a historical actor in itself. This stood in opposition to the Enlightenment (in its often-formulaic image) as based on rational, universal, and repeatable history. Meinecke and Ritter, who were conservatives but not Nazis, traced Nazism after 1945 to the negative effects of the French Revolution and the Enlightenment and to the excesses of mass democracy. Thus, in their view Nazism was not a product of German culture and society, but was instead a rupture in a healthy German national tradition corrupted by European ideas of materialism and mass politics and by the shallow utilitarianism of the Enlightenment.[11]

If for conservative German historians Nazism was extraneous to the German national tradition because it emulated the Enlightenment, liberal and left-wing historians viewed Nazism after 1945 as extraneous to European history because it opposed the Enlightenment. This view of modern German history was based on a normative understanding of modernity and revolution, notions that were themselves created by the Enlightenment and the Revolution. When the Nazis seized power in 1933, conventional wisdom viewed revolutions as coming from the left and modernity as an inexorable, onward-moving progress toward technological proficiency and political freedom. Following the revolutionaries' own rhetoric and self-fashioning, the Revolution was viewed as a fulfillment of the Enlightenment, thus creating a normative notion of European culture as based on progress and liberty. The Third Reich did not fit within this view. It is not surprising, then, that well into the 1970s leading interpretations, far beyond the confines of Marxism, saw Nazism as a counterrevolutionary and antimodern movement. This view underlined the Marxist interpretation, which utterly failed to understand the Nazi and fascist experience by viewing it as a bourgeois antiproletarian counterrevolution in the last reigning period of capitalism; this is one of the brainless interpretations of modern history.

The postwar *Sonderweg*, or special path, approach of liberal and left-leaning West German historians, such as Hans-Ulrich Wehler, Jürgen Kocka, and Heinrich-August Winkler, was also influenced in a roundabout way by Marxism. The special-path view centered on the notion of the peculiarity of German history, interpreted as diverging from the history of France, Britain, and the United States in its inability to produce a bourgeois revolution and consequently a liberal democracy. Setting out to explain why Nazism developed in Germany, this thesis applied modernization models of nation-building to German history and suggested that aberrant German nationhood was the creation of a discrepancy in German society between modern economic development and the persistence of traditional and antidemocratic social, political, and cultural structures.[12] "Normal" nationhood, by extension, was the reflection of simultaneous processes of nation-building: industrialization in the economic field, democracy in the political system, liberalism as an ideology, and the hegemony of the bourgeoisie in state and society.

The special-path thesis is an exemplary case of the dangers of imposing an explanatory ideal-type model on the vicissitudes and contingencies of historical and human affairs. It created a yardstick of historical development and then argued that German history went "wrong" because it did not conform to it. It constructed a sugar-coated history of the "West" (made up only of three countries), with slavery, colonial subjugation, and domestic injustices left out. It assumed that history proceeds in uniform political, economic, and social steps toward a well-defined target, while in fact history has no predetermined script. By asking how German history did not proceed, the historians of the special-path interpretation attempted in a sense to correct in historiography what had gone wrong in history, instead of exploring what happened and why.

Whether the Third Reich was interpreted as a negation of the Enlightenment and the Revolution or as a product of them, the final result was to separate Germany from European culture: either Nazism was an aborted German historical development, deviating from a healthy European norm, or it was a harmful European import into a healthy German national tradition. In its most radical version, this view tended to sever all ties between Nazism and European culture. This was the conclusion of Hannah Arendt (1906–1975) in her 1945 essay "Approaches to the German Problem":

What is true of German political history is even more true of the spiritual roots attributed to Nazism. Nazism owes nothing to any part of Western tradition, be it German or not, Catholic or Protestant, Christian, Greek, or Roman.... Ideologically speaking, Nazism begins with no traditional basis at all, and it would be better to realize the danger of this radical negation of any tradition, which was the main feature of Nazism from the beginning.[13]

It is astonishing that Arendt, who made ideology a backbone of her interpretation of totalitarianism, reached this conclusion, and it is ultimately to be understood in terms of an attempt to defend her intellectual identity as deriving from German culture. That Arendt resorted to such a defense mechanism is a testimony to the problem of acknowledging Nazism as a form of civilization within Western tradition.[14] I return to Arendt later for another, very different view on the links between Nazism and European history.

As a whole, from the early 1930s to the 1970s a favorable, even deferential, image of the Enlightenment and of the bourgeois, democratic French Revolution dominated historical studies: it was a narrative of the positive face of modernity and the horrible consequences of racism and totalitarianism for those who failed to follow its script.[15] This view changed after the 1960s when a combination of devastating intellectual attacks called the script into question. The change was epitomized in Jean-François Lyotard's notion of the end of "les grands récits," most notably the end of the grand narrative of the Enlightenment as promising progress, liberty, and rationality. Michel Foucault and others rejected a rational principle of human behavior and of history and saw all humanist knowledge as a mask for power. And postcolonialists criticized the

Enlightenment and its project of modernity that turned into colonial, repressive rule, all the while legitimizing itself as a universal, linear, and progressive historical movement.[16] At the same time, François Furet led a comprehensive reinterpretation of the French Revolution by demolishing the leading Marxist view that saw it as a bourgeois revolution motivated by changes in the social structure from feudalism to capitalism. The Revolution, Furet argued, was not a social event but a political-ideological one, within which the will of the people transformed from a democratic principle to repression. The Terror was thus not accidental but rather a precursor of twentieth-century gulags.

These concerted intellectual attacks on a facile view of the Enlightenment and the French Revolution were fundamental for a new understanding of the Third Reich. Nazism is now viewed not as a perverse case of antimodernism, but instead as a part of a European route to modernity. Thus an idea that a generation ago was impossible to imagine has become conventional wisdom.[17] The Nazi worldview emerged from the modern, harrowing landscapes of World War I as a culture of disorder and possibility, which are the hallmarks of modernity everywhere.[18] In shaping German society, the Nazis believed in the most modern characteristics of all – the malleability of history and the ability of human beings to shape and form twentieth-century life without the constraints of past and tradition. For, contra the formulaic rendering of the Enlightenment, modern concerns were never identified in terms of linear, progressive, rational teleology, but instead, as Marshall Berman described, "are moved at once by a will to change ... and by a terror of disorientation and disintegration, of life falling apart." To be modern is to be "both revolutionary and conservative. . . . We might even say that to be fully modern is to be anti-modern . . . it has been impossible to grasp and embrace the modern world's potentialities without loathing and fighting against some of its most palpable realities."[19] Based on this view, Nazism – undergirded by science, utopia, and revolutionary politics – was a form of modernity based on a racial-biological worldview.

A similar interpretive trajectory took place in Holocaust historiography; modernity is now viewed as a central part of the "dark continent" that was Europe in the twentieth century.[20] The sociologist Zygmunt Bauman went so far as to argue that modern civilization was a necessary condition for the Holocaust (although not a sufficient one) – this was quite a radical shift from the postwar idea that "Nazism begins with no traditional basis at all" to the idea that it stands at the heart of modernity and of European civilization.[21]

In fact, so strong has been this shift that the disillusionment with and ultimately the fall of communism, coupled with the transformation of the Holocaust into the moral signifier of modern European history, have resulted of late in reviving an old narrative that reads European history from the gulag and the Holocaust backward. Explicitly linking the Enlightenment and the French Revolution to twentieth-century terror and genocides, Jacob Talmon argued fifty years ago that during the Terror the French state became a "totalitarian democracy" in its attempt to control every aspect of its citizens' lives. Connecting Rousseau's democratic ideas with a notion of collectivism that turned dictatorial during the Revolution, he saw in the Enlightenment the ideological origins of Nazism, fascism, and communism.[22] Traces of Talmon's narrative can be found in recent interpretations. Furet, who was a fervent communist during his youth in the 1950s and became a fervent anticommunist in the 1960s, directly links the Terror to the gulag.[23] Omer Bartov views the Holocaust as "the culmination . . . of a process begun in the late eighteenth century and still continuing," a process whereby the utopian idea of perfecting humanity gave collectivities a justification for eradicating imagined enemies.[24] It is an appealing narrative, but a danger lies in the temptation to craft a story – from the Enlightenment via the project of perfecting humanity to the gulag and the Holocaust – in search of historical examples, while ignoring that the Enlightenment gave rise also to the ideas of feminism, human rights, and democracy.

On the broadest descriptive level, this long-term narrative links the Nazi regime to the Enlightenment via the notion of social engineering, in which states attempted to construct new citizens, invent traditions, and create new social or political relations and states of mind where they did not exist. These kinds of social engineering projects existed in different forms across Europe and the world – in democracies, in colonial empires, and in the radical utopias of Soviet communism, Italian fascism, German Nazism, and the American South. In itself, the idea of social engineering can mean almost anything from a national census to the physical annihilation of ethnic groups. Precisely because projects of social engineering are constitutive of the modern world, we should be careful not to jump to conclusions about direct, exclusive links between the Enlightenment and twentieth-century genocides. If we add to this the links of the Enlightenment to positive modern political traditions, then we end up with a phenomenon that connects to almost every idea of twentieth-century political thought (which in some ways it does). And if it explains everything, it ends up explaining nothing.

Differently put, Nazism, like Marxism and liberalism, could appear only in the modern political age inaugurated by the Enlightenment and the French Revolution, with their ideas of science, popular will, *levée en masse*, and a degree of egalitarianism. But the earlier set of phenomena does not lead directly to the later ones. The view that saw Nazism as not belonging to European culture should not be replaced by a mirror-image view that sees Nazism as linked to everything in European culture.

How European were the Nazis? That the Nazis opposed the Enlightenment ideas of equality, liberty, and democracy only confirms their European origins. They wanted to build a society based on principles opposed to liberal democracy and Bolshevism much as the French revolutionaries sought to build a society in self-conscious opposition to the Old Regime. The Nazis' opposition to democracy, socialism, and humanitarianism does not disqualify them from being part of European tradition, much as the revolutionaries' opposition to the Old Regime did not exclude them from European culture. There is no reason to acknowledge the revolutionaries' participation in the European tradition while rejecting that of the Nazis, apart from a desire to keep morally clean the sheet of European history. The Nazis saw themselves as Europe's saviors from the dangers of Bolshevism and Judaism. Their opposition to liberal democracy, communism, and Judaism was based on long-standing European traditions.[25] Perhaps more important, they saw themselves as eminently European, building a Europe as an alternative to Russian communism and to American liberalism and crass commercialism. Especially after 1941, the Nazis viewed their struggle as a "European defensive struggle" (*europäischer Abwehrkampf*) and a "European war of unification" (*europäischer Einigungskrieg*). In this respect, they represented familiar and genuine concerns that had been commonly expressed in debates over identity in Europe before and after 1945.[26]

If National Socialism, like the Revolution, was constitutive of European thought, it was not, unlike the Revolution, universal. The revolutionaries proclaimed their ideas as universal. The Declaration of the Rights of Man and the Citizen envisioned, in principle, a generic human being (although in practice women, blacks, and the lower classes, among others, had fewer rights than the propertied male elite), and the ideas of the Revolution could be applied (again, in principle) anywhere in the world. Human history was a narrative of progress, in which France and the ideals of the Revolution were simply ahead of the rest: imitation and emulation were not only recommended but also required. The Third

Reich presented a very different picture. Unlike liberalism and communism, Nazism was based on a vision that replaced history with biology. Nazi racial ideology opposed universal ideas because it was based on the assumption that human beings are in principle not equal. "Our National Socialism is not exportable," as Robert Ley, leader of the German Labor Front, put it.[27] The European colonial empires of the nineteenth century, based on the idea of history's linear progress, viewed the colonized as unprepared quite yet to enter history as independent agents, although that moment would eventually come. The Nazi empire was based on the radical idea that others were not worthy of leading a meaningful historical life or even, in some cases, of living at all. Himmler's plan for Poland was to exterminate its national leadership and intelligentsia, while permitting the rest no more than an elementary school education that would teach them to count to 100. This would be enough for the Poles' assigned role as subjugated people under the German masters.

But the Holocaust, to return to our specific topic, was one Nazi idea and practice that was both European and universal because the aim of exterminating the Jews had no statute of temporal or spatial limitation.[28] It extended to wherever the Nazis ruled (directly or indirectly), making it pan-European and, in theory, global. Its aim was to save European civilization and world history, not simply Germany. Hitler repeatedly used this argument in the thirteen times he publicly mentioned the annihilation of the Jews in speeches delivered or written between January 30, 1939 and January 1, 1945. A running theme in these speeches was the meaning of "Europe's crusade": "And, the hour will strike when the most evil world enemy of all times will have ended his role at least for a thousand years," described Hitler in 1942 the essence of the defense of Nazi Europe in the name of the universal fight against the Jews.[29]

The Holocaust was not a result of longstanding Enlightenment ideas nor was Nazism devoid of European traditions: the Third Reich was a variant of European civilization. It used to be unthinkable to term Nazism a civilization, much as it was unthinkable to view it as a revolutionary regime. For Nazism was not only a break in civilization but also, for many Germans, a fulfillment of a civilization. We as historians and human beings need to capture not only how Nazism limited and destroyed life, but also how it simultaneously made it possible for Germans to attain new subjective beliefs and experiences.[30]

As constitutive parts of modern European history, both the French Revolution and Nazism have been intimately linked to that global phenomenon created in Europe: colonialism. But in relation to colonialism the Revolution and Nazism differed from the perspective of both origins and outcome. We can see the difference in the fact that while the Revolution stands as one source of modern colonialism, Nazism has been viewed as its result.

When in 1967 Robert Palmer published *The World of the French Revolution*, his book included only Europe.[31] In contrast, the relation of the Revolution to colonialism has developed of late as a vigorous topic. Much of this scholarship has centered on the slave emancipation, the French Caribbean, and the Haitian slave revolt in the years immediately after 1789 and on practices of rule and of memory in the French Empire thereafter.[32] It is a measure of the influence of Holocaust studies that the war in Haiti in 1802–4 has been interpreted as "genocide," bringing into play the extermination of the Jews. (The analogy does not advance knowledge, but is another case in which an alleged connection to the Holocaust imparts legitimacy to a historical topic and to suffering of people in the past, as if some is needed).[33]

For the revolutionaries, the relation of their ideals to the world was always at center stage precisely because the Revolution saw itself as universal. But it proved extremely difficult to live up to the ideals of 1789. Slavery was abolished by the National Convention in 1794, but was reestablished by Napoleon in 1802 and was definitively abolished by the Second Republic only in 1848. The more fundamental issue was how to reconcile French colonialism in the nineteenth and twentieth centuries with the ideals of the Revolution. How are we to explain the gap between the lofty principles and their limits? The question is not whether French colonialism was the misuse of the values of 1789 but more accurately how the ideals of the Revolution had been used precisely to legitimize the domination over others. The basic issue is the place of the Revolution as an intellectual origin of colonialism.

The ideals of the Revolution lent themselves to both liberation and subjugation of colonial people. In the 1840s, Alphonse Lamartine, one of the leaders of the 1848 revolution, and Alexis de Tocqueville used the ideal of liberty to argue at one and the same time for the abolition of slavery and for the continuation of French rule in the colonies. Tocqueville wrote that French rule was needed to build "civilized, industrious, and peaceful societies . . . to familiarize [the freed slave] first [and] then bend him to the painstaking and manly ways of liberty."[34] The Revolution demolished old oppressive political hierarchies (the Old Regime first and slavery second), while erecting new ones based on the idea of *mission civilisatrice.* The universalist language of rights thus also supported exclusionary politics; colonialism was fueled by values and good will. In this sense, there were important parallels between the arguments used to exclude women in the metropole and people in the colonies: discrimination advanced itself on the idea that some people were just not ready for the masculine responsibilities of modernity and democracy. But if the Revolution's rhetoric of universal rights justified colonialism, it also subverted it, of course. In the French Caribbean in the 1790s, for example, slave insurgents who demanded rights and inclusion invoked the universalism of 1789, and women in France demanded voting rights as fulfillment of the Revolution.[35]

The Revolution, then, was a source of good and bad, and its link with colonialism, as a mainstay of European and world history, was evident, not least in the mind of the builders of the French Empire. With Nazism the story was very different, and until recently the connection to colonialism was very difficult to acknowledge. In the context of decolonization after 1945 some observers pointed to the link between Nazism and European colonialism. For black diasporic intellectuals, such as Martinique's Aimé Césaire and Franz Fanon, and America's W. E. B. du Bois, the link was obvious.[36] Césaire argued that Europeans could forgive Hitler his crimes but not his application to Europeans of colonialist procedures that had been reserved for Arabs, Africans, and others.[37] In France in particular, intellectuals on the left evoked in the 1950s the link between Auschwitz and the Algerian war. The Auschwitz survivor and author Charlotte Delbo made the connection into a running theme of her work in that period.[38] Hannah Arendt made the claim in *The Origins of Totalitarianism* that European imperial expansion helped create racism and Nazism.[39] But these insights were not pursued in German and Holocaust historiography. Césaire, Fanon, and Delbo were to some extent intellectual outsiders by virtue of their origins and experience (this is true also for Arendt, although her case is more complex). They certainly stood outside of the mainstream trends and scholars of Germany and the Holocaust in the 1950s and later. They gained their insights precisely because of their outsider positions.

There were several reasons for ignoring the connection between Nazism and colonialism. In the 1950s and '60s, when decolonization was still on course, the topic was too presentist and not historical enough. In any event, in those decades Holocaust research was not developed. After the 1970s, as Holocaust historiography began to grow, research was focused on telling the story in detail, exploring such massive topics as the machinery and administration of the extermination, everyday life, and the experience on the ground of perpetrators and victims. The sense that there was still so much to learn about the Holocaust made venturing into such apparently distant fields as colonialism seem unrewarding, if not indeed odd. Of importance, too, was the growing sense among laypersons and scholars of the supposed uniqueness and incomparability of the Holocaust. Linking such topics as colonialism to the Holocaust raised immediate (and often passionate) opposition as an attempt to trivialize and belittle the extermination.

A dramatic change has occurred in the last decade: some historians now argue that Nazism was one fundamental outcome of colonialism. I share in part this view, with reservations that are significant for the broader argument of this book. Comparative genocide studies show that the "'Holocaust' is not a separate category from 'genocide' but that the Holocaust was an extreme variant of genocide."[40] Studies of modern genocides and colonialism point out their shared features, such as a developed ideology, exterminationist rhetoric, the importance of the concepts of race and space, and an explosive historical context involving land settlement, millennial utopian thinking, security anxieties, and murder.[41] This approach, together with a growing body of work on Nazi occupation and resettlement plans in Eastern Europe, has shown that the Jewish genocide was tied up with a whole set of racial ideas that produced other genocides by the Nazis, such as against the Poles. As a result, argues Jürgen Zimmerer, "the Nazi policy of expansion and annihilation [in Eastern Europe] stood firmly in the tradition of European colonialism, a tradition also recognizable in the Nazi genocides."[42]

A narrative that links colonialism and Nazism places the Third Reich more fully within modern European history. But some problems remain. Scholars who emphasize colonialism's influence on the making of the Third Reich should explain why it was that Germany produced Nazism and genocide, whereas countries with longer colonial traditions such as Britain, Spain, Belgium, Holland, and France did not. This question is especially important because Germany had the smallest empire of the lot and no colonies at all after 1918. Hannah Arendt, whose work has been revived in the current discussion that links Nazism and colonialism, leaves this point unanswered in *The Origins of Totalitarianism*. In addition, a narrative of "from Africa to Auschwitz" that, however subtly, connects the German genocide of the Herero and the Nama in Africa in the early twentieth century to the Holocaust, runs the danger of turning into yet another deterministic story of "from Bismarck to Hitler."[43] Too many things happened in between. The pull of Nazism and the Holocaust may just create a new special-path narrative, this time of a "different" German colonial history.[44] But colonialism has a global history in which colonizers and colonized interacted transnationally. A German-centric approach to colonialism, racism, and genocide is simply inadequate.

Still, the argument that Nazi policy and genocides in the East in 1941–1945 amount to a vast colonial project remains innovative. But as much as it is innovative with respect to interpreting Nazism, it has one limitation with respect to interpreting the Holocaust. Linking colonialism and the Third Reich works very well for Eastern Europe in 1939–1945. But the notion of colonial genocide as a conflict over territory, land, and resources explains little about what motivated the Nazis to send to Auschwitz the Jews of Rome. There were no practical reasons to kill the European Jews; they had no government, army, unified leadership, or even in many cases a unified language. Colonialism fits much better the German struggle for "living space" (*Lebensraum*) in the East against Poles, Ukrainians, and Russians than the total and European-wide extermination that was based on Nazi fantasies about the Jews as an eternal enemy.

Of course, fantasy is key to any case of genocide. Even if there were practical reasons for conflicts in the case, say, of Armenians and Ottomans (small numbers of Armenians joined revolutionary movements that defied the state) or Hutus and Tutsis in Rwanda more recently (issues of land and political power), the jump from conflict to genocide always requires fantasy thinking to justify the claim that the "enemy" includes women, children, and the elderly, who also need to be eradicated.[45] The case of the extermination of the Jews was an extreme version of that fantasy thinking, and it stands squarely within the history of global genocides.

For the argument developed in this book, therefore, comparative genocide studies and colonial research are important because they bring into sharp focus the question as to what were the fantasies, hallucinations, and imagination underlying the Nazi obsession with the Jews. Historical events that belong to the same genre (revolution, genocide, and the like) are not identical; all genocides involve fantasies, but some fantasies are more explanatory than others. In exploring the Nazi genocide against the Jews we need to explain why, in contrast to colonial genocides, the extermination of the Jews did not have a statute of limitation or any practical aim ("the killing will stop when we shall conquer the land"). We also note that the Jews, as a victim group, did not share any institution in common. What they did share in the subjective understanding of Jews and Germans alike was a sense of culture and of history that made of

Jews key origins of Christian, European civilization. What lay at the core of the German fantasy about the need to destroy this part of their own historical roots and also of the roots of Europe and Christianity?

Nothing about the Nazi belief in a Jewish conspiracy to destroy Germany was based on facts. There were no practical considerations supporting such a view and no Jewish political gains that could justify the conspiracy. Nothing in the Nazi belief was driven by a desire to provide a truthful account of reality. But the stories about the Jews were nonetheless believed by many Germans and therefore were for them real and truthful. And this is essentially an interpretive problem of culture.

Finally, both the French Revolution and the Holocaust constituted a rupture in the consciousness of historical time. The revolutionaries, writes Mona Ozouf, "stepped outside history in search of a new world, an absolute beginning...from the first the Revolution thought of itself as breaking all historical molds."[46] The Revolution created the almost physically painful realization that there is no going back, that the past shall be constantly different from the present, that it cannot be recovered, and that mourning of past experience entered the essence of life – modern life. In the era that began with the Revolution, anticipation of the future was not rooted in the experience of the past. Evaluation of this state of affairs varied, but the condition could not be changed. Edmund Burke lamented at the beginning of *Reflections on the Revolution in France* that "everything seems out of nature."[47] The English poet Wordsworth felt in contrast ecstatic that nothing needed to be accepted anymore as set in the nature of things[48]:

> Not in Utopia, subterranean fields
> Or some secreted island, heaven knows where!
> But in the very world, which is the world
> Of all of us...

The editor of Hamburg's *Politisches Journal*, Wilhelm von Schirach, noted about 1789 that "the pen quivers in the hand of the historian who takes hold of it in order to try to portray the scenes of a year which seem to have surpassed human powers of description and feeling and which future generations will hardly believe actually took place...never before...has such monstrosity been so wicked."[49]

Von Schirach's words could just as well describe reactions to the Holocaust. But there is one fundamental difference in the way people understood the Revolution and the Holocaust. If both events were earth-shattering, the metaphor of earthquake captures this difference. While the French Revolution was likened by the German Romantic Friedrich Schlegel (1772–1829) to "the greatest and most remarkable phenomenon in the history of states...an almost universal earthquake, an immeasurable inundation in the political world," Jean-François Lyotard compared the Holocaust to an "earthquake [that] destroys not only lives, buildings, and objects but also the instruments used to measure earthquakes directly and indirectly."[50] The extermination of the Jews has called into question the very relations between the things that happened (*res gestae*) and the narration of the things that happened (*historia rerum gestarum*).

The problem of narration comes into sharp focus when we consider the different routes taken by the two events to acquiring the status of a foundational event. The Revolution was considered foundational immediately by revolutionaries and counterrevolutionaries, Frenchmen and foreigners. The Holocaust, as we know, acquired the status of a foundational past in Europe and North America a generation after it happened. There is perhaps no other event in history that was first relatively ignored, only to be evaluated shortly thereafter as the moral signifier of its age. This in itself is revealing about problems of narrating and explaining the event (chapter 3 discusses this topic).

In this respect, the gap that opened between what happened in the Holocaust and its narration helps illuminate the relations of history and morality. Present-day discourse about the Holocaust often warns us, as the saying goes, that we ignore its moral lesson at our peril. One wonders whether scholars really need to be reminded of it, especially when the tone of the warning veers toward moralizing. For the question is not whether morality is and should be part of a Holocaust narrative; every narrative of the Holocaust is conspicuously moral, and every narrative that ignores or denies morality has a conspicuously political motive. The immorality of the Holocaust is a given. Instead of attempting to capture the high moral ground by warning against ignoring this immorality, it is better to investigate how historians embed ethical evaluation in their narratives. It is an investigation that links history, memory, and contemporary culture.

Different periods of Holocaust consciousness offer distinct narratives of history and morality. At one extreme we have the case of those postwar West German historians who attempted to write the history of the Holocaust as an "objective," morality-free, German historical chapter. Martin Broszat (1926–1989) stands for this generation of historians who were mostly youth or young adults during the Third Reich. Broszat viewed the history of the Nazi regime as dominated by the structures and processes of radicalized state policies. As director of the Institute for Contemporary History in Munich from 1971 until his death in 1989, he also oversaw the major project of everyday-life history, *Bavaria during the National Socialist Period*, which focused on ordinary Germans and their attempt to resist the regime. But the result of this distinguished body of work was overall a history without actors: there were no perpetrators in the interpretation of the Holocaust as a whirlwind of radicalized administrative bodies searching for a solution to the "Jewish Question," and there were no Nazis in a project that privileged resistance. Broszat was a steadfast scholar of the Third Reich, but his vision of objective history was limited, designed to protect him from certain personal and professional moral considerations of the period. His historical reconstruction did not include the topic of how Germans made moral choices that led them down the path of genocide.

The gap between Holocaust history and morality is demonstrated in Broszat's reaction to the work of Joseph Wulf, a German Polish writer who survived a year in Auschwitz. In the 1950s, living in Berlin, Wulf published together with Léon Poliakov several anthologies of documents that focused on the extermination of the Jews as inherent to Nazi ideas, motivations, and regime. The titles of the volumes already had broken taboos in the stifling air of West German society, which viewed Germans as the victims, not the perpetrators of World War II: *The Third Reich and Its Helpers* (1956), *The Third Reich and Its Thinkers* (1959), and *The Third Reich and Its Executioners* (1960). Broszat rejected these books as polemical and nonprofessional, questioning "whether the collection of documents as a whole, based on the choice of documents, organization, and theme corresponds to the claims of thoroughness and methodical caution." Above all, he questioned the professional distance of Wulf from the subject matter and implied that a "scientific-historical" description of the extermination of the Jews cannot and should not be left to Jews and survivors.[51] The murder of the Jews was primarily a German, not a Jewish, tragedy. Holocaust survivors are not objective, and Jewish historians of the Holocaust are emotionally unable to study the topic scientifically. Germans, by implication, could write an objective history of the Holocaust because they did not mix morality with objectivity.

Wulf, to conclude this story, did not find support in the more progressive 1960s and 1970s. Few wanted to understand the Holocaust as actions motivated by the agency of Germans; the New Left theory of fascism, popular among the student rebels of 1968, emphasized social and economic impersonal forces and was, at any event, not really interested in the Holocaust. Fewer still wanted to listen to the Jewish story of the extermination. Wulf committed suicide in October 1974 by jumping from the fourth floor of his Berlin apartment.[52]

How far Holocaust studies have moved can be gauged by a dominant recent narrative that puts morality at the center of the historical narrative.[53] In focusing on morality the authors necessarily pay close attention to the beliefs and motivations of Germans. There is an added importance to this narrative because authors go against the discipline's bias toward not offering moral judgments and ethical statements. But this kind of narrative helps us see limits to historical reconstruction and explanation. The question is not whether this narrative is right or wrong (of course it is morally right). It is about being conscious of what can and what cannot be narrated. In viewing the Holocaust primarily as a morality tale, we run the danger of creating a grand narrative whereby history is propelled by moral considerations; however edifying this narrative is with respect to the Holocaust, this grand narrative, like all others, is inadequate to capture history's complexity. It is tautological because the moral narrative presupposes the very process it wishes to examine: anti-Semitism, persecution, genocide. The narrative reminds us of and warns us against the moral depravity of the Holocaust more successfully than it explains how the Holocaust came about.

Differently put, we run the danger of telling the Holocaust in a narrative that moralizes and pontificates.[54] The discipline of history assumes a certain neutrality of the historian; historians do have and should have a moral position about, say, slavery in the American South or Auschwitz, but in telling their story they should show that they are sensitive to the problem of voice and narration. If the author appears to impose his or her own ethical commitments on the audience, then the constant ethical reminding has diminishing returns. This is why the tone of Daniel Goldhagen's *Hitler's Willing Executioners* turned off many people (and appealed to others). A moralizing narrative is used to claim propriety and authority, to cordon off a rhetorical arena to gain a moral ground, but it creates a dissonance when the topic at hand is already considered by the reader to be morally clear.

Ultimately, a historical narrative that moralizes can end up as being too presentist. The historian always writes from within his or her own culture; it is banal to reiterate this point. But when the historian of modern Germany becomes so identified with the causes, themes, and concerns of contemporary culture and memory about National Socialism, then a delicate balance may be upset between being a critical observer of the past and being part of one's own culture. The moral narrative of the Holocaust may end up recounting history by projecting the present onto the past, whereas the concerns of people in the past were wholly different. Books based on the moral narrative of the Holocaust may seem outdated when the Holocaust is eventually seen not as a unique aberration but as part and parcel of European history. The moral narrative is a mirror image of the narrative that excludes morality from the history of the Holocaust. Historians are most illuminating when they answer ethical questions in minimalist and indirect ways. They cannot answer ontological questions about ultimate justification – such as Arno Mayer's question "Why did the heavens not darken?", which was the title of his book about the extermination of the Jews – and they cannot adequately explain by putting morality as the driving force of history.

A moral narrative of the Holocaust could have broken taboos in the 1950s and 60s, assuming someone would have listened, when the Holocaust was told in a tone of presumed amoral objectivity (if it was told at all). But precisely because the Holocaust has become a moral signifier of our time, a narrative driven by morality has an almost inescapable moralizing tone. Ultimately, the most evocative historical writings about the Holocaust use a modest tone in which the enormity of the event shines through a minimalist and guarded rhetoric. I can think of the works of Saul Friedländer, *Nazi Germany and the Jews*, and of Inga Clendinnen *Reading the Holocaust*, and of the literary works of Primo Levi and Ida Fink. What distinguishes these authors is that the voice of their work does not attempt to master the Nazi past; it seeks to understand via literary or historical means while acknowledging the incompleteness of the account that is offered. A moral narrative of the Holocaust, in contrast, often has a voice that consciously attempts to master the past or to master a historical voice that speaks about mastering the past. This is a voice that tells a story that is determined by the knowledge of what happened at the end; it thus cannot escape the script of history and of the present.

Historical narration cannot capture the horrors of the past, not only of the Holocaust but also of any past. The experience of brutality, terror, and fear is always greater than the words put together to describe it. Minimalist rhetoric works best to make a moral judgment of the Holocaust. The historian's best narrative renders the process of dehumanization and brutality without condemnation or tears but in terms that illuminate the reality of the events that took place.

2

A Dominant Interpretive Framework

The historiography of the Holocaust in the last decades has been rich, complex, and fragmented into varied fields of research, methods, and languages.[1] But similar to all historiographical bodies of work, it gave rise to several dominant conceptual categories that have informed, often indiscernibly and spanning interpretive differences, historians' arguments and use of methods; these categories have also created boundaries of interpretive common sense. In this chapter I am seeking these dominant categories. My aim is not to provide a comprehensive historiographical overview, a task that has already been done in exemplary fashion; I therefore do not include all interpretations and points of view. It is also not my intention to focus on specific historiographical debates, however significant. Rather, my aim is to cut through surface debates to the heart of how historians understand, often implicitly, the Holocaust.

To pursue this goal, I enter in this and in the next chapter into a dialogue with Saul Friedländer's magnum opus *The Years of Extermination*, which is a sort of a summa of Holocaust research and historiography of the last generation and therefore an excellent source from which to identify dominant interpretive categories.[2] *The Years of Extermination* has been received worldwide as an exemplary study that found the right balance of tone, narrative, and interpretation about the most difficult historical topic of all in the post-1945 period. The book has been a major scholarly and public event partly because it represents the apogee of an era of historical understanding of the Holocaust.[3] The Holocaust, according to Friedländer, was determined by

the centrality of ideological-cultural factors as the prime movers of Nazi policies in regard to the Jewish issue, depending of course on circumstances, institutional dynamics, and essentially ... on the evolution of the war. ... The anti-Jewish drive became ever more extreme along with the radicalization of the regime's goals and then with the extension of the war. It is in this context that we shall be able to locate the emergence of the "Final Solution."[4]

In a nutshell this statement presents the main interpretive components of understanding the Holocaust: racial ideology, radicalization of Nazi policy, and the context of war.

Scholars have agreed about the explanatory centrality of these categories. To articulate this agreement I use the excellent historiographical summaries by Ulrich Herbert and Ian Kershaw, who do not share my views about the interpretive consequences of these categories.[5] The context of the war has been viewed as the breeding ground for the extermination. Germans in occupied Eastern Europe "were living in a context in which the expulsion, even the extermination, of entire peoples was publicly discussed, a readiness to indulge in brutality and fanaticism was ubiquitously demanded, and the actions of individuals were legitimized by history and politics."[6] The war in general, but especially the war on the Eastern Front, after the German invasion of the Soviet Union on June 22, 1941, was fought as a racial ideological struggle for life or death, whose prime enemies were the Bolsheviks and Jews. The barbarization of war in the Eastern Front – a cumulative result of the scale of the fighting, geographical conditions, and ideological indoctrination – led to killing and extermination.[7]

The notion of the radicalization of racial ideology has been important to capturing contingency in the making of the Holocaust. This radicalization is no longer understood as a realization of long-term plans, but rather as the outcome of plans for the deportation of the Jews that were continually being revised and extended. The scholarly "consensus," writes Kershaw, is "that no single decision brought about the 'Final Solution,' but that a lengthy process of radicalization in the search for 'a solution to the Jewish Question' between spring 1941 and summer 1942 – as part of an immense overall resettlement and 'ethnic cleansing' program for central and eastern Europe, vitiated through the failure to defeat the Soviet Union in 1941 – was punctuated by several phases of sharp escalation."[8] It was an irregular and intermittent process governed by local circumstances and was always made to fit decisions designed to deal with problems of the moment. Moreover, plans for deportation and extermination, produced as part of the General Plan East, an overall plan devised after the outbreak of the war to restructure Eastern Europe, never included only the Jews but involved also Poles, Russians, and Gypsies – that is, entire populations.[9]

Perhaps the central innovation of Holocaust scholarship in the last generation has been the emphasis on racial ideology. Whereas once Nazi motivations were seen as emanating from longstanding anti-Semitic beliefs or were excluded altogether by emphasizing impersonal dynamics inherent in the Nazi system of government, the Holocaust is now squarely placed within the context of the regime's overall racial ideology. The "current scholarly consensus," writes Herbert, is that those who organized and carried out the extermination were committed ideologues who wanted to build a better world through genocide.[10] (Both Herbert and Kershaw use "consensus" to describe the current historiography.) Vast scholarship has shown that, well beyond this circle of true believers, the regime's racial ideology – which stands in current historiography in self-conscious contrast to the older understanding of Nazi ideas as a mixture of fuzzy beliefs, vague intentions, or sheer passion and madness – penetrated all levels of society, whether institutions (the army or the churches), social spheres (cinema, architecture, or sport), or cultural artifacts (ranging from children's board games to the Nuremberg Nazi Party rallies).[11]

Perhaps the first thing to acknowledge is the broad consensus over key categories in a historiography that has been identified by fierce debates and, moreover, that has increased in recent years to the point where it is difficult to see the forest from the trees. The Third Reich became the single most written about topic in history. A standard bibliography of National Socialism listed 25,000 titles in 1995 and a whopping 37,000 in 2000.[12] What emerged was just how complex the Holocaust had actually been. But looking at this remarkably specialized massive historiography from a distance, the big picture that also emerges is one of a broad scholarly consensus made up of the notions of the context of the war and radicalized racial ideology. The specific historiographical debates are important, not least because they often bring forth the experience of contemporaries on the ground. But they make up a whole that is bigger than the sum of its parts, and that is characterized by a certain narrative coherence.

The combination of the notions of racial ideology, context of war, and Nazi radicalization has constituted a dominant interpretive framework for understanding the Holocaust, a framework that allowed for different interpretive configurations. Although the historiography of the Holocaust is too complex to be reduced to these categories, they have dominated the two leading interpretive schools, intentionalism and functionalism (to be described shortly). The crux of each school of interpretation depended on a different combination of these categories.

Over the years, the two schools have moved closer together. Few scholars subscribe exclusively to only one school, and most choose their position, explicitly or implicitly, somewhere between the two. Christopher Browning coined the term "moderate functionalism," which recognized the centrality of Hitler's belief and role without positing an original grand design to kill the Jews. Philippe Burrin's notion of "conditional intentionalism" acknowledged the centrality of evolving circumstance during the war, but continued to emphasize Hitler's intention to exterminate the Jews.[13] Omer Bartov commingled ideology and the conditions of war. Extended research into particular topics made distinctions between the two schools inconsequential or placed them in historical context of the multiple causes that resulted in the Holocaust.[14] But even though most scholars may not think of themselves as taking a position of either intentionalism or functionalism, it has been much more challenging for them to think beyond the categories themselves of racial ideology, context of war, and radicalization.[15]

The Years of Extermination, commingling intentionalism and functionalism with a tendency toward the former, extends the interpretive framework of the Holocaust onto a larger spatial category, namely Europe, while remaining located squarely within it. Friedländer enriches the categories by crafting a story that provides "both an integrative and an integrated history" of the Holocaust, combining the history of the Germans and their collaborators, the surrounding world, and the experience of the victims.[16] The scope is a sort of a total history (in a historiographical age that repudiates it) that "penetrates all the nooks and crannies of European space."[17] He thus crafts an account that integrates the massive Holocaust research of the last generation; in terms of interpretation, he broadens the categories without thinking beyond them. In this sense, *The Years of Extermination* is a monument to a generation of innovative scholarship that produced a particular understanding of the Holocaust. As such, it may also signal that time has come to go beyond this scholarship.

Two magisterial studies epitomize the ability of the dominant interpretive framework to produce starkly different interpretations. The narrative of *The Years of Extermination* focuses on the Jews, without placing this genocide within other Nazi exterminations. Mark Mazower's *Hitler's Empire*, commingling intentionalism and functionalism with a tendency toward the latter, uses the same framework with different interpretive results: The Final Solution was "driven by Nazi ideology, and by Hitler's personal animus... what happened to the Jews of Europe grew out of the circumstances of the war and fluctuated according to its fortunes." But the meaning of the Holocaust is located in its emergence "out of even more ambitious Nazi plans for a racial reorganization of much of eastern Europe... the Jews constituted only one – albeit the most urgent – of the regime's ethnic targets."[18]

The question is whether we can think of the Holocaust beyond these categories – beyond context and ideology, in particular – and then can find new narratives that challenge our usual perceptions. Of course, there is nothing wrong in using these categories. They are and will remain central to understanding the Holocaust. But there are three points worth reflecting on. First, one result of the dominance of these categories has been that, in a historiography that is written very close to the documents, the particular characters are different but the libretto is the same, as yet another group or topic (military units, ideological manifestations) is explored within the framework of radicalized Nazi ideology. One has a sense of déjà vu. It seems that many contributions to the historiography of the Holocaust confirm yet again the well-known thesis of an influential study (the role of the Wehrmacht in mass murder, the importance of racial ideology) or validate a well-known argument in great detail based on unused troves of documents. The accumulation of facts in massive studies is accompanied by diminishing interpretive return. We know more of the same things. But what are the new questions we can ask about why they happened?

Second, it is interesting that a historiography that is considered to have fierce interpretive debates has actually been in large measure identified by several deep layers of "consensus." There is nothing wrong with broad agreements on specific issues of historical explanation as long as this explanation is insightful. The historian is not required to revise at all costs. But broad agreements may inhibit asking new questions, and they call for critical attention. The writing of history is based on the constant historiographical procedure of revision, even if revision is a tangled process that involves generational, professional, and cultural aspects. One task of the historian is to locate and question dominant set of ideas that are adopted as a given and that determine which historical questions are asked, which problems are posed, and which connections are made.[19]

Third, the problem with the categories of ideology, context, and radicalization is not that they are wrong, but that they are right in a way that obscures some important elements that made the Holocaust and the Third Reich. Using them has important consequences for method and interpretation and determines a certain way of telling the story. Part II discusses these topics in depth.

Intentionalism and functionalism, two terms and schools of interpretation that have dominated Holocaust historiography since the 1970s, deserve our attention. What are the relations between the critique advanced in this book and these interpretive trends? The terms were memorably coined, as it is well known, by the British historian Tim Mason in 1979 and have since remained important points of reference to understand National Socialism and the Holocaust. In its distilled form, intentionalism views the expressed ideological, anti-Semitic intentions of Hitler from as early as 1918 as sufficient to explain the extermination of the 1940s. According to this argument, Hitler's grand design to annihilate the Jews was subjected to momentary setbacks and expediency, but it was never in doubt as an overarching strategic goal. Intentionalists, such as Lucy Dawidowicz (1915–1990) in her 1975 study *The War against the Jews*, emphasize Hitler's beliefs.[20] In the mid-1990s, Daniel Goldhagen broadened the social base of Nazi intentions to include German society as a whole: "Germans' anti-Semitic beliefs about Jews were the central causal agent of the Holocaust... the eliminationist mind-set that characterized virtually all who spoke out on the 'Jewish problem' from the end of the eighteenth century onward was another constant in Germans' thinking about the Jews."[21]

Functionalism downplays beliefs and ideology in favor of the dynamics of administrative, institutional, and policy-making processes inherent in the Nazi system of government. Historians of this school do not doubt Hitler's anti-Semitism, but they doubt his ability to plan so far in advance and stress the contingency of the historical process as the Nazi regime looked for ways to solve "the Jewish problem." As Broszat, a proponent of this view in the 1970s and 1980s, argued, "there had been no comprehensive general extermination order at all... the 'program' of extermination of the Jews gradually developed institutionally and in practice out of individual actions down to early 1942."[22] The crux of the issue between the two schools was this: did the Holocaust emerge from an ideologically motivated plan to exterminate the Jews that had existed for some time and was put in operation in 1941 in Operation Barbarossa? Or was the Holocaust a result of a piecemeal process as an essential characteristic of the Third Reich system that led to cumulative radicalization?

The two schools have been refined over the years, losing some of their distinctions, while at the same time keeping their basic interpretive peculiarities. The categories of context and ideology that underlie them continue to structure thinking in a particular way. Studies can be grouped in one or the other camp or in both. In a historical profession that has been based on frequent interpretive changes, illustrated in the popularity of titles that promise to reinterpret and rethink this or that topic, the longevity of the categories of functionalism and intentionalism in their various modifications is remarkable. This is especially true given the tremendous development and growing sophistication of Holocaust studies in the last generation.

This longevity demands an explanation, particularly because on closer analysis the two schools posit two indispensable, although undisputed and commonly agreed-on, notions of historical explanation: intentionality, that is agency, and process, that is development in time and within context. All historical events include intentionality and process in various combinations. On a fundamental historical level, both interpretations point to an important, necessary aspect of historical explanation. On some level, in the debate between intentionalism and functionalism historians of the Holocaust were asked to select between two essential categories, and as a result many have recently chosen both and moved toward a middle ground of moderate functionalism or moderate intentionalism.

Why has this framework of interpretation, in various forms and guises, persisted for so long? The reason cannot be found only by looking at the methodological usefulness of the notions of intention and process, but also has to do with their usefulness as vehicles to internalize the Holocaust. This framework of interpretation thus made the Holocaust congruent with basic ways in which we understand modern life as a changing process marked by free and independent agents. Each school contributed a different aspect. Intentionalists emphasize human agency (over impersonal structures), while functionalists focus on process and change over time (rather than on a longstanding grand design). Both notions are important to understand the event as history. By introducing and refining basic historical elements such as context, ideology, process, and motivation, the intentionalism-functionalism framework has been a necessary step to overcome an unease in interpretation.

Another reason for the longevity of this framework is the connection between history and memory. The intentionalist and functionalist camps have reflected different claims on memory, as Dan Diner argued.

Intentionalists, interested in putting a human being in the Holocaust, are interested in who were the victims and what were the motives of the Nazis. Functionalists are more interested in how the extermination happened. Intentionalists place the victims at the center; functionalists emphasize a mostly impersonal institutional process. "The fact that the members of these two historiographical camps view one another as adversaries holding diametrically opposed conceptions does not speak well for a differentiated sense of method. Rather, it confirms the effect of diversely rooted memories." A "Jewish"-oriented memory is more likely to ask why the Holocaust happened to the Jews. A "German"-oriented memory is more likely to avoid the question of responsibility by asking how the mass murder happened as an impersonal bureaucratic process.[23] Diner's account fits better the divisions between the schools in the 1970s and 1980s than the search for common ground of the later period, but it does show some of the deep-seated reasons for the longevity of this framework.[24]

Thinking in terms of intention and process, then, makes it possible to internalize the historicity of the Holocaust, and this is one important reason for the persistence of these categories into the present, even while scholars have disavowed the relevance of the terms "intentionalism" and "functionalism." This framework fit a specific generational period and historical mode of proceeding. But as a result of the massive concentration of facts over the last two decades, the Holocaust has been historicized, and the intentions of the perpetrators and the process of extermination fully documented. It seems opportune to attempt to think beyond these concepts and methods. We should leave this framework behind not because it does not answer well the questions it raises, but because it cannot pose new questions. The point is not that intention and process are unimportant. On the contrary, they are the stuff of history; that is how historians explain. Because we now have sufficiently good accounts of what happened in these historical realities – the process of extermination and the ideological make-up of the regime – we can turn to a different central problem in Holocaust historiography: to account for what the Nazis *thought* was happening, namely, an apocalyptic, millenarian battle against "The Jew."

Differently put, the avenue suggested in this book is built on intentionalism, functionalism, and their interpretive commingling in the last generation; this is its historiographical genealogy. This avenue is built on a rearrangement of existing core categories of ideology, context, race, and contingency. The overall result of this rearrangement is not to refine intentionalism and functionalism but rather to reject their interpretive consequences and to link the persecution and extermination of the Jews to a different set of questions about culture. My argument does not add new topics of culture to the existing dominant categories of ideology, race, context, and radicalization that supported intentionalism and functionalism. Rather, culture reorders these categories and their interpretive potential. This reordering changes the ways we tell the story because new and familiar topics, cultural and not, are viewed from a different perspective.

When we consider also interpretations of the French Revolution it seems that historians have a sort of explanatory framework with which to understand brief, violent, revolutionary events. The current view of the Revolution evolved out of a modification of the work of Furet, who together with a group of other historians especially in France and the United States, demolished between the 1960s and the 1980s the Marxist-oriented interpretation that had dominated in the first two-thirds of the last century. Marxists viewed the Revolution as bourgeois in origins, as a fundamental turning point in history's march from feudalism to capitalism; it was understood essentially as a social-economic event. They did look at the specific context within which the Revolution unfolded after 1789, but interpreted that context in the keys of origins and outcome, namely of the Revolution as a turning point that replaced one mode of production with another. Historians who supported the Revolution from the left viewed its circumstances as important in explaining and justifying the Terror; they argued that the destructive elements of the Revolution were a reaction to particular internal conditions, in which the Revolution was threatened by counterrevolutionaries and external pressure, particularly the war.

First, in the 1960s and 1970s, Anglo-American historians such as Cobban attacked the notion that the Revolution was waged in the name of capitalism and suggested that it was better understood as a political revolution with social consequences. Then Furet and others advanced the thesis that it was not only a political revolution but also a revolution in conceptions of the political and in political culture. Furet launched a frontal assault on the social interpretation, calling it "Revolutionary catechism." The historical essence of the Revolution was not social, he argued, but political, and the historical essence of the Terror was not economic, or military, or circumstantial, but ideological. It was not context that produced the Terror, but rather a deadly spiraling fight over political legitimacy, in which opposing political factions could claim legitimacy by asserting to be the only authentic representative of the people; in this deadly spiral, the most egalitarian and violent group always came up on top. This view put at the center of the revolutionary process the role of political ideas, symbols, and culture, and it presented the most dramatic interpretive shift of the historiography of the Revolution in the twentieth century.

What was revolutionary in the French Revolution was the creation of new symbolic forms of political representation and power.[25] Shifting the meaning of the Revolution from Marx to Tocqueville and from social structures to political culture, this interpretation demolished the distinguished although increasingly rigid social interpretation of the French Revolution that understood it in terms of preexisting social conditions and social processes and that assumed that politics and culture were derivable from the more basic social phenomena. The new approach explored the Revolution as a popular political act and cultural creation – as the making of a revolutionary experiential political symbolism – that was not determined by the imperative of social conditions.

But the Revolution's historiography of the 1970s and 1980s left a new generation of historians with a difficult act to follow. "What's after political culture?" pondered one historian symptomatically in 2000.[26] Interpretive novelties neither changed the basic foundations of the cultural interpretation nor proposed a new method to explore the Revolution, although they did refine specific topics, some of which are important. The image that emerges is of revolutionary "acculturation and sociability [that] presents an open-ended Revolution, where new political practices and the 'apprenticeship of citizenship' may be resisted, embraced, or transformed."[27] The most important element in radicalizing the Revolution was not the self-propelled ideology promoted by Furet but the revolutionary experience and dynamic itself, the constant daily reaction to the volatile series of political events. Thus, instead of assuming the ineluctable primacy and relative coherence of discursive-ideological determinants, new studies stressed the complexity of the revolutionary process of radicalization and the time between the outbreak of Revolution and its turn toward the Terror.

The new view has thus emphasized the unfolding context of the Revolution, questioned the primacy of ideology, and shifted the focus from political representation to political action. For Furet, the Terror was not an aberration, but an inevitable result of 1789. Baker put it succinctly when he said that in 1789 the National Assembly, by virtue of its political decisions, was already "opting for the Terror."[28] Current view emphasizes contingency, as Timothy Tackett put it, the "unpredictable, unscripted character of the Revolution, with a whole series of unanticipated events impinging on political perceptions and decisions and compelling individuals both to confront problems they had never expected and to develop new solutions far more radical – and sometimes more violent – than those they had previously imagined."[29] A scholarly middle ground evolved, in which most historians accept that there is a grain of truth both in the idea of social origins of the Revolution and in the idea of political-cultural origins. The difference comes down to just how much one thinks the Terror was written into 1789 and how much one thinks that changing circumstances (war and the existence of a counter-revolution) radicalized the situation. As an interpretive approach, it does remind us of the middle ground achieved between intentionalists and functionalists in Holocaust history.

The current interpretations of the two events share an intriguing similarity in their basic narrative framework. The following text I composed can be applied equally to the French Revolution and the Holocaust: the event was not as an event at all, but a series of events. The violence that came to define it was not the realization of a predetermined plan or inherent, unavoidable ideological determinant, but instead a result of a gradual, contingent process determined by the unfolding circumstances of war. The series of unanticipated events under extreme conditions forced individuals both to confront problems they had never expected and to develop new solutions far more radical and violent than they had previously imagined.

Context, motivation (that is, culture, ideas, and ideology), and contingency in a radicalized process of unanticipated events – this seems to be the framework within which historians understand these extreme events in which human behavior and historical explanation are stretched to the limit.

Obviously, there can be no historical reconstruction of the French Revolution and the Holocaust and, by extension, of all events without the elements of context, motivation, and contingency. They are foundational for historical thinking. The question is not whether to use them, but how. If we call for their use and remind historians of their importance, we simply reiterate what should be to begin with the historian's point of departure. The methodological choice is not between context and void, but between the ways context – that is, the immediate conditions of a given society – interact with past ways of life and thought. The choice is not between ignoring or emphasizing ideology, but between the ways ideology commingle with collective mentalities and sensibilities. And it is not between determinism or contingency, but between degrees of contingency within powerful structures. With this in mind, can we think of new narratives for the Holocaust that rearrange the story in new ways?

3

Narrative Form and Historical Sensation

Thinking of ways to rearrange the story of the Holocaust means, first, exploring the possibility of narrative. We now know a tremendous amount about the Holocaust from vast, detailed studies. One problem is how to present this evidence in new ways, thereby telling different stories.

A major historical task since 1945 has been simply to describe aspects of the historical reality of the persecution and extermination of the Jews between 1933 and 1945. The basic task of all history writing – to tell what the case was – was immensely difficult. After 1945 the Holocaust was generally not considered in public and scholarly circles as a key past in European history; the term itself became synonymous with the extermination of the Jews only around 1960. Primo Levi's *Se questo è un uomo* (dreadfully translated in the United States as *Survival in Auschwitz*) was rejected in 1946–1947 by Einaudi and by five other Italian publishers for lack of interest before it was taken by a small publishing house in Turin.[1] The managing editor of Einaudi was Cesare Pavese, the famous writer, who assigned it to his assistant reader. She rejected the book, claiming it was not "right" for Einaudi's list. In 1999 the readers of the Italian daily *Corriere della Sera* selected the book as the most significant one of the century. The Einaudi assistant who rejected the book , to conclude this story, was the then young and talented novelist Natalia Ginzburg, who came from a prominent antifascist family and was married to the resistance fighter Leone Ginzburg, who was murdered by the Germans in Rome in 1944.

Few major scholarly historical works were devoted to the Holocaust until the 1970s. Raul Hilberg's monumental *The Destruction of European*

Jews, published in 1961 after much difficulties, is the exception that proves the rule. Based on a dissertation completed in 1955 at Columbia University and a recipient of a university prize, the manuscript was rejected by Columbia University Press, Yad Vashem (Israel's official Remembrance Authority of the Shoah and Heroism founded in 1953), Princeton University Press, and University of Oklahoma Press before it was published by a new, small independent publishing house in Chicago, Quadrangle Books. Princeton University Press's rejection letter of 1959, based on the evaluation of the external reader, noted that the manuscript did not "constitute a sufficiently important contribution" and "readily available" books on the subject existed "in sufficient detail for all but very few specialists." There was not much to add to the topic of the Holocaust, it seemed. The reader for the Princeton press was Hannah Arendt.[2]

Even writers and intellectuals who were Jewish and antifascist and who shared common ground, interests, and associations with the persecution of Jews had thus difficulty comprehending the historical meaning of the extermination. For historians it seemed unproblematic to narrate modern European history without the Holocaust. Gordon Craig, a distinguished historian of Germany and the 1982 president of the American Historical Association, wrote a well-received book, *Europe since 1815*, published in 1974, that did not even mention the destruction of European Jewry.[3]

Since historians finally undertook to tell the story of the Holocaust from the 1970s, and with increasing persistence and meticulousness from the 1980s, there have existed two seemingly contradictory trends. On the one hand, there have been doubts in scholarly and public discourse about the possibility of producing a historical representation of the Holocaust at all. Friedländer's view – that "[one] wonders, possibly, whether any historical approach could suffice to redeem, that is convincingly to interpret that past" – is but one expression of these doubts.[4] This state of mind was part of the epistemic crisis in Western culture created by the Holocaust.[5] On this issue historians reflected, more than they shaped, popular perceptions about the special character of the Nazi past. For a long while, it became *de rigueur* among scholars to state, "Arguably, indeed, an *adequate* explanation of Nazism is an intellectual impossibility."[6] This kind of historical evaluation worked as an emotional, moral, and professional bulwark against telling part of the story.

At the same time, Holocaust scholarship developed in a diametrically opposed direction, producing a massive number of studies about the Third Reich. The historiography continues to grow unabated, revealing how multifaceted was the history of the Holocaust. It was not simply a German event, but a European and a North African one (Libyan and Tunisian Jews were deported to camps in Europe, including Buchenwald and Auschwitz). Actually it was not an event at all, but a series of events. It did not involve only Hitler and several of his cronies, but German society, economy, and culture as a whole, as well as those of many European countries. It did not affect only the Jews, but was tied to a series of Nazi resettlement plans and murderous policies involving Poles, Russians, Roma and Sinti, handicapped, homosexuals, and others. The goal of these plans was to redraw the map of Europe. A remarkably specialized massive historiography now accounts for what happened in the period. The problem for the historian who wants to narrate the Holocaust is not that it could not be represented, but conversely that, studied in such detail, it is at times difficult to see the forest from the trees.

This body of work has been characterized by the use of substantial records to tell the story very close to the documents. That Holocaust historiography has attempted to describe the event as accurately as possible is complementary, not contradictory, to the notion of the limits of Holocaust historical representation. Precisely because of these limits, real or perceived, scholars felt – and "feeling" seems to me to be the accurate word here – that "hard facts" and evidence are the only basis for legitimate historical work. The aim of studies of the Holocaust and the Third Reich was to tell it as it really was by getting as close as possible to the period through a dense political, military, administrative, and ideological history. We can think of the major work by Christopher Browning (with Jürgen Matthäus), *The Origins of the Final Solution*, or of the grand studies on the Third Reich by Ian Kershaw and Richard Evans, who write in the British tradition of empirical, erudite histories. Kershaw's aim in his biography *Hitler: 1936–1945 Nemesis* is to tell "how it came about," whereas that of Evans in his trilogy on the Third Reich is to "show how one thing led to another."[7] One lasting contribution of the last generation, therefore, has been simply to tell what actually happened, describing in detail aspects of the military, institutional, ideological, and political historical reality of the persecution and extermination of the Jews between 1933 and 1945.

This body of work, then, answered the difficulty of narrating the story of the Holocaust by turning to massive accumulation of facts to bring the past under control and make it understandable. But this mode of proceeding also resulted in an unintended consequence that limits our understanding of the Holocaust. Historical understanding is a dialectic between the strangeness of the past and a process of familiarization, in which the historian reads documents, uses evidence, and employs methods that result in a narrative whose intention should also be to elucidate – not to do away with – the past's strangeness. But because historians viewed Nazism as already possessing intrinsic problems of explanation and representation, they saw their aim as reconstructing the history of the Third Reich in order to suspend disbelief: they measured their success by their ability to undo the strangeness of a racist and murderous world. When Broszat called in the late 1980s for historicization of the Third Reich and the Holocaust he also implicitly meant it was time to take the strangeness of the Nazi past away from the event and to tell it by "scientific, empirical" methods producing a logical story of military, social, political, and ideological history.[8] Recent approaches that placed the Holocaust squarely within modernity, racial scientific thought, or the dynamics of Nazi administrative process have also ignored, at times inadvertently, the strangeness of the Nazi past. They gave both modernity and Nazism, in spite of contrary intentions, a false sense of coherence: for what the Nazis showed was precisely that modernity was fashioned from rational elements mixed up with fantasies, memories, and dreams of redemption that could not be reduced to racial ideology and administrative processes.

What has been lost in these historical reconstructions was precisely the strangeness of the past. My point is not that the Holocaust is strangely unique and incomprehensible; for the historian, all pasts are strange. Rather, my point is that the historian ought to elucidate the strangenesses of the past, not attempt to overcome them. By "strangenesses of the past" I mean those elements that can be captured through an analysis of culture, mentalities, and sensibilities. It is precisely the task of the historian to capture the mental horizons of these strangenesses. Yet for the most part Holocaust historiography has seen the strangeness of the past – for example, the difficulty that contemporaries had with grasping the reality of the extermination – as something history writing has to overcome, instead of seeing it as a historical sensation of the period that shaped the event as a subjective experience of contemporaries. This enormous body of work characterized by an almost positivist attachment to facts banished from the story of the Holocaust the strangenesses of the period instead of integrating them into the narration of how things were.

When Holocaust historiography provides a detailed account of the unfolding events in the context of their military, institutional, ideological, and political historical reality, it exhibits a very particular view of historical reality. It misses the historical sensations of the period dominated by sentiments of incredulity in the face of mass murder, of ideas of redemption and existential national anxiety, of fears and exhilaration evoked by the unspeakable breaking of taboo. These historical sensations exist in some Holocaust studies (most often on the margins and as an embellishment) but not as key narrative strands. They have been mainly perceived as a trace to confirm and illustrate an argument, but should instead be explored as mentalities that are part of the story, that expressed and shaped collective intentions and actions. They too were the way things were.

A different way to consider this topic is to note that, although historians have shared and reiterated the idea that the Holocaust is difficult to represent, this concern did not result in a new narrative form of historical writing or a different way of rearranging the story compared to other historical cases. A common practice has been instead to begin one's study on the Holocaust by asserting its uniqueness, while proceeding to narrate and analyze it just like any other historical event.[9] In contrast to literature, poetry, and other arts, history did not find a new form of narrative to express the problems of Holocaust representation and the perception of contemporaries about the strangeness of the event. Of course, it is difficult for historians to reconfigure the conventional – that is, typical – historical narrative that is based on the need to present the evidence in a logical, orderly, clear way, to keep (some sort) of chronology, to respect relations of cause and effect, and to demonstrate with pertinent sources who did what to whom and why.

But we can attempt to rearrange the story by taking the strangenesses of the past not as a given or as a reflection of more important developments happening elsewhere, but as subjective experiences of contemporaries that shaped the event. A place to start thinking about new narrative possibilities is Friedländer's *The Years of Extermination*.

The Years of Extermination is an illuminating narrative because it recounts the political, military, administrative, and ideological history of the Holocaust, while at the same time it also recounts the elusive historical sensation of disbelief as part of the way things were. Friedländer's study of the Holocaust is an integrated story of the policies of the perpetrators, the behavior of the surrounding European societies, and the world of the victims. At the same time, this book was written by a historian and intellectual who has been most influential over the last several decades in arguing for the limits of representation of the Holocaust. His words, halfway between a *cri de coeur* and a theoretical observation, are known to all scholars of the Holocaust, and beyond: "Does an event such as the 'Final Solution' allow for *any kind* of narrative, or does it foreclose certain narrative modalities? Does it perhaps escape the grasp of a plausible narrative altogether?"[10] Consequently, Friedländer's historical reconstruction of the Holocaust in the book exists in tension with his view that the Holocaust resists a plausible narrative. How, then, does Friedländer commingle in one narrative the story of the Holocaust and the doubts about the possibility of telling this very story? How does the doubter of a plausible Holocaust narrative narrate the Holocaust?

Friedländer himself articulates this as the main challenge of the book. The introduction ends with the following words: "The goal of historical knowledge is to domesticate disbelief, to explain it away. In this book I wish to offer a thorough historical study of the extermination of the Jews of Europe, without eliminating or domesticating that initial sense of disbelief."[11] His aim is to write a historical narrative of the Holocaust that *both* offers explanations of the unfolding events in their context and conveys the most powerful sensation about the event, during the period and since – that it is beyond words.

For him, the "sense of disbelief" is not simply a problem of historical reconstruction and is not something the historian has to overcome to be able to portray the period better. Instead, it is a defining characteristic of the period and an element the historian has to integrate into his or her narrative.

The Years of Extermination tells the familiar political, military, administrative, and ideological story whose aim is to overcome the strangeness of the past, but it has also another story to tell. The book is best seen not for its interpretation of the Holocaust; this interpretation is new, but not that new. It is important in this specific historiographical moment, but interpretations come and go. Instead, the book's most important contribution is the way it embeds its interpretation within a specific form of describing, finding a new way of representing the evidence and telling the story by commingling the narratives of what happened and the historical sensation of disbelief (what people understood that happened). This book cries out to be perceived and understood formally, as a historical narrative that combines evidence and a poetic act.

The narrative of the *Years of Extermination* is characterized on first sight by unity, order, and coherence. It is strictly chronological, aims at providing the "totality" of the Holocaust, and has a clear organizing and explanatory principle in the notion of redemptive anti-Semitism. But in fact this narrative is fractured at its core and does not follow the usual mode of historical writing.

Friedländer's narrative is distinguished by the use of Jewish individual testimonies interspersed throughout the chronological history of the extermination. He argues that often the victims' voice was perceived as "a trace left by the Jews that bears witness... and illustrates their fate." He uses the voice of the diarists differently: "[B]y its very nature, by dint of its humanness and freedom, an individual voice suddenly arising in the course of an ordinary historical narrative of events such as those presented here can tear through seamless interpretation and pierce the (mostly involuntary) smugness of scholarly detachment and 'objectivity.'"[12]

The result is a narrative marked by violent dislocations and interruptions. On one level, there exists the chronological, political, military, administrative, and ideological story of the extermination; it follows the typical modes of historical accounts. But on a different level, this narrative is pierced through by diarists' voices that are used not to bolster empirical evidence or to strengthen arguments about historical causality, but to insert a human dimension that "facts" alone cannot quite capture. These voices create images in short stories and vignettes, which are not so much connected to what comes before and after as they are startling in their visualness. Different diarists follow one another; they appear, disappear, only to reappear again hundreds of pages later in a loosely joined narrative. The regular historical account acts like the necessary context, the outward reality to the deep, genuine, existential meaning of the story.

Thus, following an ordinary historical discussion of the events in Holland during its occupation (the policy of the military administration, the reaction of the public, etc.), Friedländer turns to the diary of young Etty Hillesum. Her experience is not narrated as a means to explain, exemplify, or provide proof for the previous discussion. Friedländer does not introduce the short page on Hillesum with a commonly used historical phrase such as "The travail of occupation is exemplified in the story of Etty Hillesum." Instead, he starts by "Etty (Esther) Hillesum was still a young woman student in Slavic languages in Amsterdam University during these spring months of 1941."[13] Her story is not offered to provide evidence for a given argument; its meaning lies in speaking at all, in existing. For the Nazis, observed once George Steiner, the crime of the Jews was the crime of being; the meaning of Hillesum's voice is that of being. Her story does not require the historian's justification ("this source illustrates well my argument that..."). She is part of the narrative in much the same way as protagonists in a novel are (and that is why we accept without question her next appearance 200 pages later and again for less than a page).

The historical narrative of *The Years of Extermination* has qualities of a literary narrative. While the literary and poetic aspects are widely accepted as constitutive parts of historical narrative, the kind of ruptures and breaks inserted by Friedländer are devices associated with works of fiction, and historians do not *usually* use them.[14] They are anomalous in historical studies. It should be noted that not only the relationships between the historical narrative and the diarists' poetic narrative are marked by dislocation but this is also a characteristic of the book as a whole. The reader is alerted to the narrative of dislocation, characterized by moving from one scene to another, by the ubiquitous double space that separates the scenes. This book is not a tight monograph. Consider the studies by Browning, Evans, Hilberg, Kershaw, Longerich, or any other monograph on the period. (At the same time, Friedländer's narrative is possible in part only because there now exists a massive literature that accounts in detail aspects of what happened). *The Years of Extermination* is a loosely jointed narrative bounded by strict chronology and the overarching plot of Nazi policies and ideology of extermination.

Some diarists' stories have the air of literary episodes. The diarists speak, and only rarely does Friedländer interject with the authorial voice of the knowledgeable historian, who by virtue of hindsight knows more than the people in the past.[15] He recounts the reactions of David Sierakowiak, a Jewish youngster, scarcely fifteen, to the persecution of the Jews shortly after the Nazi invasion of Poland. "And at that point," writes Friedländer, "the young diarist added a puzzling question: 'is this evidence that the end for the Germans will probably come soon?'"[16] Friedländer leaves the question hanging in the air and moves on to the next topic. What is the meaning of this question, I noted in the margins when I first read it. But the literary pattern emerged as I went on reading. He suspends the episode in its particular historical time, holding back from the usual practice of historians, which would be to add a comment that places it in a larger context. The aim is to represent a truth expressed by Sierakowiak without the interference of the "smugness of objectivity" and of historical time that is measured in years and decades.

The attempt to capture Sierakowiak's subjectivity in this specific instant, while History swirls around him, reminds me of Ida Fink's notion of time in her story "A Scrap of Time": "I want to talk about a certain time not measured in months and years.... This time was measured not in months but in a word – we no longer said 'in the beautiful month of May,' but 'after the first "action," or the second, or right before the third.' We had different measures of time . . . during this time measured not in months nor by the rising and setting of the sun, but by a word."[17]

The Years of Extermination is a total history of the Holocaust that is aware of itself as partial; this awareness forms the formal essence of the text. Friedländer posits the historical totality of the Holocaust as an integrated and integrative story, while at the same time he uses a narrative form that intimates that this history cannot quite be captured. It is a historical narrative against itself. The power of this work is the fundamental ambivalence at its heart, a book built on its own contradiction: describing the past as history and at the same time setting the limits to that describing.

"Style is the bridge to substance," observes Peter Gay in an essay about Jacob Burckhardt.[18] Friedländer's book has a distinct composed tone, without moralizing and pontificating. The reader discovers the style as he or she goes along; Friedländer does not alert the reader to it. Only once does he make clear his rhetorical choice, in a footnote on page 757, in which he discusses Janusz Korczak, who walked at the head of the row of children of his orphanage, as they all marched together to their death in the Warsaw ghetto on August 5, 1942: "[T]here have been many descriptions of this march, and quite a few 'literary' embellishments were added to the bare facts, which certainly do not need any added pathos."[19] His style contrasts with writings that see fit to remind readers about the morality embedded in the Holocaust. Friedländer's moral presence emerges from his minor tone.

At the same time, it should be noted that Friedländer tells a story in black and white, of the entire continent on one side and the victims on the other. His is a story without "gray zones." The story focuses on the complexity of the extermination project and of the Jewish experience, but because it does not explore the construction of a genocidal culture and the psychology of the perpetrators it therefore largely avoids the dilemmas faced by Germans and bystanders. The book's focus on ideology as the main motivation for the Holocaust is conventional and at times even too simple an explanation. At issue is to offer a description, and not at all an explanation, let alone justifying the explanation via evidence and argument, while leaving the moral consequences of the tale to the moral imagination of the readers. This is the ultimate impact of the book even if Friedländer might view its interpretation, explanation, and evidence as profoundly important. *The Years of Extermination* is concerned with bequeathing to the historical account the moral essence of the event (in contrast to historical narratives characterized by the smugness of "objectivity").

The intellectual origins of *The Years of Extermination* are to be found in *Probing the Limits of Representation*, a book edited by Friedländer and published in 1992, that explored the representation of the Holocaust against the challenge of postmodernism that rejected the possibility of a firm reality beyond the self-referentiality of linguistic constructs.[20] Twice in the introduction to *Limits of Representation* Friedländer cites a sentence by Pierre Vidal-Naquet quoted from Carlo Ginzburg's essay "Just One Witness": "I was convinced that... everything should necessarily go through a discourse... but beyond this, or before this, there was something irreducible which, for better or worse, I would still call reality. Without this reality, how could we make a difference between fiction and history?"[21] *The Years of Extermination* provides a total history of the Holocaust as an irreducible reality by using not just one, but many witnesses.[22] At the same time, Friedländer also intimates in the introduction that "a precise description of the unfolding of events... [and the] impact of empirical evidence" cannot by itself "carry its own interpretation, its own truth."[23] And he ends by saying, "But the truth aimed at by history's, as opposed here to fiction's, specific form of discourse needs the maintaining of other convergent paths as well... it does not kill the possibility of art – on the contrary, it requires it for its transmission."[24] The book's narrative commingles two aspects, which are only seemingly contradictory: its language is tied to reality through a detailed history of the event and the voice of the witness, while its form alternates, characterized by a violent dislocation that is uncommon in historical studies.

Taking a long view of Friedländer's own perspective on the Holocaust over the years, the narrative form of *The Years of Extermination* both originates and departs from it. In the 1980s and 1990s he, on the one hand, argued that "The 'Final Solution,' like any other historical phenomenon, has to be interpreted *in its historical unfolding* and *within the relevant historical framework*," while, on the other hand, questioned whether "an event like the 'Final Solution' allows for *any kind* of narrative, or does it foreclose certain narrative modalities? Does it perhaps escape the grasp of a plausible narrative altogether?"[25] What seemed twenty years ago to be two opposing positions commingle in the book into one narrative. Friedländer tells the story of the Holocaust in its historical framework, but he also recognizes that this history in itself is not enough to capture the period. Its power lies in the combination. This narrative act reveals a certain element of the past that is not quite knowable through ordinary historical narrative, although it clearly existed and is indeed essential to understand the period.

We can now go back to the notion of narrative and the relationship between explanation and description. A prevalent opinion among historians favors analysis over description, but this is surely a mistake. "Historical description" is far more complex and fascinating than a theoretically unaware perspective recognizes. It is certainly not separated from explanation. *The Years of Extermination* fits well with Allan Megill's elegant words that "upon descriptions, explanations arise. Descriptions and explanations presuppose an interpretive perspective, and in the best histories they modify and enrich such a perspective."[26] Friedländer turns the event we call the Holocaust into a vast collection of settings, happenings, actions, characters, and experiences. He provides explanations for precise problems (for example, the role of Hitler, the timing of the decision of the Final Solution, the responsibility of the Catholic Church). But the overall explanation that arises from the description is that the historical method can grandly tell about the Holocaust, while it also requires an additional component to get to a deep human element embedded in it. This imparts to the book a certain feel – of the period, of contemporaries, of the victims, of suffering, of what we call the past – that is remarkable.

What are the broader implications of our discussion for historical writing? On one level, it seems that Friedländer's specific narrative form does not lend itself to wide application. A fractured narrative pierced with testimonies will hardly illuminate topics such as "Nazi school policy in Nuremberg" or "the Nazi film industry as propaganda and entertainment." Historical narratives are resistant to change, and the narrative form of this book is not a blueprint for imitation. Moreover, although Friedländer is careful not to argue this explicitly, the underlying tone of the book is that the Holocaust stands apart as a historical case. The individual voices that pierced the historical narrative "would hardly be necessary in a history of the price of wheat on the eve of the French Revolution, but it is essential to the historical representation of mass extermination."[27] The book's narrative form seems to fit the particular case of the Holocaust and potentially other mass exterminations.

I would like to propose an alternative reading. Far from being based on a special method for a special historical case, I view *The Years of Extermination* as a model of the mode of proceeding of historical sensation described in the introduction. While the narrative form of the book is particular, the interpretive benefit is general. It captures the historical sensation of disbelief of the period in a way that distinguishes it from other books about the period. It reconstructs it through a close reading of diaries, chosen and used according to strict historical method, which endows the book with (what we feel is) a presence of the past. This historical sensation is not at all fuzzy, but is based on the materiality of the written page, the pen, and the act of writing in the direst circumstances. Huizinga was inspired to write *The Autumn of the Middle Ages* after looking at a painting of Van Eyck. He claimed that in some cases objects of the past can preserve "an aura of the past *itself*" and that the past maintains a certain presence in artifacts (such as paintings, furniture, everyday objects, or a book).[28] We can legitimately question this claim, while acknowledging that the diaries transmit a sense of the past itself as if it had survived.

Friedländer was able to craft his narrative because he made the strangeness of the past – embedded in this case in the sense of disbelief – part of the history of the Holocaust; doing so enabled him to capture a human element that was part of the period. But this narrative form, I would like to suggest, is not a particular mode of proceeding that fits only the case of the Holocaust. Friedländer observes that the individual voices that pierced the historical narrative would not be necessary in a history of the price of wheat on the eve of the French Revolution. But this example is not a good one; no one would deny that the topic of the price of wheat demands a different sensibility from that of the Holocaust. The question is whether it would demand a *fundamentally different* mode of historical proceeding; the answer to this question is surely "no." The Holocaust is a special event; we feel it, and we feel correctly. But it demands a different sensibility not because it is an event that goes off the charts of regular historical analysis, but because the stakes of interpreting it are higher for human morality and history than the price of wheat. (It would be a different story in a case in which a deliberate human action changed the price of wheat in order to cause massive hunger and death.) Indeed, it is not that one encounters special problem of representation with the Holocaust, but rather that the Holocaust makes problems of historical representation especially clear.[29]

Friedländer's narrative strategy is successful not because it fits only the Holocaust but because, by capturing the historical sensation of disbelief, it reveals a certain element of the past that is not quite knowable through ordinary historical narrative, although it clearly existed and is indeed essential to understanding the period. The observation to make about Friedländer's commingling of irreducible reality and the possibility of art is not that it is not historical enough, but, on the contrary, that it is too limited: to my mind, this is a sensibility that belongs to all historical understanding. His argument – bounded by personal experience, by public and scholarly perceptions of the Holocaust, and by (some) conventions of the historical craft – needs to be set free to apply to all historical understanding.

I referred earlier to Lyotard's observation that the Holocaust was an earthquake that destroyed the very instruments used to measure earthquakes, thus calling into question the relations between the things that happened and the narration of the things that happened. One can see this state of affairs as unique to the historical case of the Holocaust, or one can see it, as I propose, as a general condition of history writing that was made evident by the Holocaust. Because historical sensation is part of all historical reconstruction we see the accomplishment as well as the limits of *The Years of Extermination*. Historical sensation permeates the book. But in terms of method Friedländer presents sensation as separate and opposed to "thorough historical study"; for him, only an extreme case such as the Holocaust demands such a narrative form. But in fact historical sensation and historical method are united, together comprising historical understanding. In this respect, *The Years of Extermination* only reveals more plainly in the case of the Holocaust what is an essential element in all historical understanding.

Based on this observation, what are the concrete implications of Friedländer's narrative for Holocaust historical writing? Paradoxically and unintentionally, the narrative form exposes interpretive limits of the current political, military, administrative, and ideological history when it stands by itself as the account of what happened; this history can be refined, specific questions can be revised, and new information about particular issues can be found, but as a whole – precisely because we know now so much about the Holocaust – it cannot at this stage of the historiography fundamentally challenge our understanding of the event. The narrative form of *The Years of Extermination* reveals the boundedness of the book's interpretation because it shows the potential of embedding a historical sensation such as disbelief within the interpretive framework based on radicalized racial ideology in the context of the war. It is here that we can think beyond *The Years of Extermination* and the dominant interpretive framework by integrating other cultural representations into the Holocaust narratives.

Let me give an example of the possibility of a new narrative by keeping to the topic of disbelief. The most frequent way that contemporaries

described the extermination was as something indescribable and unprecedented. After the German invasion of the East began, a German soldier
observed in a letter, "Emil wrote of the starving children he recently saw
in the Warsaw ghetto . . . the truth is worse, more cruel, more bestial than
any fantasy."[30] Avraham Lewin, a Zionist, a religious Jew, and an educator in the Yehudia private high school for girls, wrote in his diary in
the wake of the great deportations from the Warsaw ghetto that started
on July 22, 1941: "Our language has no words with which to express the
calamity and disaster that has struck us. . . . This is a slaughter the like of
which human history has not seen. . . . Those who are far away cannot
imagine our bitter situation. They will not understand and will not believe
[it]."[31] Shortly after the Germans shot 33,700 Kiev Jews in the Babi Yar
ravine near the city, a Ukrainian inhabitant Iryna Khoroshunova wrote
in her diary, "I only know one thing, there is something terrible, horrible
going on, something inconceivable, which cannot be understood, grasped
or explained."[32]

After 1945, the sentiment of uniqueness came to identify the Holocaust
in history and memory. Some took this sentiment at face value, as attesting
that the event was indeed unexplainable and unrepresentable. Others,
including some historians, viewed it as one proof that the Holocaust
was fundamentally different from other historical events. But historians
commonly construct their histories of the Holocaust by bypassing this
sentiment: studies account for what happened, where, and why, but do
not engage this mentality as part of the explanation.[33] Friedländer's *The
Years of Extermination* is an exception that nonetheless fits within the
general pattern: he uses the sentiment of disbelief as the narrative key
of the book, embellished with individual voices of Jewish diarists, while
accepting the notion itself as such without exploring how it emerged
and fit within what happened.[34] It is part of his narrative but not of the
explanation.

But what happens when we treat the sentiments of disbelief and uniqueness as mentalities, as subjective images of the world that shaped and were
shaped by the actions of mass murder? In this investigation we are interested neither in whether the Final Solution was historically unique (it was
not, if by "unique" we mean it had characteristics that fundamentally
distinguished it from all other historical events) nor in finding similarities
to other genocides and probing whether it was part of a century of genocides (it was). For Germans, Jews, and other Europeans the extermination
seemed special, and therefore, for the historian of culture, this perception
has to be accounted for and explained. Imagining during the war what

happened to the Jews as unprecedented was a cultural artifact and, as such, for the historian, a vehicle to make sense of how people made sense of the events around them.

By thinking about the extermination as something unprecedented, contemporaries used a notion of historical time ("something like this never happened before in human history"), linking Jews and what was happening to them to a sentiment of historical origins. This way of putting the relationship between the extermination of the Jews and perceptions of historical time opens up new interpretive possibilities. I would like to suggest that the extermination of the Jews was imagined by Nazis, other Germans, Jews, and Europeans as an act of creation, in the sense of genesis, in which the Jewish world would be destroyed to make space for the Nazi one. As an act of creation, it was perceived as producing a cosmic result, either salvation or eternal damnation; as being a human experience that lacked historical precedence, which every creation is by definition; and, as such, as a transgression, in the sense that it was a violation of all past known practice. The notion of creation, as is evident from the earlier quotations, was the organizing metaphor used by victims, perpetrators, other Germans, and Europeans to make sense of what was happening to the Jews after 1941.

But where did this connection between Jews, Germans, and historical time come from in the Third Reich? This investigation demands that we conduct a cultural study of Nazi ideas of time as represented in the persecution and extermination of the Jews; this study would be premised on exploring, first, the intimate links that connected the extermination to the culture of the earlier years of the Third Reich, and, second, the perceptions of time common in German society embedded not only in racial ideology but also in the ideas of Christianity, nationhood, and history.

The interpretive potential of this approach is significant. It allows historians to explore how people made sense of the extermination by viewing the sense of disbelief as a constructed historical mentality. The notion of creation allowed contemporaries to make sense of the extermination as a radical rupture, because a genesis has no roots in the past, while also fitting within the Nazi ideas of historical time that underlay the persecution of the Jews since 1933 as registers of time. It thus enables us to close the unacceptable gap, in terms of the historical method, between the years of persecution and the almost unimaginable extermination by showing that however radical the extermination was, it did share, via the notion of creation that made it imaginable, cultural continuities with German society that preceded it. But this narrative is possible only when we are open to rethinking the interpretive validity of the notions of racial ideology, radicalization of Nazi policy, and the context of the war – and of the centrality of Auschwitz – in explaining the Holocaust. This rethinking will enable an exploration of how Germans came to imagine a Germany, and later a world, without Jews in a Nazi culture conceived as a work in progress. In the chapters that follow I develop the case for such a perspective.

PART TWO

THRESHOLDS AND LIMITS OF HISTORY

4

Beginnings and Ends

Thinking about the French Revolution and the Holocaust requires placing these brief, violent, and radical events within narratives of beginnings and ends. Linking the events to what came before and after is crucial to the interpretation of what actually happened. Scholars are faced with explanatory temptations. One is to stress the events' long-term origins, whereby origins stand in these explanations as markers of historical significance. The historian thus "discovers" large patterns and regularities in the development of historical events. It is comforting to think that a momentous event, such as, say, the Russian Revolution, was not the result of contingent actions that led to unintended consequences and unpredictable outcomes, but was rather part of a long historical script in which the "road to the Russian Revolution" started with Ivan the Terrible, Peter the Great, the 1825 Decembrist revolt of young military officers against Nicholas I, or the 1881 assassination of Alexander II by an anarchist. Another temptation is to stress the events' unprecedented nature, whereby historical rupture stands as a marker of significance. Uniqueness becomes the hallmark of the event, as ties to the past are severed. In the case of the Holocaust this view serves, among others, to assuage our anxiety that it was an inherent part of our civilization. A final temptation is to read the event in the key of an outcome: in this case what really happened is less important than what a given historical script predetermined. Marxists saw the French Revolution as the beginning of the bourgeois historical epoch. Quite dramatic, no doubt, but this view ascribed to the actors of the Revolution results they never intended and it ultimately explained their behavior by factors beyond their control.

These temptations are known to historians. In a period when leading principles of historical understanding are contingency, complexity, and ambiguity, historians are aware of their fallacy. Nonetheless, events such as the French Revolution and the Holocaust have always attracted narratives of beginnings and ends, of origins and outcome. Historians are part of their society, and it is all too human to explain the world in terms of "unity and symmetry at the expense of experience," as Isaiah Berlin wrote in his essay "Historical Inevitability."[1] Historians can never reach a cultural Archimedean point from which one can interpret the world from the "outside." They are always "inside" culture; they are a product of the intellectual tradition and historical mentality of their society, while attempting at the same time to explain and criticize it. The temptations are known, but the idea that history is governed in some way, even in a reduced and minimal way, by large patterns or regularities is also attractive. How to capture the antecedents of the Revolution and the Holocaust without crafting a narrative of origins? How to capture their tremendous rupture without losing sight of historical continuity?

Some of the most celebrated understandings of the Revolution and the Holocaust are narratives of origins and outcome. Marxists saw the Revolution as a crucial point in history's long march from feudalism to capitalism to communism: it was bourgeois because its genesis and consequences were bourgeois. For Tocqueville and more recent scholars the Revolution was a crucial point in the march of the modernization and centralization of the French state. When viewed as a vehicle of aggrandizement of state power between Louis XIV and Napoleon, the Revolution shrank: "All that the Revolution had done, would have been done, I have no doubt, without it," wrote Tocqueville.[2] Lynn Hunt framed her analysis of the unfolding experience of revolutionaries' political culture against these interpretations that took preconceived ideas of origins and outcomes as the real meaning of revolutionaries' actions.[3] It is important to point out that historians of Marxist and Tocquevillian persuasions did explore revolutionary intentions, but these did not alter their overall interpretation because they presupposed the very intentions they set out to explain. Before the inquiry started, these historians had already restricted the field of vision to a given interpretive field. The notion that history obeys regular patterns means that every event is an element in a necessary pattern.

It would be a mistake to relegate these kind of narratives to a bygone era of grand narratives or to specific historical methods. The danger of historical inevitability lurks also for those who decidedly reject any notion of it and for those who pay close attention to intentions, culture, and experience. Furet and Baker thus viewed the ideology of 1789, the political choices made by the National Assembly, and the ambiguities of the Declaration of the Rights of Man and the Citizen passed in August 1789 as directly "opting for the Terror."[4]

In Holocaust historiography a simple rendition of intentionalism is the most common interpretation that stresses origins. Goldhagen, for example, sees the Holocaust as the result of endemic exterminationist anti-Semitism existing since at least the end of the eighteenth century (and perhaps before – the book starts with the birth of Christianity). He does look at the intentions and experience of the perpetrators by keeping the story close to the ground and to the everyday life of the killers, but his attitude is profoundly anti-empirical: he presupposes the very motivations he intends to explore. Isaiah Berlin observed on the "metaphysical origins" embedded in a teleological outlook: the idea that people are endowed with characteristics that are "internal to their possessors, so that every entity has a 'nature' and pursues a specific goal which is 'natural' to it."[5] This was Goldhagen's portrait of German anti-Semitism from the end of the eighteenth century to 1945. The important point is that one can pursue a historical investigation that is based on close examination of people's intentions and experience – "agency" in current historical parlance – while at the same time producing a perfectly nonhistorical, metaphysical study.

Perhaps it is to be expected that given the centrality of the Holocaust in contemporary culture it has been placed within a twentieth-century identity narrative of origins and outcome. Bartov represented a common view when he argued that the "Holocaust is at the center of a crisis of identity . . . [that] has in many ways become the characteristic feature of the twentieth century."[6] This is an attractive interpretation in a society that sanctifies the notions of identity and of Holocaust memory. But it seems to reflect better current scholarly discourse and popular culture about the Holocaust than the ways people in the past perceived their life. It reads the history of the Holocaust from the present day backward, ignoring that many people did not view the Holocaust as fundamental during its unfolding and in the decades immediately following 1945.

The relations between the Holocaust and a presumed twentieth-century "crisis of identity" can be illuminated by thinking in analogy about the relations between the Enlightenment and the French Revolution. The classic interpretation claiming that the Enlightenment produced the Revolution may have inverted the logical relations between the two: did the Enlightenment invent the Revolution, pointedly asked Roger Chartier, or did the Revolution invent the Enlightenment by attempting to create legitimacy, justification, and roots in a body of texts and a group of authors who criticized the Old Regime? There is the risk, he observed, of "proposing a teleological reading of the eighteenth century that seeks to understand it only in relation to the phenomenon deemed to be its necessary outcome – the French Revolution – and to focus only on the phenomenon seen to lead to this outcome – the Enlightenment."[7] In claiming that an identity crisis produced the Holocaust, we invert the logical sequence: Did an identity crisis cause the Holocaust, or did the Holocaust produce and accelerate identity concerns? We should not confuse significance with provenance: the fact that an identity crisis resulted from the Holocaust does not mean that an identity crisis also produced it. And we should not seek to understand the twentieth century only in relation to the phenomenon deemed to be its necessary outcome – the Holocaust – and to focus only on the phenomenon seen to lead to this outcome – identity.

To have a perspective of origins and outcome assumes that the object of investigation is chronologically well defined. But it is precisely this assumption that we should reflect on with respect to the Holocaust. Periodization is important to make sense of a historical event, especially for the Holocaust and the Revolution that constituted ruptures of historical continuity. Of value here is thinking with the work of Tocqueville and Furet, who himself famously used Tocqueville to test one of the "fundamental concepts which the French Revolution has given rise to and which in consequence dominates its whole history: this is the concept of the before and the after, separated by a radical break."[8] "The year 1789," wrote Furet, "is the key to what lies both upstream and downstream. It separates those periods, and thereby defines and 'explains' them ... the Ancien Régime is thought to have an end but no beginning, the Revolution has a birth but no end."[9] If we do not quite know when the Revolution ended – 1794, 1799, 1804, 1814, in 1978, or 1989 – we do know when it began – in 1788 and 1789 – with the financial crisis of the monarchy, the jostling for power between the king and the nobility, the election for the Estates-General that was last convened in 1614, drafting of *cahiers de doléances* (grievance lists), stalemate over the political role of the Third Estate ... and the rest is history.

As for the Holocaust, we know when it ended – on May 8, 1945 – with the total defeat of the Third Reich, which had continued to implement its policies to exterminate Jews right up to the end. But when did the Holocaust begin? In 1933 with the Nazi seizure of power? In 1935 with the Nuremberg Laws? Or in 1938 with the Night of Broken Glass, which one scholar of Germany evaluated as "that infamous night [in which] the genocide campaign began in earnest"?[10] Perhaps the war was the crucial turning point, but when exactly? After September 1, 1939, with the herding of Polish Jews into ghettos? After June 22, 1941, as the killing squads following the army in Operation Barbarossa began shooting tens of thousands of Jews? Sometime between late 1941 and early 1942, between the constitution of death camps and the first gassing of Jews in Chelmno in December 1941 and the Wannsee Conference convened on January 20, 1942, to prepare the "Final Solution of the Jewish question in Europe"?[11]

The answer to the question, when did the Holocaust begin, is clear and vague at the same time because the word *Holocaust* hides various stages, policies, and intentions. On the one hand, there is an abundant literature about the decisions made and actions taken between June 1941 and January 1942, when the systematic extermination of the Jews began on the ground and was planned as a state project. Scholars have covered this decision-making process with hair-splitting detail. But on the other hand there is also a general sense, not wholly mistaken but historically unspecific, that the Holocaust was the more broadly defined and chronologically longer process of the persecution of the Jews in Nazi Germany. The Holocaust is sometimes defined, at times by the same scholar, as the "persecution and murder" of European Jewry during World War II – that is, as happening between 1939 and 1945, if not before – and also as "the systematic mass murder of European Jewry by the Nazis," that is, as taking place between the second half of 1941 to 1945.[12]

One way to define the object of study, to provide a coherent narration of the events, is therefore to start from the end because 1945 provides a firm point in the story. From this perspective, bringing together diverse current bodies of work on the Holocaust, the following story emerges. The rupture that was the Holocaust, or the Shoah, is the decision and implementation to exterminate systematically the Jews all over Europe. The Holocaust took place between the autumn of 1941 and May 1945 – more concretely, between the mass murder committed by the SS and special Task Forces (*Einsatzgruppen*) in the East and the beginning of the death marches at the end of the war.[13] The plan was to make not only Germany but also Europe and indeed the world free of Jews (*Judenrein*). The mentality behind this was that Jews were mortally dangerous, that the struggle between Jews and Germans reached its

apocalyptic battle for life and death, and that therefore the implementation of the plan to annihilate them, by setting up special death camps in
the East, must be immediate, during the war and often at the expense of
the war effort.

This definition accounts for the arrest and deportation of the Jews in
the remote island of Corfu on June 9, 1944. It was a premeditated act
planned some time in advance that could not assist the military effort.
Its "justification" was not determined, strictly speaking, by contingent or
contextual motives, but by the plan and desire to exterminate Jews wherever they happened to be. It neither altered the local military scene nor
assisted in the major battle of the day, the Allies' invasion of Normandy
three days earlier. Indeed, the operation hurt the military effort because
it required special petrol for the boats, which was very expensive. But a
combination of local factors – on June 7, 1944, the Allies entered Rome,
and the German hold on the island, which had been occupied by Italy at
the beginning of the war, seemed short-lived – and an apocalyptic vision
about a Jewish–German battle for survival sent the Germans on Friday at
5:00 a.m. knocking on every Jewish door at the island. The entire community, 2,000 people, was assembled in the main square. Allied planes
hovered above, but the Germans continued. The Jews were forced to sur-
render their valuables and hand over the keys of their homes, which were
later looted by the Germans who sold what they did not need. Several
days later the Jews were placed on barges pulled by motorboats, and from
the Greek mainland they were deported to Auschwitz.[14]

The Holocaust was a genocide characterized by a total, universal extermination with no expiration date. It was preceded by a smaller scale genocide from September 1, 1939 to the autumn of 1941. The two periods
characterize different stages of the variegated phenomenon of historical
genocide. For the sake of clarity, I use the term "Holocaust" to identify
the phase of total extermination and the term "genocide" to identify the
years 1939–1941. At times I use "Holocaust" to mean the general period
of the persecution and extermination in the Third Reich or to note the
field of study; I trust that the meaning will be clear from the context.

The term "genocide" was coined on the pages of the *Washington Post*
in 1943 by Rafael Lemkin, a Polish Jewish refugee lawyer, who was later
instrumental in the approval of the United Nations Genocide Convention
on December 9, 1948. According to Lemkin, genocide is the "destruction
of a nation or of an ethnic group. . . . Generally speaking, genocide does
not necessarily mean the immediate destruction of a nation. It is intended
rather to signify a coordinated plan of different actions aiming at the
destruction of essential foundations of the life of national groups, with

the aim of annihilating the groups themselves."[15] Killing members of a social group is only one way of committing genocide. According to the UN Convention, there are four other genocidal acts: preventing births within the group, causing sustained physical harm, intentionally creating conditions of life to destroy the group in whole or in part, or forcibly removing children of the group to another group. In this respect, the Nazi rule in Eastern Europe, viewed in terms of imperial and colonial policies, committed several genocides: against Slavic peoples in occupied Poland and Ukraine, against Russians, as well as against the Jews.[16]

The years 1939–1941, which have been often viewed simply as an antechamber to the total extermination that followed, were a period of open-ended Nazi policy to extinguish Jewish life. It is difficult to conceive of a policy of genocide that is open ended and inclined to twists, turns, and contingent changes. But that was the essence of this period, in which the Nazi were adamant on creating a German world without Jews. The final aim was clear; the means to achieve it were flexible. The immediate aim of German policy was to get rid of the Jews in a variety of methods, using a combination of deportation, killing, starvation, and forced labor; the final aim was to have the Jews wither away sooner or later.

More than a half-million Jews died in Poland between September 1939 and the invasion of the Soviet Union. The beginning of the war was thus a decisive moment in the Nazi plan to remove Jews from normal life not only in Germany but also in occupied Europe. Several plans floated in the air for the creation of a separate Jewish territory: the idea of a Jewish reservation near the Polish city of Lublin emerged immediately after September 1939; then in 1940, after the fall of France and its colonial empire, there was a plan to deport the Jews to Madagascar; and in early 1941 ideas were raised about a reservation farther to the east in a (soon-to-be conquered) Soviet territory. Jews were not systematically killed during this stage, but they remained alive only momentarily, until Germans decided how to get rid of them, or because of their utility to German aims, but not as independent human beings.

In Poland, Jews lost any claim to humanity, as described in a secret army report from Posen:

In Truck three SS-vehicles under the guidance of high SS commanders rode through the streets on October 30, 1939, hitting [Jews] indiscriminately on their head with horsewhips and long lashes.... Eventually, a number of Jews were driven into the synagogue. They were forced to crawl through the benches singing, while the SS men continuously hit them with lashes. Then, they had to take off their trousers and were hit on the naked buttocks. One Jew, who defecated out of fear, was forced to spread the excrement on the face of the other Jews.[17]

The Holocaust was preceded by a genocide, and the genocide was preceded by persecutions from 1933 to 1939.[18] Göring characterized the essence of this period in a speech given on December 6, 1938: "The Jew cannot live in Germany."[19] The Nazi persecution was not designed merely to discriminate or humiliate, although these were immediate products of the policy: it was meant to make Jews leave Germany, thus creating a Germany without Jews and Judaism. Various solutions to the Jewish question were discussed during those years, including emigration, relocation, and extermination, although the main aim was to persecute, not to kill.[20]

For Jews, life became impossible. They were excluded from their professions, from education, and, what shocked and hurt them the most, from participating in public life as equal social beings. They were banned from theaters, museums, concert halls, and swimming pools, lost their passports and driving licenses, and were forbidden to own a radio. Non-Jewish acquaintances could not fathom the depth of Victor Klemperer's crisis. By August 1937, he lost hope in the distinction between evil rulers and good Germans: "I believe ever more strongly that Hitler really does embody the soul of the German people, that he really stands for 'Germany'.... And if the government should change one day: my inner sense of belonging is gone." On February 23, 1938, he summed up his incredibly deep loneliness as "the greatest isolation."[21]

This narrative from 1945 to 1933 is good and coherent. It assigns the periods of persecution and genocide a logic of their own before the period of total extermination. They were neither mere background to a more significant plot that followed nor first acts in the main play to come. They were the plots, distinct entities that nonetheless were connected to what came thereafter. This narrative follows step by step the changing, ever-radicalized Nazi policies and plans to solve the "Jewish question," while emphasizing the role of Nazi ideology and the context of the war in the Holocaust. It opens up different possibilities for the development of Nazi anti-Semitism. Still, this narrative should be refined because even now it is too neat, too logical, reflecting our needs for order and organization to make sense of the past. Life is more chaotic, beliefs and actions commingle, mix up, and are messed up in ways that are not reflected sufficiently in this narrative.

Now that we have crafted a narrative of the events, let us look at it from its beginning, from 1933. There is an implicit assumption of causality in this narrative, in which one stage begets the next. Even with all the emphasis on changing Nazi policies and aims, this is a narrative of a radicalized, forward-progressing ideology that ultimately ends in Auschwitz.

But it offers little sense of the cultural construction of a world without Jews for those Germans for whom the center of Nazi anti-Semitism was not Auschwitz but, for example, the decision of the German state from January 30, 1933 on to cleanse Germany of Jews: a moral, historical, post-Enlightenment break was made then, not by planning extermination, but by imagining that a German world without Jews could be a reality, somehow.

At the same time, the three periods, too clearly defined, are isolated one from the other: the result is a severing of the Holocaust from the genocide, which is severed from the persecution. This creates an explanatory gap between the periods of persecution and extermination. But what made possible in prewar German life and imagination the extermination of the later war years? The three periods should be regarded as heuristic devices, categories used to make sense of the story, not as having an inherent meaning. In reality, the ideas and motivations that made them possible blended and mixed. This blending comes into sharp focus when we consider that, in terms of the culture and memories motivating the persecution and extermination of the Jews, the narrative described earlier is closed within itself: racial ideology begets motivations between 1933 and 1945. What are the connections of racial ideology to other ideas in German society in the period, and what are the links between Nazi anti-Semitism and pre-1933 traditions, symbols, and memories? Differently put, the extermination of the Jews in 1941–1945 should be placed within the symbolic universe of Germany between 1933–1941, and this should be placed within that of prewar Germany.

Viewed from this perspective, it is not Auschwitz that stands at the center of the historian's study of Nazi anti-Semitism, but the making of a German world without Jews. This world would have been created with or without Auschwitz; its creation was under way from 1933. A narrative of Germany without Jews does not require the notion of radicalization to move the story forward because the assumption is not about the story's final destination (the extermination beginning in 1941), but about its starting point in January 30, 1933, when the German state adopted its policy against the Jews. The shadow of the Holocaust obscures the fact that the Germans' attitude toward the Jews between 1939 and 1941 would not have left many Jews alive even had the Holocaust not happened. In Poland Jews were uprooted from their homes, stripped of their possessions, denied their livelihoods, driven to overcrowded ghettos with poor sanitary and food supplies, sent to forced labor, and executed.

Oskar Rosenfeld was deported from Vienna to the Lodz ghetto on November 4, 1941. He kept a remarkable diary until July 28, 1944, shortly before his deportation to Auschwitz. What he identified in May 1942 as the essence of the sealed ghetto was true from the moment of its creation in November 1940:

Every community will breathe, flourish, grow, create. It's part of the animal instinct, law of nature. To come into being, to grow, to pass away, every renewing life, parallel to nature...ghetto the exception. People...are granted just enough air to vegetate. They don't plant crops...you cannot produce. When the suit becomes worn, you have to walk in rags.... The bolts get rusty, the colors fade...there is no growth, everything falls apart step by step. And without work, starving here are the engineers, chemists, mathematicians, botanists, zoologists, pharmacologists, physicians, architects, teachers, writers, actors, directors, musicians, linguists, administrative officials, bankers, pharmacists, handicraftsmen like electricians, woodworkers, carpenters, metal experts, upholsterers, house painters, furriers, tailors, shoemakers, textile manufacturers, turners, watchmakers.[22]

Between 1939 and June 1941, the Germans had made up their mind that Jews did not deserve a human existence in territories under German control, but they did not set out to exterminate them outright.[23] "Now I judge everything as a Jew because it is at the heart of National Socialism," wrote Klemperer on April 16, 1941.[24] Should this sentence be understood as a precursor to the total extermination? This is the wrong question. Instead of attributing Klemperer intentions he could not have had, we can see the genocide he did describe. A people without a future do not need a past: "I am virtually ravaging my past," he wrote several weeks later on May 21, 1941, as he was "burning, burning, burning for hours on end" all his possessions of his past life in preparation for the move to a new quarter at the recently instituted "Jews' House." The mentality behind the German policy was that Jews did not deserve to live, although there was no urgent necessity to kill them. The shadow of Auschwitz diminishes the revolutionary aspect of this policy for European civilization.

In this sense, I follow Tocqueville who argued that "All that the Revolution had done, would have been done, I have no doubt, without it." Auschwitz accelerated the realization of a world without Jews that would have been created without it.

Let us return to the "concept of before and after, separated by a radical break," with which we began this discussion, and consider it based on the narrative of the Holocaust as preceded by a genocide that was preceded by persecution. I pose a question by way of a thought experiment: what was more historically improbable – the emergence of the Holocaust from a background of genocide and persecution or the emergence of the Terror from a background of the Declaration of the Rights of Man and the Citizen (assuming one does not subscribe to the thesis of Furet and Baker about the inherent link between the Declaration and the Terror or view the Enlightenment and the Declaration as engines of repression)? Obviously, this is an impossible question, an ahistorical one. It would be useless were we seeking an answer and a certainty, but we are seeking neither. Instead, we are after new connections and ways of thinking about a historical event whose monstrosity often blocks the imagination.

Consider the following passage from Timothy Tackett's essay "Interpreting the Terror":

The Terror... remains one of the most enduring mysteries of the entire Revolutionary period... historians have made considerable progress in illuminating the psychology of Revolutionary violence among the peasantry and the urban working classes... but the actions of the educated segments of French society – men and women steeped in the Enlightenment values of reason, justice, tolerance, and humanitarianism – seem far more enigmatic. How did individuals who had only recently passed the Declaration of the Rights of Man and the Citizen, a document that would be a model for liberal reform throughout the world, come rapidly to create a totalitarian and eminently intolerant regime in which thousands of people were sent to the scaffold through a travesty of the judicial system or were summarily executed without trial?[25]

On one level, the Nazi decision to exterminate all the Jews is a most extreme form of genocide; you cannot go further. This may result in viewing the Holocaust as historically standing apart. But on the level of intentions, the Nazis believed from the beginning that Jews should be removed from Germany, and although the Nazis did not adopt extermination as a policy after the seizure of power, it was part of a variegated discourse about solving the "Jewish problem"; after September 1, 1939 it was tangibly in the air. The contrast with the intentions of the revolutionaries is that they did not intend to produce the Terror, and the values of the Declaration stood in contradiction to the Terror. The novelty of the Holocaust in 1941–1945, then, must be linked to manifestations in German society between 1933–1941. The point is not to create another teleology or a narrative of historical inevitability. Putting the Terror and the Holocaust in relationship makes us conscious of hidden assumptions in the way we disconnect the Holocaust from what preceded it. The challenge is to connect the Holocaust to earlier Nazi and German culture without making it inevitable, to construct the Holocaust historically not as a teleology but as a possibility, not as an inevitability but as an eventuality.

The thesis of Furet and Baker – that the Terror was central to the revolutionary process and had already been embedded in the Declaration – can illuminate this mode of proceeding. Furet saw the Terror as semiotically predetermined in the language of 1789 and as emerging from a concept of political sovereignty that owed its characteristics to the Old Regime's public space and political culture. He and Baker based their argument not on what revolutionaries wanted to do, but on what the discourse of the general will made them do. If the Terror is central to the Revolution, even though the intentions of the revolutionaries were diametrically opposed to it, it follows that the Holocaust as thought and practice was central to the Third Reich. Historians needed to rescue the Revolution from this determinism and to show the liberal culture of the Enlightenment and the contingency of the revolutionary process. In thinking about the Holocaust our problem is different: when we perceive the Holocaust as overdeterminedly unprecedented, we a priori sever the extermination from cultural manifestations that preceded it.

Differently put, the extermination is connected to German society between 1933 and 1941 along the lines charted by Baker when he wrote that historians should explain "how the Revolutionary script was invented…from within the political culture of the absolute monarchy."[26] How was the Holocaust conceived in the Nazi culture that preceded it? If we can find links between two opposites such as the Terror and the Enlightenment, we should be able to find links between the extermination and the earlier culture of the Third Reich. On the one hand, finding these links has been impeded by difficulty in internalizing the Holocaust, by notions of uniqueness and incomprehensibility, and by resistance to placing the Holocaust as a much more resolute part of the early years of Nazi Germany than as a short period of war frenzy. On the other hand, the historiography of the last several decades has convincingly forged these kinds of links by emphasizing the role of racial ideology; I discuss this role later. But above all, forging these links means decentering Auschwitz in the narrative of the persecution and extermination of the Jews in the Third Reich.

This way of putting the relations between the Holocaust (1941–1945) and the Nazi period that preceded it does not sit comfortably with the view of the Holocaust as an irreducible radical rupture. On one level, this rupture is undeniable: "As I sit writing at the table," to recall Primo Levi's words, "I myself am not convinced that these things really happened." The sense of rupture has been shared, in various ways, among victims, perpetrators, and following generations. In terms of method it means that the Holocaust's momentum and dynamic had no proper origins because its meaning lies in the unfolding of events that had no precedent. But historians also know that every historical event has antecedents: how much of a rupture was it, then, and what kind?

The idea of the Holocaust as a rupture is canonical. It exerts an enormous strain on the modern imagination to explore historical links between the Holocaust and the previous years of the Third Reich because doing so requires juggling rupture and continuity in tense relations. We can identify this tension in an opinion articulated in the mid-1980s by the German philosopher Jürgen Habermas: "There [in Auschwitz] something happened that up to now nobody considered as even possible."[27] At first sight this sentence seems evidently true and unproblematic, but on a closer look it bears an ambiguity embedded in the word "considered." "Nobody considered [Auschwitz] as even possible" means that nobody dared breaking the taboo of violating the basic shared dignity of all human beings. This is what Habermas says in the following sentence: "There [in Auschwitz] one touched on something which represents the deep layer of solidarity among all that wears a human face." At the same time, "nobody considered [Auschwitz] as even possible" also means that something happened there that no one could have imagined or conceived or put into words because it was not part of the mental horizon of society. There is an unresolved tension between these two meanings: one implies that people could imagine a Holocaust but did not believe that this taboo would ever be broken, while the other implies that a Holocaust was not part of the imagination of the age and therefore speaking about its representation in the period that preceded it amounts to anachronism. Both meanings should be questioned. If a society can imagine a taboo, it must also imagine the breaking of it; imagining breaking a taboo is constitutive of the taboo. If an event happened in history, it must have been imagined beforehand. Rupture is not a sufficient concept to understand the Holocaust.

Thinking about the Revolution as a historical rupture, Furet posed the following question: "How can we think simultaneously of the Revolution as a radical rupture and as an essential continuity? What kind of process of continuity is it which takes the road of Revolution?"[28] It was Tocqueville who challenged the idea of a revolutionary break with the past: "It would, however, be deceiving ourselves strangely to believe that there arose out of it [the Revolution] a French people entirely new, and that an edifice had been erected whose foundation had not existed before."[29] His interpretation, which was taken up by Furet, was radical because it was contrary to the Revolution's own idea of itself as an event that cut the flow of history between old and new.

This kind of a historiographical challenge needs also to be applied to the Holocaust: our histories of it reflect too closely the expressed beliefs of contemporaries about the rupture. One hesitates to write this because this mode of proceeding may seem to silence the victims and their memories. It does not. It puts the subjective understanding of contemporaries in the complex context of the time by exploring "the process of continuity that takes the road" of revolutionary change. This mode of proceeding will allow us to understand why contemporaries of the Holocaust experienced rupture out of continuity.

The subjective opinion of contemporaries should be a lightning rod for historians as they attempt to understand a given period, but it cannot be the ultimate arbiter of historical interpretation. Contemporaries often have a limited understanding of the relations between their present and the past. Think about the link between Nazism and the Enlightenment. The Nazis saw their movement as undoing the work of the Enlightenment and as having no relation to it; today, we view Nazism as one heir of the Enlightenment idea of social engineering. In addition, contemporaries have no knowledge of the relationships between their present and the future; hindsight is sometimes a virtue in historical understanding. Survivors and contemporaries often described the Holocaust as an indescribable event beyond the power of words. This was a genuine sentiment, but has been a common mode of expression in modern history and especially in the twentieth century, when the twists and turns of history were extreme. The experience of Verdun, for example, was regularly referred to in the writings of participants as *inénarrable* (untellable) and *indescriptible* (indescribable).[30] Germans who were driven from their homes in Eastern Prussia and Czechoslovakia at the end of World War II repeatedly described what happened as "scenes out of which no words exist."[31]

In fact, Habermas was wrong in arguing that "there something happened that up to now nobody considered as even possible." Recent scholarship has shown that what made the Holocaust thinkable was prior extermination by Germans of the Herero and Nama.[32] The genocide in Africa showed that wiping out a people was indeed a possibility: visions of their own superiority, together with viewing people as superfluous and inferior, which prevailed in the colonial context, linked the German genocides in Africa and those committed forty years later in Eastern

Europe. "This ultimate breaking of a taboo," noted Jürgen Zimmerer, "– not only contemplating the extermination of whole ethnic communities but actually executing such a plan – was first committed in the colonies."[33] In its violence and racism, Nazi imperialism thus based its rule also on European colonial precedents.[34] Isabel Hull took this argument a step further in her study of the modes in which German military culture sought extreme solutions, including the possibility to "destroy whole peoples.... The continuities between colonial and European warfare are not due ... to Europeans learning evil lessons in the colonies and then applying them at home.... Rather ... the colonial situation merely provided the opportunity to practice on Africans and Chinese what the military experts took to be the immutable precepts of warfare."[35]

Other studies made further connections between the Holocaust and the imagination of total destruction. A wide-ranging extinction literature has existed since the nineteenth century, written by anthropologists, physiologists, biologists, Social Darwinists, and others; it claimed the right of the modern, civilizing state to remove allegedly primitive and inferior races. The need to take control of evolutionary laws by exterminating a whole group of people was linked to inferior races in the colonies and to the Jews in Europe, for example.[36] World War I was a cauldron of genocidal images of war and violence, as "one of the most striking aspects of battlefield descriptions in Great War literature is the extent to which they resemble accounts of the Holocaust."[37] Work by Götz Aly and Susanne Heim has shown how the idea of breaking the taboo of humanity was articulated in German plans for resettlement, deportation, and extermination in Eastern Europe that circulated among population experts and other governmental offices before 1939.

Habermas's view represented the bounded Holocaust consciousness and historical knowledge of his time. The extermination of the Jews – not the specificity of the gas chambers in Auschwitz but the idea of severing Jews from the human family – must have been imagined before it occurred. The Holocaust happened only because there were words, images, and concepts to articulate and conceive of it. There was more continuity than we usually assume in the rupture that was the Holocaust.

The historical meaning of the Third Reich as a genocidal regime was defined before 1941; the Holocaust added to this meaning, but did not create it ex novo. The Holocaust was part of a larger attempt, of other genocides, to create a Nazi way of life. National Socialism already existed as a revolutionary genocidal regime by mid-1941, with its racial plans of resettlement, forced labor, the withering away of European and world Jewry, the practical enslavement of Poles and Russians, and the creation of whole groups of people without rights. In the years before the total extermination of the Jews there existed discourses and representations of extermination that made imagining a world without Jews possible. Ultimately, any approach that stresses the rupture of the Holocaust without taking into account the imagination that made it possible is bound to be unsatisfactory. It severs the Holocaust of 1941–1945 from the work in progress that was the making of Nazi Germany and from its common values, shared expectations, and collective mentalities and sensibilities.

5

The Totality and Limits of Historical Context

For all their subsequent historical importance, the French Revolution and the Holocaust were fashioned by human beings who acted close to the ground, amid the circumstances of unfolding events. From the perspective of origins and rupture we move in this chapter to the specific context that makes history. "Always contextualize!" is an often heard refrain among fellow historians. As an essence of historical explanation, it is an inseparable twin of "always historicize!"[1] There is no doubt about the value of either imperative, but this only begs the question. For historians the question is not "to contextualize or not to contextualize." Historians historicize and contextualize: this is what they should do for a living. Rather, the question is, What are the promises as well as the limits of historical context as an explanation? What can the context explain, and what can it not explain?[2]

The issue of context has been at the center of the debates on the violence of the Terror and the Holocaust. It is quite remarkable to note the multiple associations that exist in the rhetoric, explanatory dilemmas, and mode of argumentation among historians of both events. Some of the associations are subterranean, others are more explicit, while still others demonstrate a touch-and-go state of semi-awareness. Take for example the following text of Robert Darnton from *What was Revolutionary about the French Revolution*:

Historians have succeeded in explaining much of [the Terror] . . . as a response to the extraordinary circumstances of 1793–1794 . . . circumstances account for most of the violent swings from extreme to extreme during the revolutionary decade. Most, but not all – certainly not the slaughter of the innocents in September 1792. The violence itself remains a mystery, the kind of phenomenon that may force one back into metahistorical explanations: original sin, unleashed libido, or the cunning of a dialectic. I confess myself incapable of explaining the ultimate cause of revolutionary violence...these massacres took on the character of a ritualistic, apocalyptic mass murder.[3]

These are considerations and language from the workshop of Holocaust studies: apocalyptic mass murder, violence that remains a mystery, metahistorical explanations, original sin, the explanatory power and limits of circumstances to make sense of extraordinary violence. Darnton does not explicitly make the connection between the Terror and the Holocaust – perhaps because he did not want to appear to be trivializing the Holocaust, perhaps because he did not want to link rhetorically Nazism with the Revolution, which he admires, or perhaps he was not fully aware of the connection (I doubt that). At any event, the association between the Nazis and the Revolution lurked somewhere in his mind because he makes a comment that is meaningful precisely because it stands conspicuously out of context. Several pages before the text just cited, Darnton discusses the revolutionary cult of virtue that produced a new understanding of family life. "Saint-Just," he writes, "the most extreme ideologist on the Committee of Public Safety, wrote in his notebook: 'the child, the citizen, belong to the fatherland.'"[4] And Darnton adds the following comment: "It would be anachronistic to read Hitlerism into such statements." This appears to be a gratuitous remark: it adds little to the understanding of Saint-Just's ideas, it is not followed by an analysis of the possible links between the Jacobins and modern dictators, and it is not clear why he mentions Hitler and not any other tyrant-ideologue in the last two centuries who believed that citizens belong to the fatherland (such as Mussolini, Mao, Stalin, or Pol Pot). The sentence is conspicuous because Darnton is a fine writer of well-crafted narratives. Is this a case of displaced association, in which the disturbing violent analogy between the Terror and the Holocaust figures as an issue of duties to the nation?

The explanatory value of context, to look more closely at the historiography of the French Revolution, does not contradict the narratives of origins and outcome. Marxists looked at the specific context within which the Revolution unfolded after 1789, but only to interpret it as fundamentally a series of social changes and developments that moved France from feudalism to capitalism. If Marxist historians were not interested in the course of the Revolution in order to find out its meaning – they had already presupposed this meaning before the investigation got under way – they were very interested in the circumstances that led to the Terror. For the historians who supported the Revolution from the left – Alphonse Aulard (1849–1928), Albert Mathiez, Georges Lefebvre (1874–1959), and Albert Soboul, who together held the Sorbonne Chair in the field for close to a century – the circumstances of the Revolution were fundamental to justifying the Terror. They argued that the destructive element of the Revolution was a reaction to the particular threat posed by counterrevolutionaries and the invading foreign armies about to attack Paris after the outbreak of war in April 1792. Aulard, the first historian to be named professor of History of the French Revolution at the Sorbonne and who sympathized with the Third Republic, wrote in *The French Revolution: A Political History* published in 1901:

The Revolutionary Government as a whole is often called the *Government of the Terror*.... But... there was nothing systematic in the creation of the Revolutionary Government. Nearly all the facts... go to prove that this government was not the application of any system or any preconceived idea.... The Revolutionary Government was an expedient of warfare, and it was always given out that it must have come to an end with the war.[5]

Furet launched a frontal assault on the idea of circumstances as an explanation for the Terror, criticizing historians for accepting the revolutionaries' claim that the Terror was a reaction to specific circumstances. Not context produced the Terror, but a deadly fight over political legitimacy:

The theory of "circumstances" transfers historical initiative to the forces hostile to the Revolution; that is the price to be paid for relieving the Revolution of responsibility for the Terror.... The truth is that the Terror was an integral part of Revolutionary ideology... every history of the Revolution must therefore deal not only with the impact of "circumstances" on the successive political crisis but also, and above all, with the manner in which those "circumstances" were planned for, prepared, arranged and used in the symbolic universe of the Revolution and in the various power struggles.[6]

But is it really an option for historians to ignore circumstances? Viewing the Terror of 1793 as directly connected to the Declaration of 1789 is a historical determinism. It rejects the fact that the circumstances of the Revolution changed minds, constrained choices, and opened unimaginable possibilities. It was none other than the ideologue Saint-Just who observed that "the force of circumstances may perhaps lead us toward consequences that we could not have imagined."[7] Maurice Agulhon

observed that those who tie 1789 to 1793 insist excessively on the active
role of ideas in history. One needs to take into account "everything which
was thought... [but also] everything which took place." Circumstances
are made of both ideas and actions: "Circumstances, at bottom, are history itself."[8] Recent scholarship has reinstated a sense of context to the
interpretation of the Terror by questioning the primacy of ideology and
the supposed direct link between 1789 and 1793.[9]

The interpretation of the Terror has followed a dialectic that began
with an evaluation of context as a justification for the Terror, evolved
into a rejection of context in favor of the Revolution's direct ideological
responsibility for the Terror, and has now settled on a view of the Terror
as the outcome of ideas and actions in context. The difference has been
the political valence attached to each interpretive stage. The Marxists
elevated the notion of circumstances to justify, and thus minimize the
importance of, the Terror within a framework of a deterministic interpretation of the Revolution as chiefly a social event. Furet attacked the
notion of circumstances, thus making the Terror inherent to the Revolution, within a framework of an interpretation of the Revolution as
chiefly a political event. The dominant view today is of the Terror as a
product of circumstances but without the political baggage of previous
interpretations. In this sense, the Revolution is over.

In Holocaust historiography, the context of war has been of late a main
interpretive field of vision. The deportation and extermination of the
Jews are now seen as part of overarching Nazi plans to redraw the map
of Europe by enslaving and killing whole groups of people. These plans
were not determined by an all-encompassing blueprint, but were governed
by general racial ideas modified according to local circumstances. This
view has focused on the actions of individual Germans and is therefore
important because for years explanations for the Holocaust have emphasized impersonal forces, such as modernity or the bureaucratization of
killing. Now, finally, enter the German killers.

The most famous rendition of this view is the acclaimed book of Christopher Browning, *Ordinary Men*, that describes the experience of
German soldiers in a genocidal war: "The fundamental problem is to
explain why ordinary men – shaped by a culture that had its own par-
ticularities but was nonetheless within the mainstream of western, Christian, and Enlightenment traditions – under specific circumstances will-
ingly carried out the most extreme genocide in human history."[10] His
answer was that the circumstances of war transformed Germans into

killers much more than did their Nazi experience between 1933 and 1939 or a presumed atavistic anti-Semitism that went back hundreds of years: "[W]artime brutalization, racism, segmentation and routinization of the task [of killing], special selection of the perpetrators, careerism, obedience to orders, deference to authority, ideological indoctrination and conformity" – these were the factors that made the soldiers of Reserve Police Battalion 101 into killers.[11] In particular, scholars have emphasized conditions on the Eastern Front that led to the brutalization of the German army: the scale of the fighting, the climatic conditions, and the clash of ideas between Germans and Russians.[12]

The context of the war has thus been a crucial element in understanding the Holocaust, with June 22, 1941 viewed as ushering in a qualitative change in German policies toward the Jews. The importance of this date is confirmed by the prolonged scholarly debate over the Nazi decision-making process that led to the policy of extermination in the months after the invasion of the Soviet Union: scholars work within this framework by providing more detailed evidence about what happened during this period, without challenging the interpretive framework itself. The reconstruction of the unfolding of the German war of annihilation reminds us that, on a profound level of historical explanation, "context, without which there can be neither meaning nor understanding, is the world," as George Steiner has observed.[13]

But confronted with the explanatory totality of context, historians should pause and turn skeptical. The question is not whether the context of a brutalizing war is important to understanding the Holocaust (of course it is), but in what way and what does it explain.[14] Based on innovative studies from the 1990s we now have a growing body of work on the conditions of the war (especially in the Eastern Front) and its impact on the soldiers.[15] There is no doubt of the "catalytic impact of the war itself."[16] But perpetrator studies of the Holocaust, often exploring in ever-greater detail case studies of the local, ideological, and military context of the extermination, tend to confirm what we know already from other studies.[17]

In terms of method, moreover, in reconstructing the context one describes the circumstances within which something happened, not necessarily why it happened. Neither peer pressure nor wartime brutalization tells us much about sentiments and beliefs that existed before 1939 and that shaped what happened during the war. It is not that the war conditions alone created an exterminatory mindset, but that the pre-1939 years created the conditions that made this context possible to begin with. This is one of the insights provided by Claudia Koonz's *The Nazi Conscience*: "The Final Solution took shape not on the distant eastern front nor as a series of fiats issued after the invasion of the Soviet Union in June 1941. Rather... a genocidal consensus [was formed]... prior to Germany's invasion of Poland in 1939."[18]

Differently put, historians face here the problem of how to use the notion of "context" to ascertain "experience." "Situation" and "context," however extreme they may be, cannot account by themselves for human actions. The way people act and think cannot be extrapolated and subsumed only within the immediate circumstances because habits of mind then become in effect a mere reflection of the surrounding context rather than elements in the making of this context. In this mode of understanding the notion of "experience" thus describes a situation but not something out of which the individual's sense of self emerges. But a "context" does not simply exist out there, and people do not simply exist as passive sounding boards of a "context." A context conditions people's thoughts and actions, but it is also constructed by people as they go along. Assuming that the war context provides an explanation for the Holocaust severs the extermination of the Jews from the Nazi prewar years and from those historical factors that made it possible because it was imaginable.

Nothing enables us to explain the frenzy of killing by starting from the context of the war. It is a problem of culture and of beliefs, and of relationships of the "context" to the past. The Holocaust cannot be reduced to context and circumstances. There is in the Holocaust, to use Furet's observation about the Revolution, "a new type of historical praxis and conscience which are linked to a type of situation but are not defined by it."[19]

The war-context interpretation of the Holocaust has been linked to the argument about the radical shift in the policy toward the Jews that took place after the German invasion of the Soviet Union. According to this view, in contrast to the Nazis' brutal but not exterminatory treatment of Polish Jews, the invasion launched extermination on a large scale by members of the SS and special Task Forces assisted by the German army. But this view has now been revised.

The genocidal policy against the Jews began not in 1941 but in 1939 after the invasion of Poland in Operation Tannenberg.[20] The terror of the German army did not result from the barbarization of war in the Eastern

Front after June 1941; the true radicalization of the German army started right at the beginning of the war. (And in this sense was not a radicalization at all: it was the modus operandi at the outset.) A central group that planned and perpetrated the policies against the Jews was concentrated at the SS Reich Security Main Office (RSHA) headed by Reinhard Heydrich. Its members perceived themselves as revolutionary activists whose aim was to construct a future society based on racial, grand-scale genocidal ideas for the reconstruction of Eastern Europe. Their ideas preceded the war, and their qualitative evolution happened in Poland, once they had the opportunity to test and carry out their social experiments in an environment that lifted legal and moral restraints.[21] The year 1941 did not usher in radically different behavior under circumstances of extreme war conditions, but witnessed an intensification of a genocide begun two years earlier in Poland. Extreme war conditions on the Eastern Front did not result in weakened moral values, but on the contrary, immoral values helped create these extreme war conditions.

The war-context interpretation that focuses on events after June 1941 runs the danger of being closed within itself. Genocides and ethnic cleansings usually take place in the context of war. Under the extreme conditions of war, soldiers cling to what is familiar and what enhances group identity; peer and ideological pressures intensify, partly as a defense mechanism that helps the group maintain its unity. German soldiers were no exception in behaving in these ways. Consequently, focusing on the circumstances under which brutalization occurred may become a psychological model in search of examples. These examples will be found because they exist; they prove that extermination happened within a context of brutal war. But they do not tell us how this context was shaped by soldiers' beliefs formed earlier, thus obscuring what connected this period to the preceding years. The context of war had a context too.

But are we not creating a chain of contexts without end, thus falling into a tautology of origins? I do not think so. Not all contexts are explanatory in the same way. The immediate context is perfectly sufficient to understand why Helmut Kohl won the 1982 German elections or why West Germany and not the magical team of Hungary won the soccer World Cup in 1954. But some historical problems are more complex. By choosing the context within which to understand a given event, historians define the event; the choice, which determines issues of chronology and method, involves an interpretation. Understanding the Holocaust in the context of post-June 1941 war defines the event within chronological boundaries that isolate the Holocaust from what happened before. And by viewing a military event as the cut-off date and military conditions as paramount, this construction of the context overlooks continuities of mentalities and habits of mind that are less visible but no less profound.

The totality and limits of context are illustrated by a distinguished interpretation of the Holocaust that reveals more clearly hidden assumptions, as well as the weaknesses and strengths of using the notion of context as an explanation.

The work of Götz Aly has been groundbreaking in enhancing our understanding of the Holocaust. He called attention to the role of Nazi population experts and their attempt to reorder the ethnic map of Eastern Europe according to racial ideas. The logic of National Socialist policies was driven by plans geared toward change and territorial expansion.[22] In his interpretation Aly emphasized extreme contingency and circumstantial situations. Hitler gave no single order to commit genocide, but this occurred in the context of plans of massive population transfer, economic exploitation, and mass murder. A key group in the project was the technological intelligentsia, including demographers, race and population experts, and others, who were driven by rational considerations and bureaucratic motivations to solve problems of resettlement. Solutions were devised on the local level, in Poland and not in Berlin, which led to deportation that led to annihilation. Aly's work thus places the extermination of Jews within a framework of Nazi plans for racial reorganization, and his work has the merit of pointing out the importance of the early war years, 1939–1941.

A group of historians has significantly added to this picture by arguing that genocide in the Galicia District, Byelorussia, and Lithuania was mainly a result of local initiatives driven by immediate practical considerations. The murder of Byelorussian Jews, it was argued by one scholar, was primarily a result of food supply issues. Bureaucrats in the ministry for agriculture had to look for solutions to the problems of the shortage of food in the Reich and the supply of adequate food to the German army in the Soviet Union. Regional authorities decided to reduce the demand for food by annihilating that part of the Jewish population unable to work.[23] Similarly in the case of Lithuania, the genocide arose within the context of a starvation policy that was "an important, and possibly a decisive, factor" in the decision to exterminate the Jews.[24]

This way of deducing motivations from practical considerations is not without problems. These interpretations explain by using extreme notions of context and contingency. The problem is not the scale of observation, namely, that they explore what happened on the local and regional level as opposed to what happened in Berlin. In fact, this local focus is a virtue of these studies, which illuminate local pressures, constraints, and motivations in the extermination of the Jews. It reminds us of the advantages of micro-history, in which, to recall the assessment of Giovanni Levi, one of the founders of the approach, "phenomena previously considered to be sufficiently described and understood assume completely new meanings by altering the scale of observation."[25]

But the point of micro-history is to provide a more realistic description of human behavior within relatively narrow dimensions as a basis to draw far wider generalizations. The studies mentioned do provide general implications, but in fact, the hegemony of situational events and practical considerations explains significantly less than what was intended. Countries that have problems of food supply, even under emergency situations of war and famine, do not usually solve the problem by killing tens of thousands of possible eaters. Circumstances and practical considerations cannot necessarily tell us why people choose one moral action over another operating under the constraints of normative systems. They cannot provide sufficient answers about how people came to believe that killing thousands is a moral duty or help us understand the interior world of the killers. People are not machines, and their behavior is also determined by freedoms beyond the constraints of a given situation: even if they kill for what they believe are practical considerations, they still need to justify, rationalize, suppress, lie, and redeem their actions.

In terms of argumentation, these studies invert relations of cause and effect. It is not that Germans killed Jews because of specific, contextualized resettlement or food problems. Solving these problems by killing Jews did not cause the belief that the Jews were evil; instead, that solution arose from a system of belief in which Jewish life was deemed worthless, with or without resettlement and food supply problems.

When we consider the Holocaust as a European event, the historian's construction of the war context in the East reveals another explanatory limitation. Circumstances of resettlement and practical problems illuminate the reasons for killing Jews in the East, but they cannot explain why Germans sent to Auschwitz the Jews of Corfu or of the small French village of Izieux, where there were no resettlement or food problems. In Izieu, in the middle of the mountains between Lyon and Chambery in the Loire region, forty-four Jewish children were hiding in a remote house. On April 6, 1944, the Gestapo led by Klaus Barbie came to take the children and seven of their leaders. All were deported to Auschwitz. Only one adult survived, one child was able to escape, and one was released because he was not Jewish. This event shows the premeditated nature of the Final Solution; it had, strictly speaking, no contingent or contextual motives.

"Context stinks," tells the professor to the astounded student who came to seek advice about his dissertation in Bruno Latour's hilarious dialogue, "On the Difficulty of Being an ANT."[26] But why should I deny myself contextual explanations? asks the desperate student. You can keep them, answers the professor, but do not believe they explain anything. If your explanation is good, then by elaborating on more parts of your picture you simply add new elements to the description, and if the explanation is not good, then you are adding something irrelevant. Your task, he tells the student who is by now totally distressed, is to provide a description, for I have never seen a good description in need of an explanation.

The professor thus reaches a conclusion that is not far, in terms of method, from the evaluation advanced earlier with respect to Friedländer's narrative – that descriptions are themselves interpretive. It has implications for our discussion on the narrative and explanatory role of context. I would read Latour's brusque judgment, which is delightful in its counterintuitive chutzpah toward historians' reflexive extolling of context, in the following way. Defining historical context as the interconnected conditions in which something existed or occurred, we can observe that reconstructing a context constitutes the descriptive essence of history, for the portrayal of these interconnected conditions provides a narrative of people in their world. This is the stuff of all historical writing. But this description in itself is not automatically explanatory.

It is a paradox that, although it has become *de rigueur* for historians to begin their studies by observing that they place their topic in a broader context, they then often write their history without bothering to articulate what defines that context. Its interpretive power is regarded as self-explanatory, almost an incantation. There are four points to be made about the context of World War II and the interpretation of the persecution and extermination of the Jews. They are specific to this case, while having broader implications for the role of context in historical reconstruction.

First, there is no such place called context. The context is a result, not simply a cause. Our job is to set the historical context as a relationship among many different threads (political, cultural, economic, and the like) that is both the creation of people's action and at the same time makes a new situation that sets limits on, as well as opens up new possibilities for, these people. If we dig ever deeper into the context of World War II, we shall find in greater detail what happened on the ground, but we shall not be necessarily wiser as to how this "context" came about as a result of beliefs, representations, and conditions that preceded it and made it happen. Only by multiplying the connections of the context of the war with what made it possible in the preceding period can we grasp how this context came about, was perceived, and enabled a certain human action. To paraphrase Wittgenstein who said "a doubt without an end is not even a doubt," a context without an end is not even a context.[27]

Second, by reconstructing the context historians may simply provide a broader picture of what they know already and are setting out to "prove." The historian who sets out to put in broader context the extermination that she views as a result of radicalized racial ideology in a brutalizing war may end up simply providing more information, however multi-faceted it may be, that confirms the initial hypothesis because the context had already been reconstructed interpretively before she began the investigation. That is why many recent studies confirm what we know already, because they operate within a certain dominant idea of what was the context of the Holocaust during the war. Before we leap into reconstructing the context, we should be clear on whether we had not preconceived it in such a way as to merely seek evidence to prove it. Questioning the dominant interpretive framework of the Holocaust is the first step to rethinking how to reconstruct historically the context of the extermination in different ways.

Third, if the persecution and extermination of the Jews are viewed as produced by the military, political, racial ideological conditions of the war – defined as "the context" – we end up excluding cultural elements that shaped these conditions. It is significant that cultural representations that cannot be reduced to Nazi racial ideology are in the main not considered part of the current historiographical picture of the "context" of the war. This is not because ideas are not taken seriously, for Nazi racial ideology is an essential part of this image of the context. It is rather because only certain ideas are taken seriously in a "context" that is defined very specifically.

Fourth, there is no Context with a capital C, but rather contexts. No doubt, the context of the racial war existed, but it was only one part of a larger historical reality, or rather it was one specific context within a multitude of interconnected ones. Historians can never reconstruct *the* context, but only *a* context. I use the term "historical reality" purposefully. For my critique of the way historians trust too easily the notion of context is not a poststructuralist argument that doubts the ability of history to reconstruct the past. On the contrary, I call for more reality in the reconstruction of the past by acknowledging the multiplicity of contexts and of the historical factors that go into reconstructing them.

"There is no virtue, there are only circumstances." This sentence was expressed by Eugene de Rastignac, the fictional contemporary of Adolph Thiers. Thiers was born in 1797, two years before Napoleon's coup of Eighteenth Brumaire ended the Revolution. He defeated the Paris Commune, perhaps the last revolutionary gasp of 1789–1799, and had no love for the Revolution: circumstances, opportunism, making the best of evolving conditions were his beliefs. And this is also the danger for the historian – that in venerating circumstances we shall forget what human beings bring with them when they act in them: virtue and the lack thereof.[28]

Ultimately, a context that explains must close the gap between human intentions and consequences. This is why Furet's explanation of the Terror by obliterating circumstances in favor of an ongoing march of a discursive ideology is unconvincing. The context of the revolutionary war, the internal strife between Jacobins and Girondins, and the fear of counterrevolution makes much more historical sense as an explanation for the Terror because – as an argument – it is sensitive to the gap between liberal intentions in the 1789 Declaration of the Rights of Man and the Citizen and the ensuing dictatorial consequences, and therefore to the unfolding circumstances that led from one to the other.

In Holocaust historiography, the problem with privileging the context of the war in 1941–1945 is that it creates too wide a gap between anti-Semitic intentions in 1933–1941 and the radical consequence of total extermination. This interpretive gap should be closed, without arriving at an argument about a one-directional, inevitable road to the Holocaust, while taking into account that intentions existed right from 1933 to create a Germany without Jews, that the language of extermination was one of the available rhetorics to solve the "Jewish problem," and that a genocide had taken place in 1939–1941.[29]

The Third Reich did not wait for the context of a world war against the Soviet Union and the United States to come to a belief that Jews had no right to live. The more we know about the Third Reich, the less convincing remains an interpretation that views the Holocaust through a lens of extreme contextualization of war conditions. The Nazi regime enjoyed widening legitimacy after 1933, as the economic recovery, its foreign policy successes, and internal stability grew. Hitler was largely successful in retaining the backing of most Germans well into the war years. Nazi terror alone can explain neither how the Third Reich came into being nor its staying power. The consensus around Hitler was not uniform, but most Germans supported the repression and persecution of outcast groups.[30] Far from being hidden, the terror characteristic of Nazi Germany was openly propagated before the war; there was continual public dissemination of information about the punitive, repressive side of the regime. Before and during the war, as recent scholarship has abundantly shown, a wide circle of collaborators participated in the thinking about and ultimately realization of the extermination of Jews, Russian prisoners of war, mentally ill patients, and other victims: this wide circle included physicians, psychologists, lawyers, academicians, various race experts, geographers, officials in local, regional, and national administrative offices, policemen, soldiers, and employees of the security services. The expanding circle of collaborators in the implementation of the prewar persecution of the Jews shows the limits of an interpretation that focuses on the war because it does not account for the culture and imagination that produced it.

The nexus between circumstances and imagination is important. In the case of the Terror, the circumstances that brought it into being were a commingling of real and imaginary threats. There were the real threats of war and foreign armies poised to crush the Revolution, as well as of domestic rebellion at the Vendée and counterrevolutionary activity by nobles and the king. And there were imaginary threats, which exaggerated the perceived danger of counterrevolution and of conflicts between revolutionaries themselves.[31]

In the case of the Holocaust, the mix of real and imaginary threats was not quite the same. German perpetrators faced threats that were part of war, but none of them came from Jews (Jewish partisans fought against the Nazis years after the persecution had began; their actions cannot be seen as a result of the Nazi policies against the Jews). The German perception of Jewish threat was wholly imaginary: Jews had no political party or unified leader, they neither rebelled nor fought as a unified force, and they possessed no army. Even if Germans assumed that Jewish men controlled the world economy and/or international communism, Jewish children certainly did not. The revolutionaries' sense of angst was based on a kernel of reality, but the Nazi idea of the Jews was a matter of the imagination. Here, ultimately, is the limit of the interpretation that focuses on the context of war: this interpretation is essential, there is no understanding of the Holocaust without it, but it is not sufficient because it tells us little about the cultural making and receiving of the phantasmagoric idea of Jewish threat.

6

Contingency, the Essence of History

"The new semester does not begin until May 7.... But why worry about what happens after May 7? Is it so certain that we shall still have the same government on May 7? The comparison with the Jacobins is popular just now. Why should the German Jacobins last longer than the French ones?" March 19, 1934

"I am reading the first few pages of the Tocqueville [*The Ancien Regime and the French Revolution*], which Frau Schaps gave me in 1924. No one, not even the most significant and knowledgeable contemporaries, anticipated the course of Revolution. Every page of the book surprises me with analogies to the present." September 29, 1939

"Once I would have said: I do not judge as a Jew.... Now: Yes, I judge as a Jew ... because it is central to the whole structure, to the whole character of National Socialism and is uncharacteristic of everything else." April 16, 1941

Victor Klemperer[1]

Were the Terror and the Holocaust inevitable parts of the French Revolution and National Socialism? Anyone with a background in historical understanding would immediately reject inevitability and embrace contingency. The notion of contingency has become a mainstay of historical analysis. The disciplinary demands "Always contextualize!" and "Always historicize!" are joined by "Reject inevitability!" It follows, therefore, that to learn more about the role of contingency in historical explanation we should take its importance as a point of departure.

The predicament for the historian is to show the Revolution and the Holocaust as, to use Chartier's words written about 1789, "not pure accidents produced by chance circumstances nor absolute necessities whose

moment and modalities were logically inscribed in their very causes."[2]
It is not an easy task. Post-1945 West German historians such as Meinecke and Ritter explained away Nazism as a chance circumstance that
said nothing significant about German culture and society. Aulard saw
the Terror in much the same way. Others opted to explain the Terror
and the Holocaust as an absolute necessity. Historians had a field day
with Goldhagen's interpretation – an easy target, uncomplicated in its
argument for centuries-old sentiment of "exterminatory anti-Semitism"
among all "willing executioners." The classic intentionalist view of the
Holocaust had strong deterministic elements, as did the classic functionalist school of impersonal dynamic propelled by cumulative radicalization
inherent within the Nazi system of government. The Marxist view of the
French Revolution is a *locus classicus* of historical determinism: since the
Revolution fulfilled its historical destiny of ushering in a bourgeois mode
of production, there was nothing more to explain, and no human actions
or follies could alter its predetermined course.

The notion of contingency is as elusive as it is desired. The relentless
assault of the Nazi state and society against the defenseless Jews right from
the beginning of the Third Reich makes the task of capturing contingency
most difficult for historians of the period. Is it possible at all to write an
unscripted narrative of the Holocaust given the predominant agency of
the Nazis in moving events forward?

In current Holocaust historiography, the element of contingency is captured within a dominant narrative of National Socialist anti-Semitic policy as a gradually radicalizing process in search of a solution to the
"Jewish Question." According to this narrative, there was no predetermined plan to exterminate the Jews and no innate exterminationist
anti-Semitism in German culture.[3] The relationships between the anti-
Semitism of the regime and ordinary Germans were complex. The image
of the regime as controlling the German population by violence and coercion is no longer tenable. Instead, it is becoming clear that large sections of
the German population supported the regime, and even among segments
of society that rejected the Nazis before 1933 disapproval changed into
tacit approval after the regime's extraordinary economic, foreign policy,
and military successes.

The regime's Jewish policy was not popular among large segments
of the population, so the narrative goes. But neither was it a subject of
concern; in comparison to Hitler's successes, these excesses were excus-
able. The rabid anti-Semitism of the regime thus linked with the passive

anti-Semitism that was common in German society and that was not committed to a specific goal or solution, certainly not to extermination. And yet, for all its criticism of excesses, the public was ready to accept the radical program of the Nazis when it was provided legally by the government in a context of growing legitimacy of the regime. More than anything else, it was the indifference and readiness to accept the persecution of the Jews and to ignore it as unimportant that characterized the attitude of ordinary Germans.

The radicalization of anti-Jewish policy was a result of various factors, according to this narrative. On the most immediate level, the very daily experience of persecuting the Jews – the boycotts, the discrimination in school, at work, on the bus, and near the ice cream parlor – led to more radical behavior and the removal of moral inhibitions. Fundamental to moving the process forward was the role of the true believers, a group of Nazi ideologues who shared extreme anti-Semitic views. Mostly born in the decade before 1914, university educated, and of middle and upper class origins, they held leadership positions in Heydrich's Reich Security Main Office and, after the beginning of the war, could be found in the police forces and the special Task Forces that initiated the deportations and killing of the Jews. They shared an ideological conviction that a racial reconstitution of German society was vital to the future of the nation.[4]

During the war, the Nazis did not have a predetermined goal to annihilate the Jews; at every stage of the way they found themselves doing something that a year ago, or even a month ago, would have been unimaginable. The removal of inhibitions was a process. Ulrich Herbert articulated the scholarly consensus of this narrative:

The necessary precondition for such developments was not the formulation, sooner or later, of an intention to murder all Jews. What was required was rather a framework of ideological justification that ruled out a humane solution in every case and was explicitly prepared to brush aside all opposing points of view whether pragmatic, political, or ideological in nature. It is precisely when we recognize the process that set the genocide in motion as one of cumulative radicalization that the issue of the ideological justification and motivation of the perpetrators becomes especially acute, because it is not the pursuit of a predetermined goal that needs explaining but rather the continuous, persistent readiness repeatedly to represent one's actions to others and to oneself as "harsh, but unavoidable" given the ostensibly urgent circumstances.[5]

This is a worthy narrative. It combines the functionalist view of the process of cumulative radicalization of the Nazi regime with the intentionalist view of the primacy of anti-Jewish ideas among leaders and party followers.[6] It replaces the radicalization of impersonal administrative forces in the classic functionalist view with the radicalization of personal ideological ideas. It explains by commingling a basic ideological commitment with the impact of war circumstances. It refuses to read the Holocaust backward by emphasizing change over time in the policy against the Jews. In short, by combining ideology and context, it proposes a sensible way out of the predicament of accounting for contingency.

But does it capture a sense of contingency? The notion of contingency is often represented in narratives of the Holocaust by the idea of a dynamic process of radicalization. The assumption is that by describing a process that is dynamic we capture possibilities and unpredictability. But radicalization and contingency are not interchangeable, and the notion of radicalization in itself does not safeguard against the danger of tautology. Let us think about this problem by associating it with the work of Furet, who ascribed important meaning to the radicalization of the revolutionary process: "Each successive political group [the Girondins, Jacobins, etc.] pursued the same objective: to radicalize the Revolution, by making it consistent with its discourse [of pure democracy].... The Terror... [was] inherent in the ever-escalating rhetoric of the various groups competing for the exclusive right to embody the democratic principle."[7] For Furet, the revolutionary dynamic of the Terror was self-propelled, indifferent to the vicissitudes of political changes and human action. The "ever-escalating dialectic of rhetoric" has quite the same impact on his narrative of the Revolution as the "radicalized dynamic process of racial ideology" has on the narrative of the Holocaust: it is not a guarantee against a narrative of inevitability, but in fact produces it.

Indeed, in current Holocaust narratives the function of the idea of radicalization is often rhetorical, namely, it moves the story forward. Historians thus "finesse a difficult question of contingency with their most powerful tool: narrative," as Edward Ayers, the historian of the American South, observed in a different context.[8] No doubt there was a process of radicalization in the making of the Holocaust, and narratives pay attention to changes in Nazi policies and Germans' actions. But the danger is that radicalization produces a narrative, if unintentionally, of the inexorable spiral ahead of ideology and war conditions: necessarily forward, toward ever-extreme conditions and states of mind. The notion of radicalization describes a condition and in itself explains little. It should not obscure the fact that it was not a cause, but a result; radicalization did not emerge automatically but was deliberately brought into being. Radicalization can well presuppose a built-in consistency, an unstated assumption that there is some sort of essence that consistently unfolds more fully. The challenge for the historian is to capture not "radicalization," but a sense of the present, at any given time between 1933 and 1945, that could not anticipate the future. This sense was poignantly captured by Klemperer at the outset of this chapter: "I am reading the first few pages of the Tocqueville.... No one, not even the most significant and knowledgeable contemporaries, anticipated the course of Revolution. Every page of the book surprises me with analogies to the present."

Why is it so difficult to tell a story of the Holocaust made up of many different possible outcomes, a story in which many different narratives interacted, while one became a historical reality? Why do narratives of the Holocaust often read, against the intentions of scholars, as a self-propelled process that leads inexorably to extermination? One reason emerges when we think of the French Revolution.

The Revolution was a drama with a range of independent, forceful historical actors who vied for power and influence, an event with several active sides, each of which could change the course of history. Opposite the revolutionaries were the powerful forces of counterrevolution: the king, the aristocracy, and European rulers who launched wars to crush the Revolution. The first proposal to take violent action came from the counterrevolutionaries in July 1789 as they convinced Louis XVI to launch a coup d'état against reforms. In addition, various revolutionary groups – Robespierre's Jacobins, Danton's Girondins, Babeuf's Society of Equals, and others – exercised power on the course of events. All this adds up to a story dependent on many events and actions that coalesced in a particular way and into a particular result. Small changes by one of these groups could have produced a different result: with so many different historical actors who could influence the events, contingency is waiting to be recovered.

What if the nobility agreed in 1788–1789 to a compromise on the ways to solve the financial crisis of the state? If the Assembly of Notables did not push to convene, for the first time since 1614, the Estates-General, thus introducing a national representative assembly into the absolute monarchy? Or if they had agreed, as suggested by a group of mostly Parisian noblemen, to change the voting procedure of the Estates-General, which was based on one vote for each of the separate orders, representing the clergy, nobility, and everybody else, which put everyone else at a fundamental disadvantage? What if Louis and his family were not stopped in

Varennes, but succeeded in crossing the border and reaching the Austrian army?[9] Given the wave of unity among otherwise factionalized revolutionaries in Paris, might a republic have been declared after Varennes and the Terror avoided? What if the king had refused the pressure of the counterrevolutionaries, remained in Paris, and became a model citizen-king?

Multitudes of small events coalesced to produce the Holocaust as well, but in one fundamental respect it was very different from the Revolution. It was an event that pitted one side that was all mighty and had all the initiative against another that was powerless to influence events in any crucial way that could have changed their course. Every history of any event is one of reciprocal relationships and negotiations, and the history of the Holocaust is of course one of perpetrators and victims; the Jews must be made part of this history. But relationships of power tilted dramatically in favor of the Nazis. Jews alone could not change their fate once the Nazis decided to drive them out of Germany, persecute them, and ultimately exterminate them. With no state, army, or overall organization the Jews could do little against the onslaught. To capture the contingency of the persecution and extermination of the Jews the historian thus has less elements to consider because there were few powerful actors who could have changed the course of events.

The reactions within Germany with respect to policies against the Jews are instructive. Unlike the Revolution, which turned against its own sons, the persecution and extermination of the Jews did not produce political and moral opposition or anything close to internecine wars or inner Terror against factions opposing either of the anti-Jewish stages. Germans accepted the Nazi language about the Jews after the Nazi seizure of power. No organized groups of apostates in German society, or the churches, or the army opposed the anti-Jewish measures. Neither was there serious opposition in friendly or occupied European countries. Opposition to the persecution and extermination simply did not play an important part in the history of the relentless Nazi machine that rolled over the Jews.

To be sure, the Holocaust as a contingent event was determined by a host of factors such as the progression of the war, the Allies' decision not to bomb Auschwitz, the public stance of the Pope, and organizational struggles within the Nazi state. Local conditions in specific countries were also fundamental, as in the case of Bulgaria's King Boris who, although he was Hitler's ally, surrendered to public pressure and refused to hand over "his" Jews to the Nazis: Bulgarian Jews were all saved.[10] Everyday conditions on the ground determined life and death: a good neighbor or a good stranger could save a life. But the fundamental story was that which made these historical situations possible to begin with: the actions of the Nazis.

The radicalization narrative does capture contingency, but it is a particular contingency. In historical narratives, contingency is bounded by the historian's choice of the structures within which possibilities of action might develop. These structures – they can be economic and political, they can depend on gender, the diplomatic balance of power, or on social relations – each explain some things and conceal others. They predetermine the conditions within which historians consider possibilities and contingency. Some narratives capture contingency better than others, depending on the framework within which they let historical actors imagine and realize their aims.

Marxist historians of the Revolution, for example, did study social and economic choices of revolutionaries, but they did so within an overall schema of the Revolution as bourgeois in nature; revolutionaries' possibilities thus existed within these limitations. Functionalist historians of the Holocaust did study Nazi anti-Jewish policy choices and changes, but they did it within the overall schema of the extermination as an impersonal dynamic of cumulative bureaucratic process. Goldhagen, a representative of the intentionalist school, did analyze the choices perpetrators made, but he did it within the overall schema of willing executioners endowed with exterminatory anti-Semitism. In these examples, there is one key condition within which historical actors could act, think, and be interpreted.

The narrative of the Holocaust as a dynamic process of radicalization captures a contingency framed by racial ideology and conditions of war. It tells us about ideological decisions, choices, and possibilities with regard to solving the Jewish question (such as the option of emigration between 1933–1939, the plan in 1940–1941 to concentrate the Jews in a Lublin reservation, or total extermination) that Nazi institutions and individuals spiraled to an extreme. It captures in detail the decision-making process between June 22, 1941 and the Wannsee Conference that led to the Final Solution.[11] But can we craft different narratives of contingency beyond the one underscored by radicalized racial ideology?

Capturing historical contingency accounts for the combination of two elements: the different possible developments and the sense of open-endedness and malleability of human action and thought inherent in any historical situation, on the one hand, and the constraints imposed by the period on these possibilities, on the other. Edward Ayers describes it as the task of capturing "a sense of contingency and possibility even within powerful structures."[12] From this perspective, I would like to suggest, Nazism was a work in progress set to build a German world without Jews.

Nazism as a racial civilization was not a given reality but a work in progress, "a model," to use Eugen Weber's words on the making of the French nation after 1871, "of something at once to be built and to be treated for political reasons as already in existence."[13] The search for Nazi ways of life permeated the revolutionary upheaval in post-1933 German society. From the beginning, the Third Reich was meant to be a racial society, but what kind of racial society was still to be determined. The general racial principle comprised many possible developments. The Nazis had few clear ideas of how exactly to build the racial society and what precisely it meant. They did not have a body of great books to instruct them, no "Communist Manifesto" or Marx and Engels to show the road ahead. They made themselves up as they went along. Indeed, on the race issue, the racial experts of the regime knew better than anyone else how flimsy the category of race was.[14] Peter Fritzsche captured the essence of this condition when he talked about the process of "becoming" and of "conversion" that made individuals into a "race minded German...., [as] they grappled with questions about the importance of fitting in, the convenience of going along, and the responsibilities the individual owed to the collective."[15] The overriding sentiment among Germans in the tumultuous years of 1933–1945 was that the story of the Third Reich was uncertain about how it would evolve and where it would lead to.

But an open-ended narrative of the search for Nazi ways of life was bounded by the Nazi project of a Germany without Jews: this project determined the Nazis' intentions and the policy of the German state from January 30, 1933 onward. Contingency – the different opinions and sentiments about the project, its complexity, probability, and uncertainty – made sense only within this powerful structure. Humane solutions (to a Jewish "problem" invented by the Nazis to begin with) were immediately cast aside.

I propose to think of this problem through the metaphor of the whole and its part. Let us think by association about the construction of the idea of nationhood. A nation is a work in progress in which different ideas about its identity coexist in relationships of opposition, disagreement, and conflict, and yet, there exists a national whole that is greater than the sum of its parts. The idea of a Germany without Jews worked much the same way. Some supported it, some opposed it, some were left indifferent, but it was and remained a goal of the leadership of the Third Reich from the beginning, a whole larger than the sum of Germans' views about the Jews.

Crafting a narrative in which the persecution and extermination of the Jews in the Third Reich could have unfolded differently gives meaning to the earlier claim that it is not Auschwitz that stands at the center of the historian's study of Nazi anti-Semitism, but rather the making of a German world without Jews. One core of this narrative focuses on the making of a moral community by shifting attention from Nazi policies and ideology to Germans' values and sensibilities, to acculturation and sociability that made sense of the idea of a Germany without Jews. We find offensive the Nazi claim to provide a better life for Germans and to found a racial civilization. But these claims and ideals motivated Germans, making them dream, plan the future, and kill. We cannot dismiss them just because they were morally wrong, but instead should put them at the center of our story. This perspective shifts our attention from the contingency of the decision-making process about the Final Solution in the fall and winter of 1941–1942, about which we have substantial knowledge, to the contingency of the prewar years when these genocidal possibilities were imagined.[16] It is in this respect that a narrative of Germany without Jews does not require the notion of radicalization to move the story forward, because the assumption is not about the story's final destination (that is, Auschwitz), but about its starting point in January 30, 1933, when the German state adopted its anti-Jewish policy.

With few adjustments and contingent changes, the history of the total extermination of the Jews in 1941–1945 could have ended differently. For the total extermination, as it transpired in Auschwitz, was an improbable event, many small currents, events, opportunities, and chances had to happen for this unfolding to take place. Small changes in what happened could have brought a different outcome. Stephen Jay Gould explains in his popular book *Wonderful Life* the course of evolution by associating it with the course of human history. Both are based on contingency, "the central principle of all history": they are dependent on "an unpredictable sequence of antecedent states, where any major change in any step of the sequence would have altered the final result ... but wind the tape of history back ... let it run again with just a few small and judicious changes (plus their cascade of consequences), and a different outcome, including the opposite resolution, might have occurred with equal relentlessness past a certain point."[17]

This is true about the way the extermination happened between 1941 and 1945. But it is not quite true about the idea of a Germany without Jews, which had been in the making since 1933. Jews had already lost their right to live before 1941. In this respect, Auschwitz was contingent on the unfolding of the war, but it could become a reality only because a world without Jews had been already imagined before the war. In a Europe dominated by the Nazis the Jews would have withered away one way or another.

The persecution and extermination of the Jews came in spurts and outbursts interspersed between periods of balance of forces. Persecution and extermination did not come gradually, like a gathering storm, nor did it follow a steady, progressive escalation or a lengthy, gradual process of radicalization. It came in a series of earthquakes interspersed with periods of quiet. Each earthquake opened up unprecedented and unpredictable new possibilities of development and of thinking, while being nonetheless interrelated to the past. History is (at times, although not always, because there is no one way to describe History) a balanced ensemble of human forces that is interrupted by abrupt tremors, which open up, but give no indication of, the unanticipated violence, imagination, and future that lie ahead. People do things they could not even imagine doing, they change their mind overnight, they don new beliefs and enter a "threshold of revelation" that they themselves had ridiculed a fortnight ago, but all these actions are still linked to existing mentalities and imagination.[18] Gould terms the process of history interspersed with radical moments "punctuated equilibrium."[19] I use the term as a metaphor for historical change and obviously not as a literal description of human affairs in the past, which risks letting determinism in through the back door.

Four moments punctuated the equilibrium of the Third Reich with respect to the Jews. The first was state policy and public support for the total removal of Jews from German life in the early years of National Socialism. Historians, knowing with hindsight the end of the story, often interpret 1933 as the beginning of a gradual process of discrimination and prosecution. In fact, it was more like an avalanche. The Third Reich began not with a slow increase in violence against Jews, but with a massive, explosive attack on their civil, legal, and human condition in precisely the places of everydayness, where one thinks he or she is most secure, be it the bus, the home, the workplace, or the body. The idea of negating civil liberties to Jews and limiting their (perceived) role in society and culture received deep public support from all walks of life across Germany. It was accompanied by callous everyday behavior and acts of violence, whose message was to deny Jews companionship in the national community they had considered theirs. The revolutionary meaning of this policy was to repeal the emancipation laws and the integration of Jews into German society that had been on course since the Enlightenment. It was the first state-organized plan in centuries to expel Jews from a European country.

Betty Scholem wrote on April 18, 1933 to her son Gershom in Jerusalem: "A small event: The Zernsdorf bus normally stops on our street *before* the bus stop, so we don't have to walk so far. This time, someone called out to the driver as he lowered the steps for us: 'So, for this pack of Jews you're making an extra stop!!' Now do you understand why I've been getting migraines?"[20] An angry crowd broke into jail and lynched a young Jew who shot an SS man in a fight during the boycott of Jewish businesses in Kiel on April 1, 1933. A small pogrom took place on Palm Sunday 1934 in Gunzenhausen in central Franconia, when inhabitants entered the homes of their Jewish neighbors, dragging more than thirty Jews to jail; later reports stated that one Jew was found dead and another committed suicide by driving a knife into his heart. In 1935 the town of Harpstedt refused to sell food to the three local Jewish families, who therefore needed to travel to Bremen to get their daily bread.[21]

The persecution of the Jews in the early years of the Third Reich was tied up with an anti-Marxist and antiliberal vision of modernity shared by many Germans and Nazis. This vision was not antimodern, but rather proposed a different modernity built on the ruins of communism, liberal democracy, and Jewish influences. If it had any clear delineation in those early years of the Reich, it proposed a united national community devoid of class and party political strife and of aristocratic and big-wig privileges and enjoying the benefits of technology, communication, and modern science in the service of the people; a national will embedded in a charismatic leader to regain Germany's leading position in Europe; and support for a form of representational art. But it is important to capture the sense of the immediate post–seizure-of-power moment: Germans then did not think of war, racial civilization, or genocides. Images of the future were nebulous, and no one had a clear idea of what the racial state would mean, if anything at all. Instead, what concerned the Nazis and their supporters was the present, namely, overcoming the recent decline of Germany by demolishing all that Weimar stood for. They pinned their hopes on a transformation in current politics, culture, and identity, and the Jews were at the center of this transformation as the originators of (these or those) pernicious elements that had to be eliminated to redeem Germany.

For it was the Jews who represented the overall meaning of the Nazi revolution, the crushing of one modernity and the making of another, because only they represented in the minds of the Nazis and other Germans at one and the same time different and often opposing enemies: Marxism and liberalism, democracy and Bolshevism, communism and cubism (not quite the artistic style for social realists). They represented the whole that was bigger than the sum of its parts. Of course, not all Germans and Nazis linked Jews to all these attributes. But that is precisely the point: the Jew symbolized different enemies of a German regeneration to different people. The power of the symbol of the Jew was precisely that it could mean different things, while still providing a common denominator of redeeming Germany from its present decline.

In terms of contingency, the greatest possibilities for changing the policy of Germany toward Jews presented themselves in the early months and years of the Nazi regime. For change to occur, the German elites had to play a decisive role. But in the crucial days of the boycott of Jewish businesses on April 1, 1933, no bishop, synod, church dignitary, or organization made any public declaration in support of the Jews. No intellectual and scholar (with few exceptions), or academic body publicly condemned the dismissal of Jewish professors and students, the national burning of books in May 1933, and the targeting of a defenseless minority. Wide sections of the population supported the persecution of the Jews. Although many others opposed it, the project to rid German society of Jews moved forward unabated and became a way of life.

The second moment of punctuated equilibrium happened on Kristallnacht, the Night of Broken Glass on November 9, 1938, which demonstrated that for the Nazis the enemy was not simply the Jews – these had already been removed from German culture, economy, and society beginning in 1933 – but Judaism. On that night, 1,400 synagogues were set on fire in the Reich. And there was more to it. In Hindenburg (Upper Silesia) SS men played soccer with the Torah scroll in the synagogue's courtyard, laughing that "we are stronger than your Jehovah"; a seven year-old girl and an eleven-year-old boy were paraded in Dinslaken (North-Rhine Westphalia) with a cord tied around their necks; the "Aryan" school director in Zeven (Lower Saxony) ordered his students to watch a synagogue set ablaze, and all were photographed at the spectacle; the Jews in Regensburg were forced to parade through the town holding a sign "Exodus of the Jews" (*Auszug der Juden*), while at the synagogue Dr. Flehinger, a community leader, was ordered to read aloud passages from Hitler's *My Struggle* (*Mein Kampf*), after which Jews who needed to relieve themselves were forced to do so against the synagogue walls; and all Jewish men in Baden-Baden were forced to march through the streets to the synagogue holding a sign reading "God does not forgive us."[22]

Why did the Nazis, set on constructing a *racial* civilization, burn the synagogues, which are *holy, religious* symbols? This is a good question to pose in a historiography that sees racial motivations behind every Nazi action. In these acts the Nazis perceived historic Judaism as soiling the new Germany. No trace of Jewish past existence in Germany was to survive, and all across Germany synagogues, Jewish community centers, and Jewish cemeteries were completely erased. The anti-Jewish actions of 1933–1938 were an outcome of the political constitution of the Reich and were aimed at removing Jews from German life and, via immigration, from German territory. But in 1938 these ideas had become articles of faith in German society; they surprised no one and were accepted (with various degrees of conviction) almost everywhere. Jewish modernity, with its elements of Bolshevism, democracy, and a host of other attributes, had been defeated, making space for Nazi modernity, while Jews had been leaving in great numbers since 1933. At any moment the Nazi state could have devised additional means to speed up their departure. The meaning of Kristallnacht was not about pushing more Jews to leave, but about exorcising – physically, emotionally, and culturally – any presence of something Jewish, past and present, from German life.

Herr Marks, a Jewish owner of a butcher shop, was arrested on Kristallnacht. "The SA men were laughing at Frau Marks who stood in front of her smashed plate-glass window [with] both hands raised in bewildered despair. 'Why are you people doing this to us?' She wailed at the circle of silent faces in the windows, her lifelong neighbors. 'What have we ever done to you?'"[23] Kristallnacht was not about Jews as individuals, but about Judaism. That is the answer to Frau Marks's question. She and her husband did nothing to the Nazis. They were persecuted not because of anything they did, but because of what they symbolized in the imagination.

From this perspective, the range of possible Nazi policies toward the Jews began to narrow because burning the synagogues was not targeted at Jews as liberals, Bolsheviks, or potential emigrants from the Reich, but instead at Jews as possessors of an inherent quality that contaminated

German identity, history, and life. This belief still left open some possible policies toward the Jews in case war broke out, but not that many.

The third moment of punctuated equilibrium followed the outbreak of the war. This period is important for evaluation of the notion of contingency, because it is often simply seen as a time of transition from prewar persecution to post-June 1941 total extermination. Between 1939 and June 1941, the Nazis devised several plans to solve the "Jewish problem." Already on September 21, 1939, Heydrich, by now chief of the RSHA, ordered the commanders of the Task Forces to concentrate all of Poland's Jews in larger cities, "as first prerequisite for the final objective" that should be kept secret. By "final objective" he probably meant the deportation of the Jewish population from the various Polish regions and their concentration in a reservation near the city of Lublin.[24] Shortly thereafter the plan was not that secret anymore, showing how fast moral mental barriers fell. A few days later, on September 27, Heydrich mentioned in a conference of the RSHA another idea, approved by Hitler, namely, to expel all Jews over the demarcation line to the Soviet Union.[25] Theodor Schieder, the Königsberg historian, proposed a different creative plan. In a memorandum submitted to Himmler, he suggested increased German settlement in Polish areas, the expulsion of Jews from German cities, and, overall, a "total de-Judaization of remaining Poland" with the aim of sending the entire Jewish population overseas.[26] (He was later to become a key historian in postwar West Germany). The next plan picked up on this original idea. After the fall of France in May 1940, it was suggested that all European Jews be sent to Madagascar, which fell to German hands as part of the French Empire. Hitler talked about it, and the RSHA wrote memos to that effect. Hans Frank, the Governor-General of occupied Poland, was elated because the last thing he wanted was to have the Jews dropped in his Lublin backyard. We shall ship them, he described on July 12, 1940, to an exceedingly amused crowd in Lublin, "piece by piece, man by man, woman by woman, girl by girl."[27] And when the plans for invading the Soviet Union were in full swing, Himmler raised the idea of expelling the Jews to Siberia after the victory.

Some scholars view these plans as evidence of contingency in a period of Nazi experimentation to find solutions for the "Jewish problem"; these plans show, so the argument runs, the radicalization of thinking from September 1939 to June 1941 when the Nazis still had no blueprint for the extermination of the Jews. There are elements to recommend in this view, such as the emphasis on contingency and on the lack of a clear-cut plan, but it also gets some things wrong. It is not sufficient to argue that the Nazis did not have a clear idea of Jewish total extermination in 1940. The question is, Which idea (as opposed to an administrative plan) did they have? Which options for treating the Jews did the Nazis really view as possible, and what were the bounded structures within which contingency made sense to them? Furthermore, to argue that this period of persecution was one of experimentation implicitly assumes that the next period of extermination was not. This argument is based on the historian's hindsight knowledge of the Final Solution, which contemporaries did not have at the time. In fact, every period is experimental in its own particular way. The Final Solution was an experiment in annihilating a whole people that the Nazis undertook on the way to founding a racial civilization and that they would have probably implemented later with respect to other peoples. The months from September 1939 to June 1941, then, were not simply an antechamber to the period that followed. The Nazis made sense of their new anti-Jewish actions based on their experiences and imagination that had been recently created in the Third Reich.

From this perspective, the various Nazi plans seem to represent not a process of radicalization but instead, as one historian noted, of "maturation."[28] All these plans assumed that Jews did not deserve to live: contingent factors – such as the development of the war, the international situation, public opinion, or the plan to settle Germans in Poland – operated within this framework. In the historical discipline the notion of contingency evokes agency, possibilities, and a potential for change, all of which often implicitly carry positive connotations, and so it may be difficult to acknowledge that in certain historical cases contingency is extremely constraining and its potential is all dark. These plans are proof of contingency insofar as we interpret them as different expressions of the will to destroy Judaism by forces of nature instead of by guns and gas.[29] The essence of all these plans was the expectation that the Jews would perish by the combined measures of forced migration, starvation, overcrowding, disease, hard labor, lack of sustainable economic development, and sheer violence, be it in Lublin, Madagascar, or somewhere beyond the Urals. In the meantime, the regime continued officially also to promote emigration. Holding onto various policies at the same time was not contradictory. In any event, no Nazi seriously thought that emigration to Madagascar was intended to secure Jewish prosperity. The Nazis wanted the Jews to emigrate so they could die out far from their sight. The territorial solution was always a fiction, a Nazi metaphor to get rid of the Jews.

This fiction was understood by Germans and Jews. In a letter to a friend Eduard Koenekamp recorded his impressions after a visit to several Jewish quarters in Poland in 1939 as a member of the Stuttgart Institute for Foreign Countries (*Auslandsinstitut*):

The extermination of this subhumanity would be in the interest of the whole world. However, such extermination is one of the most difficult problems. Shooting would not suffice. Also one cannot allow the shooting of women and children. Here and there one expects losses during deportations.... All agencies which deal with the Jewish Question are aware of the insufficiency of all these measures. A solution of this complicated problem has not been found.[30]

Koenekamp was not perturbed by his call to exterminate the Jews but by how to reconcile this action with his own sense of moral self. It was fine to exterminate, he seemed to be telling himself, but we should find a way to do it that would not offend our sensibilities.

The Nazi policies toward the Jews reflected the idea that the Jews were a people that sooner or later would disappear. All over Poland, Jews were isolated from the rest of the population, forced out of their homes into designated urban areas called ghettos. Their property was seized and disposed of as the Germans saw fit; some Jews were made to work for the German war economy. Between 1939 and 1941, during this "mild" phase of anti-Jewish policies (compared to the systematic killing after June 1941), more than a half-million Polish Jews died in ghettos and labor camps. Many starved to death, many died of diseases, and others were shot. A visitor to the Warsaw ghetto described the conditions: "[O]n the streets children are crying in vain, children who are dying of hunger. They howl, beg, sing, moan, shiver with cold, without underwear, without clothing, without shoes, in rags, sacks... emaciated skeletons, children swollen with hunger, disfigured, half conscious, already complete grown up at the age of five, gloomy and weary of life."[31]

The creation of the sealed ghettos was a key to understanding the Nazi mentality of the period. The sealed ghettos' primary psychological meaning pointed beyond an experimentation measure or a stage in a process of radicalization. Rather, they manifested a state of mind that envisioned a German world made free of Jews not by killing them outright but by setting an undefined expiration date on their existence. This was radical enough. The Lodz ghetto was established in April 1940, and on May 1 the Germans hermetically sealed the ghetto and its 163,000 inhabitants from the world. Warsaw Jews were also ordered to move and live in one part of town. On November 16, 1940, the Warsaw ghetto was sealed. Three days later, Emmanuel Ringelblum, the historian who established the Oneg Shabat archive of the Warsaw ghetto, wrote in his diary, "A wave of evil rolled over the whole city, as if in response to a nod from above."[32] This action separated 338,000 Jews from the world and crammed one-third of the city's inhabitants into 2.4 percent of its territory. In early 1941 the population swelled to some 445,000 people as a result of the influx of Jews from surrounding areas. The death rate among Jews in Warsaw rose from 1 per thousand in 1939 to 10.7 in 1941. In Lodz, the number was 43.3 in 1940 and 75.9 in 1941.[33]

"Logically, we must die out," wrote Chaim Kaplan, a Zionist, Hebraist, and educator in Warsaw, in his diary in 1940. "According to the laws of nature, we are doomed to destruction and total annihilation. How can a whole community feed itself when it has no anchor in life? There is no occupation, no profession that is not limited and circumscribed for us! . . . Total segregation from all life's professions. Segregated and separated from the world we shall atrophy in our poverty, suffering, hardship, and filth, we shall rotten until our end will come."[34]

It was not simply that between September 1939 and June 1941 the Nazis destroyed the traces of the Jewish present and past on German and occupied territories. The sealed ghettos created Jews who were (still) alive but without a past, present, or future: a people without time. In October 1940, the entire Jewish community of Baden and the Saar-Palatinate was deported to Vichy, the nonoccupied zone of France. The Jews of Alsace-Lorraine had already been expelled to Vichy on July 16, 1940. Seven years after coming to power, the Nazis succeeded in making the first free-of-Jews regions in Germany. More than the deportations of Polish Jews into the ghettos and of German Jews into Vichy France, more than the deaths by slave labor, shooting, and starvation, the sealing of the Jews from the world, from human time, indicated the Nazis' conscious and unconscious intentions. Nazi contingent plans had meaning within these powerful structures.

The fourth moment of punctuated equilibrium was the move after mid-1941 to mass murder and then to exterminate all the Jews of Europe.

I started this chapter with the notion of contingency as the essence of history, and I end it with a somber, restricted vision of the role of contingency in the extermination of Jews in the war years. This is not a contradiction. The idea that at a certain juncture a given historical case presented the possibility of few historical outcomes does not mean that we create a narrative driven by inevitable, predetermined results. It means that the notion of contingency is not a free-floating device in the hands of the historian; it does not apply similarly to all historical cases, and it carries different explanatory weight according to circumstances. Some historical cases are governed by a restricted contingency, and it is important to note this in a profession and a general culture that have made the term "contingency" sacrosanct.

We prefer to believe in the free will of the individual to change things, in our autonomy to shape the world, and therefore in the moral responsibility attached to our actions. All this is correct. But it is also correct that at times societies bring themselves to a situation in which only few real choices for actions are available. This is where German society brought itself in September 1939 after six years of relentless anti-Jewish measures. In six short years (this was not at all a long, gradual process, coming to think of it), Nazis and other Germans drove Jews away from civil society and demolished any sign of Judaism in Germany. It can be observed with certainty that many Germans participated in the persecution of the Jews, while many others, indeed German society as a whole, did not oppose the regime's anti-Jewish initiatives. No group in German society firmly rejected the Nazi assault on Jews and Judaism.

What did Germans create and enable by these stances of participation and nonopposition? The issue is not only to what degree some Germans really believed in Nazi ideology (or acted out of opportunism or indifference). This position assumes that culture is a reflection of what people think and that intention is a reflection of ideology. It also may assume that fixed, real Nazi ideology existed out there that was in turn really believed (or not). But Nazi ideology and intentions changed with time. Rather, another interpretive direction is to use culture as denoting what was available to Germans for thinking. Not all Germans agreed on the meaning of Nazi anti-Semitism – of a German world, wherever its territory would be, without Jews and Judaism – but the meaning became for many a social practice and for all a recognizable, internalized image of their world. Between 1933 and 1939 the revolutionary achievement of the Nazis was to make this imagination possible.

What did German culture enable Germans to imagine about the Jews in August 1939? Germans could imagine a world in which extreme violence was applied to get rid of Jews and eliminate Judaism. How exactly this world without Jews would come about in the future, in the looming war, they did not know, and many did not interrupt their life to think about this issue. But, then, no one in Germany knew in 1939 how exactly this world would materialize, not even Hitler. The key issue is not about knowledge, but about sensibilities – for Germans had already been able to imagine between 1933–1939 some version of a world without Jews and Judaism and thus were making it their own.

On the eve of the war most Germans failed to think deeply about the short- and long-term consequences of this new imagination. They avoided thinking about the long-term consequences of building a new humanity based on violently eradicating across Europe a tradition that inextricably belonged to their own culture. The time for this reckoning would come only after 1945. The emergence of this awareness, which came as a shock, is one reason the Nazi persecution of the Jews has become a foundational event. But in the very short term, many Germans had already mistreated, humiliated, profited from, brutalized, killed, and denied the legitimacy of existence (or consented to all this) to their "own" Jews – German citizens who looked and talked like them, who were distinguished members of society. How would they treat, then, East European Jews in a war that loomed ever closer? Those Jews looked and talked differently, were viewed as primitive, filthy, Bolsheviks, if not subhuman, and were significantly more numerous than German Jews. At a minimum they would receive the treatment of "our" Jews. To cause these Jews to vanish from existence, what options had Germans left for themselves apart from exercising harsher violence? On what terms should these Jews be allowed to live in the conquered territories, if at all?

"During the morning hours of the first of September, 1939, war broke out between Germany and Poland," described Kaplan in his diary at the beginning of the war. "We are witnessing the dawn of a new era in the history of the world. . . . Wherever Hitler's foot treads there is no hope for the Jewish people."[35] His evaluation could have been shared by Germans as well: the war would be momentous, and Jews had no place in the new Nazi empire. A German world without Jews was not a consequence of the context of the war. Rather the means to bring about this world between 1939 to 1945 – the various Nazi plans to get rid of the Jews, culminating in Auschwitz – these were the consequences of the context of the war. Every period provides its framework of contingencies available within powerful structures. To build a racial empire, a new humanity, free from the shackles symbolized by the Jews, these Jews would have to disappear, somehow. Contingency would play out within these powerful structures.

The three passages by Klemperer at the beginning of this chapter convey accurately this idea of contingency as possibilities existing within structures. There were always possibilities for different choices and developments, as Klemperer wrote in 1934 and 1939, but they existed within a framework of ideas that gave them meaning, as he realized in 1941.

The persecution and extermination of the Jews are events in which the search for contingency is constantly bouncing off powerful constraints: the relentless anti-Semitic drive of Nazi policy and the hegemonic role of Germans' actions. It may help to consider that historical events do not have a contingency with a capital "C," but several intersecting threads of contingencies. There are different registers of contingency, with different impacts on individual histories and social structures.

In terms of Nazi policy and ideology toward the Jews, the initial threshold was a Germany without Jews. There would be no changes in this policy; it had twists and turns, but also a clear, unambiguous direction. A narrative of radicalization is one way to capture the development of this policy and ideology in the Third Reich. Another, suggested here, is to shift perspective by exploring how Germans came to imagine the possibility of a Germany without Jews, by way of exploring what made the idea stick and the Nazis tick. In an attempt to capture contingency, recent historiography has emphasized that the idea of killing all the Jews was not yet firmed up in September 1939 or even in mid-1941. This is correct. But what needs to be explained as well is how the idea that Jews have no right to live had already been firmed up by that time and with what possible consequences.

The structure of Nazi anti-Semitism was shot through, however, with elements that could change and indirectly alter the regime's anti-Jewish policy. Hitler could have been killed in a car accident, an event that might have opened different historical possibilities that could have influenced the sort of the regime and the fate of the Jews. The basic unknowability of the future that is tinged with hope, especially in dire circumstances, is the meaning of Klemperer's observations, "why worry about what happens after May 7?"

History is ultimately made by human beings, whose sense of possibilities is very different from the historian's impersonal structures. Most arresting in the search for contingency are the individual acts that tear through the powerful structures and broader history. Their actions cannot always change History, but they make a profound difference for the individual, for his or her immediate surroundings as well as for the larger community. A refusal of a German soldier in Police Battalion 101 to shoot Jews could not have stopped the rolling Nazi killing machine, but it would have made a world of difference for the morality and identity of the soldier, of those around him, and of the ways Germans would remember the crimes years later.

Kurt Gerstein, a profound religious Protestant, who served as a disinfection expert in the hygiene unit of the SS, witnessed the gassing of Jews in Belzec on August 2, 1942. It wholly shattered his conscience. On the train journey back to Berlin, he confided in a Swedish diplomat. During the weeks that followed he attempted to inform the papal representative in Germany and the Swiss embassy, even while continuing to deliver Zyklon B to the camps. On March 5, 1944, he wrote his father, a judge and staunch supporter of the regime:

> However tight the limitation on a man may be . . . he must never lose his standards or his ideals. He must never exonerate himself before his conscience and before the higher order of things to which he is subject by saying: that is not my business, I can do nothing to change things . . . that *is* my business. I am involved in this responsibility and guilt, having knowledge of what is happening and a corresponding measure of blame.[36]

He hanged himself in a French prison on July 25, 1945.

These kinds of moral choices are part of any search for contingency, of individual agency, and of historical paths chosen and not chosen. Not all choices are that burdensome and weighty. But everyday personal choices give history its human inflection and moral depth.

Finally, for individuals, chance occurrences and sheer contingency determine life. With the end of the war near, on February 12, 1945, the remaining Jews of Dresden were ordered to report for labor duty three days later. The destination was probably Theresienstadt. Klemperer was not included in this transport, although he was one of those who delivered the orders. Among those summoned were children under the age of ten. Everyone knew that the summons meant death; Klemperer expected to be included in the next transport. But on the night of February 13, an Anglo-American air raid reduced Dresden to rubble, including the Gestapo headquarters – all its offices, files, and lists. Most city Jews survived the attack. They removed their yellow star and destroyed documents that identified them as Jews. "I sat in restaurants," Klemperer wrote on February 19, "I traveled by train and tram – as a Jew in the Third Reich all of it punishable by death. I constantly told myself, who could recognize me."[37] The link between summoning the Jews and bombing Dresden was not a contingency case of major historical importance, but for Victor Klemperer on that day it meant the world.

7

Ideology, Race, and Culture

La coeur a ses raisons que la raison ne connâit pas.
Blaise Pascal

For the history of civilization the perennial dream of sublime life has the value of a very important reality.... There is not a more dangerous tendency in history than that of representing the past as if it were a rational whole and dictated by clearly defined interests.
Johan Huizinga[1]

Historians shifted in the last generation their view of the role of ideas in the French Revolution from the social interpretation to the political-cultural one. According to the social interpretation, ideas were a reflection of a social structure determined beforehand; the rise of the bourgeoisie happened independently of revolutionary ideas. According to the political-culture interpretation, revolutionary ideas, culture, and experience were constitutive to the historic meaning of the Revolution as the first attempt in modern democracy. This political culture – made up of expressed and hidden meanings within revolutionary texts, symbols, holidays, images, and collective mentalities such as the obsession with conspiracy – was about a political imaginary world where no one had ever been and to which the Revolution wanted to lead, as much as it was about concrete interests, struggles for power, and ideological control. So far this political-cultural interpretation has not yet been fundamentally challenged. Interpretive debates are occurring mostly within this framework rather than outside of it. Following a period in which revolutionary politics was interpreted in symbolic and ideological terms, most recent historians view the period's conflicts as contested efforts to deal with real problems and interests.[2]

The meaning of Nazi anti-Jewish ideas, to turn to the Third Reich, cannot be seen as social or economic because Jews were not targeted as members of a particular class, but as members of a race. Jews from all classes were victims, and so the Holocaust reveals the limits of Marxism. The meaning was also not strictly political because there were no defined political interests in exterminating the Jews, who had neither a political party nor unified political vision. Interpretations that saw National Socialism in political terms, such as fascism and totalitarianism, failed to account for the Holocaust. Friedländer correctly observed that totalitarianism and fascism fit much better National Socialism "once the 'final solution' is *not* included."[3] The Holocaust cannot be seen as simply contextual either: an event that was, as Klemperer wrote, "central to the whole structure, to the whole character of National Socialism and is uncharacteristic of everything else," can be modified and shaped, but not wholly determined, by the context.

The meaning of ideas in understanding the Holocaust comes into sharp focus when we associate it with the Revolution. Lynn Hunt divided her book on revolutionary political culture into two parts: "the poetics of power" and "the sociology of politics." In the French Revolution political imagination commingled with concrete interests, a battle for power, and ideological domination. But the Holocaust evinced none of these elements. It was not about ideological control, because the Jews did not possess a single, unitary worldview. It was not a struggle for power, because the Jews were powerless. It did not deal with real social, economic, or political problems, and it did not promote concrete interests: the murder of the Jewish children of Paris, Rome, Sarajevo, and Kiev did not answer any real, specific problem for Germans in, say, Tübingen. The Germans' perceived deadly Jewish threat did not exist in the reality of things, but it did exist in the imagination. The Holocaust was a result of quintessential imagination. Ideas mattered – but which ideas and how should the historian capture them?

To capture Nazi ideas, the notion of Nazi ideology – a more or less systematic set of ideas about racial superiority and anti-Semitism – has in the last generation dominated understanding of the Holocaust. Through ideology – which stands in contrast to a mixture of fuzzy ideas, vague intentions, states of mind, or sheer passion and madness – the Nazis aimed to build a racial state, society, and way of life: "When National Socialism has ruled long enough," observed Hitler, "it will no longer be possible to conceive of a form of life different from ours."[4] Nazi ideology was elaborated by professional and managerial groups such as physicians, scientists, psychiatrists, demographers, and geographers; supported by the cultural intelligentsia in the arts, academia, and literary circles; refined and legitimized in research institutes and universities; and maintained by German bureaucracy and technology.

Nazi racial ideology was arranged in three concentric circles. The inner circle concerned the transformation of German society by eradicating those regarded as "alien" or "unfit." A memorandum circulated by the German Ministry of Interior on July 18, 1940 gives an idea of the radical plans that were envisioned, which called for the rearrangement of German society based on racial fitness and social and economic performance. Society was to be divided into several groups that ranged from healthy to sick. The lowest group constituted "asocial" elements who would be denied any social assistance; they would be treated according to "measures of negative population policy," namely, starvation, deportation, forced labor, and ultimately extermination. The second lowest category consisted of those deemed "bearable"; the possibility of their sterilization was considered.[5] The memorandum did not simply chart plans for the future, but also reflected existing policies: 70,273 institutionalized mentally and physically disabled persons were murdered at six gassing facilities between January 1940 and August 1941.

The second, wider circle of ideology encompassed Nazi ambitions to restructure Europe, especially Eastern Europe, along racial lines. A war of racial domination meant creating "people without rights" who would exist in relation to their utility to the German economy and production.[6] Societies such as Poland and Russia would not be allowed to have any form of cultural, artistic, and creative life. Deportation, forced labor, and starvation were standard policies, preparing Eastern Europe for a massive resettlement of Germans. Finally, the widest circle on a universal scale included the struggle against the Jews, humanity's eternal enemy, as an essence and goal of Nazi racial ideology.

It is hard to believe that several decades ago scholars and laypersons regarded the Nazi regime as a movement without ideas and denied the very existence of Nazi ideology. This was also the opinion of scholars who contributed to the understanding of Nazism. Franz Neumann, the German Jewish political scientist who perceptively analyzed National Socialism, argued in 1942 in his classic *Behemoth: The Structure and Practice of National Socialism* that "National Socialism has no political theory of its own... the ideologies it uses or discards are mere *arcana dominationis*, techniques of dominations."[7] Hannah Arendt, as we have seen, viewed Nazism in 1945 as owing "nothing to any part of Western tradition," although other parts of her work anchored the movement squarely within modern European history.

The conceptual move to consider Nazi ideology seriously was therefore a fundamental change. It was a shift of historical consciousness – from viewing Nazism as alien to European history and to "real" ideologies such as liberalism and communism to viewing it as having a body of ideas that had been integral to European history. It is now commonplace to view twentieth-century European history as an ideological struggle between liberalism, communism, and National Socialism not because they serve as a good map to finding truth in history, but because people believed in them and were ready to die and kill for them.[8]

The contribution of this approach has been enormous. The Holocaust has been interpreted as a commingling of the context of the war and the belief in racial ideas, of circumstances and ideology. German troops perceived the reality of the Eastern Front, so runs the dominant argument, influenced by a combination of the conditions of war and the considerable ideological indoctrination of the regime: "Indeed these issues were closely connected... [the soldiers] accepted the regime's perception and image of the war as an ideological struggle in which they were duty-bound to destroy the 'enemies of humanity,' Bolshevism, 'Asiatic barbarism' and the Jews."[9] The scholarly consensus – backed by sustained research on ideology in every sphere of life in Nazi Germany – is that, as Yehuda Bauer put it, "without a guiding ideological motivation and justification, mass murder generally and the intent to annihilate the Jewish people in particular, would have been unthinkable. Ideology is central."[10] Even historians who marginalized the role of ideology, such as those who viewed the Holocaust as an answer to immediate practical considerations, assign ideology some role. Ultimately, all attempts to understand the Holocaust as caused by institutional and policy-making processes inherent in the Nazi system of government, by the inner logic of National Socialist policies geared toward resettlement and expansion, or by the need to solve immediate pragmatic problems – that is, all attempts that fundamentally ignore the beliefs and values embedded in the acts of the perpetrators – are bound to end in an interpretive cul-de-sac.

But the ideology argument itself seems to have reached a cul-de-sac. It was a historiographical corrective that is itself now in need of a corrective.

Similar to the argument about the explanatory hegemony of the context of the war, the problem is not that the ideology argument is wrong, but rather that it is right in a particular way that obscures important aspects of life and death in the Third Reich. About ideology, the simplest argument is the following: the point is not that ideology is marginal to understanding the Holocaust, but that as a guide for values and beliefs it is insufficient. The historiography is dominated by a hegemonic view of ideology as the organizer and arbiter of motivations in the Third Reich, of mentalities and sensibilities. This view provides an interpretive certainty for a historical problem that cautions against hermetic explanations. Viewing the Holocaust as a combination of war conditions and Nazi ideology is an attractive explanation, indeed too attractive and too neat. If ideology and context clarify why the extermination happened, it begs the question, What else is there to explain? Scholars' assertion "to take ideology seriously" has now the sound of déjà vu based on a historiographical reflex, not on a critical evaluation.

I suggest taking ideology seriously by diminishing its explanatory role. A broad, indeed very broad, view of ideology is illustrative of a historiography in which it can designate anything, from Goebbels' reflection in his diaries to medical experiments in Auschwitz. Of course, on one level, ideology is everywhere and can designate anything. And yet, if it is everything and everywhere, it explains nothing. If ideology is everything, there is no ideology. It has become such a catch-all notion about motivations in the Third Reich that it is difficult to discriminate between ideology, on the one hand, and ways to think outside, alongside, against, underneath, and above it.

The focus on ideology has generated valuable attempts to complicate its role in German society and culture. Geoff Eley, responding to Daniel Goldhagen's one-dimensional use of ideology, suggested using an "*extended* understanding of [Nazi] ideology, as being embedded in cultural practices, institutional sites, and social relations."[11] Peter Fritzsche explored ideology in his evocative *Life and Death in the Third Reich* as a composite of Nazi ideas and the personal process of "becoming a National Socialist, a comrade, a race-minded German." Ideology is understood here as something produced not by the regime and imposed from above, but by a process shaped also by individuals who ultimately changed their most intimate beliefs: the outcomes "varied from person to person, but the *process* gave them an ideological inflection."[12] Topics that explored the construction of ideology (in contrast to those that explored simply its representation and political meaning) made substantial contributions. The history of Nazi morality, still in its early stages as a topic of research, is a case in point, as evident by recent studies based on the idea that the "road to Auschwitz was paved with righteousness."[13]

And yet the hegemony of ideology as an explanation of the culture, beliefs, and motivation of Germans in the Third Reich remains undiminished because although the notion of ideology has been made more complex and differentiated, it is often still the framework within which culture, beliefs, and motivation are understood. An extended understanding of ideology may simply add more items to the list of what we understand under the term, while the point is to understand the Third Reich by putting ideology in relation to other forms of thought within German culture. It is appealing to think that by complicating the notion of ideology we also provide a more complex and nuanced interpretation of German culture, and therefore can maintain ideology's interpretive hegemony. The work of Louis Althusser is at times used to support such a move because he saw ideology as a dynamic social force representing dominant beliefs and values. But he also viewed it as created by the repressive state apparatus and, ultimately, as so pervasive that it was impossible to escape its influence or exist outside of it.[14] We are at square one: the problem is not to make ideology more complex but to acknowledge that it is not the world; it is simply one of the forms of thoughts in society. This may not be an easy task. After all, the notion of ideology has been such a familiar, useful, and convenient element in the scholar's explanatory toolbox of the Third Reich and indeed of modern history that it may be difficult to think of German culture in the period beyond it. But that is exactly what we need to do.

There were many truths in German society beyond ideology, without which it is impossible to understand how the ideology was believed and constructed to begin with. Germans' collective mentalities existed before, during, and after Nazi ideology. "Ideology" cannot exhaust the world of emotions and mentalities that was German culture because Nazi ideology had to interact with different and older collective representations, such as Christianity and nationhood. As a statement about the mental horizon of the Third Reich, ideology seems intellectually undemanding: it is too cerebral to encompass people's ways of thought in the past. Historical actors are not always aware of what they are doing, and they are not always able to articulate why they do what they do; they are sometimes unaware of the full significance of their creations. Irrational motives, obsessions, emotions, and nightmares are part of what drive people. Motivations cannot be reduced to circumstances or to ideology. Ideology is part of culture, but it is not the thing itself. It is only one part of the web of symbols and meanings with which people understand and act in the world.

It is worthwhile thinking of the role and limits of ideology in explaining the Holocaust by associating that with the role and limits of ideology in explaining nationhood. As a modern idea that began in the era of the French Revolution, nationhood has since attached itself to every ideological creed, be it liberalism, fascism, Nazism, communism, Muslim fundamentalism, and anything in between. This is precisely the reason, implied Benedict Anderson in *Imagined Communities*, that we should not treat the nation as an ideological construct. No specific ideology can explain why the idea of nationhood spread the world over. The meaning of nationhood was not that it was liberal or fascist, but that it was imagined as a community that made it possible for people to kill and die for the nation: "These deaths bring us abruptly face to face with the central problem posed by nationalism: what makes . . . [it] generate such colossal sacrifices?"[15]

As a case of genocide, the Holocaust cannot be understood without the ideology that carried it. Similar to other modern genocides, and in contrast to a pogrom that is short-lived and unmethodical, the Holocaust was justified by a systematic body of ideas. But Anderson's move to disconnect ideology from the object of study (nationhood or in our case the Holocaust) is instructive: because there can be no genocide without ideology, racial ideology was as much an essential component of the Holocaust as a defining cause. Accordingly, it should be a starting point of our investigation, not the concluding answer. The central question is not whether anti-Semitism and racial ideology had a role in the Holocaust (of course they had). And it is not what kind of a role ideology had in relation to situational factors such as conditions of war and immediate local considerations (there was a mixture of factors, including ideology, circumstances, and local conditions). Rather, what needs to be explained is the transformation of consciousness that made thinkable the idea of a Germany without Jews, so that it helped produce as well as make sense of the situation of war and extermination. Why and how did particular cultural artifacts, such as the notion of the apocalyptic battle against the Jews, arouse such deep attachments? What made anti-Jewish imagination generate such colossal sacrifices and brutality in such a short time?[16]

During World War II Marc Bloch reflected on what history is and how to explain the contemporary historical whirlwind:

There can be no psychology which confines itself to pure consciousness. To read certain books of history, one might think mankind made up entirely of logical wills whose reasons for acting would never hold the slightest mystery for them. . . . Does anyone consider that the oppressive moral atmosphere in which we are currently plunged comes only from the rational parts of our minds? We should seriously misrepresent the problem of causes in history if we always and everywhere reduced them to a problem of motive.[17]

To move from the ideological to the cultural is not only to enlarge an investigation or change its topic. It means casting doubt on two ideas: that actions can be inferred from ideology that authorize or justify them and that ideological expressions reflect reality and experience at the same time. But it is precisely the tensions among reality (the conditions out there, whatever they may be), experience (how the individual perceives that reality and puts his or her actions and feelings in a narrative form), and the expression of ideology (how a state, a party, or an organization constructs a narrative of legitimacy and identity) that structure social life.[18] These tensions provide an opportunity for historians not only to understand motivations but also to identify sensibilities. For ideology was not reality and could not stand for all manifestations of meaning in Nazi society; people gave multiple meanings to their life in ways that included, reflected, parceled out, reinterpreted, ignored, and opposed "ideology." Mentalities are more complicated than ideology, but ideology is what historians are worried about.

Just as the explanation based on the primacy of context runs the danger of explaining behavior as determined by external forces, so an explanation based on the primacy of ideology runs the risk of reducing beliefs and mentalities to extraneous forces determined by the regime. Michael Geyer observed that "caution is necessary in putting ideology into the history of the war, lest it appear as some extraneous principle or dogma that is handed down to a hapless officer corps, a conscript army, and the German nation. The image of ideology as imposed dogma misses the reasons that ideology got into the armed forces in the first place and was able to become such an important and deleterious force in the conflict."[19] The picture of Germans who made up their mind about the world because of a combination of external pressures – the battles, peer pressure, barbarization of war, and Nazi ideology – is incomplete, indeed uncomplicated. All people are also the authors of themselves, as the anthropologist Barbara Meyerhoff noted.[20] Imagination cannot be reduced to ideology.

In Nazi culture, expressed ideas often did not represent reality. Let us consider two Nazi texts. The First Ordinance on the Exclusion of the Jews from German Economic Life of November 12, 1938, issued several days after Kristallnacht, finished whatever source of livelihood still existed for Jews. The Thirteenth Ordinance of the Reich Citizenship Law of July 1,

1943 left no legal institutions to which Jews could appeal for redress. But the 1938 ordinance was issued after the Jews had already been deprived of their legal status and material existence, while the 1943 ordinance was issued after millions of Jews had already been murdered. The texts shed no light on the actual relations between Germans and Jews. Reality had superseded the texts. The important meaning lay in what was done, not in what was said, and there was no congruency between the meaning of the decrees and the reality they dealt with. Nazi language at times represented reality and at times disguised it.[21]

Self-conscious, public expressions of Nazi ideology get us so far in illuminating Nazi ideas, but it is less successful in getting us the rest of way to examine Nazi culture and mentalities. Consider the following evidence. Although public expressions of anti-Semitism were prevalent between 1933–1939, they were significantly absent in specific situations. Newsreels barely mentioned concrete anti-Semitic policies during the Third Reich, while anti-Jewish measures were mentioned only three times between 1933–1939, even though they were in full swing in Germany during this period. Hitler himself did not often address the Jewish question.[22] He hardly said a word about Jewry after his seizure of power, and after authorizing the April 1933 boycott against Jews, he publicly distanced himself from it. He then said nothing about Jewish policy until the imposition of the 1935 Nuremberg Laws. Only on three occasions between April 1933 and September 1939 did Hitler express directly his obsessive racism: in a speech to the Reichstag at the 1935 Nuremberg Rally, again at the Nuremberg Rally in 1937, and at the Reichstag speech on the sixth anniversary of the seizure of power on January 30, 1939.[23] And yet, Hitler's central role in the anti-Jewish policy is beyond doubt. Nazi language can thus hide as much as it reveals. There is an element of Nazi anti-Semitism that cannot be captured by a literal, ideological reading of public expressions and stated intentions.

In one sense Nazi ideology was supported by a sophisticated arrangement, one provided by industrial, scientific, modern society. Biological racism was institutionalized by the state apparatus: it was legitimized by science, researched in hospitals and universities, and implemented in government offices that attempted to find a "rational" solution to the "Jewish problem." The "spirit of science" made Nazism into a project of utopian modernity.[24]

There is no doubt of the interpretive value of the view of the Holocaust as a modern, utopian, social engineering project expressed in the language of scientific racial biology. But is it enough? We would still have to grasp what is essential to the Holocaust and, I would argue, to every genocide, namely, how to account for the mixture of modern elements of mass murder with old and new sensibilities, imagination, and images of the past. In this sense, this view has some limits. If the Holocaust was a result of "rational" demographic planning for racial rearrangement in the East, why did the Nazis choose to exterminate the Jews of Corfu who had no relation to this project? If the Holocaust was essentially a utopia of modernity, it still needs to be explained why did the Nazis chose as their main enemy the Jews, an ancient people with a long history and fundamental role in Christian, European, and German society, an important player (real and perceived) in the making of modernity, as well as the source of a long tradition of positive and negative moral, religious, and historical symbols? And why did they target this group as the only one that was hunted all over the continent, as a sort of a spaceless and timeless enemy, while other racial enemies, such as, for example, the mentally ill or asocial groups, were not considered existential threats that demanded deportation to Auschwitz from Thessalonica or Rome?[25]

Perhaps more important, an exploration of the emotional and aesthetic sensibilities of the perpetrators that is not reduced to ideology fits very well recent research that has challenged the most famous and popular image of the Holocaust, that of mass murder as a cold, anonymous process of administrative, factory-like killing. This image is simply not accurate: 1.1–1.3 million Jews were killed from September 1939 to December 1941, before the introduction of the death camps, by shootings, mass executions, and the Nazi policies of ghettoization, starvation, and slave labor. Another million and a half Jews were shot in 1942 and 1943. Altogether, close to 50 percent of the victims of the Holocaust were killed at close range in face-to-face contact. Ulrich Herbert could thus argue that

> the image of a "clean" death by gassing does not apply to much of the genocide. On the contrary, the Holocaust meant, to a considerable degree, exterminating human beings in very traditional, even archaic, ways, with a correspondingly high number of direct perpetrators. The notion of modern "industrial" genocide...is clearly an attempt to represent the mass murder as an abstract, even metaphysical, mass death of nameless victims.[26]

Consequently, we have to ask whether the interpretation of the Holocaust as a modern, industrial project does not confuse the form with the substance of Nazi goals: was the Nazi quintessential goal to create a society based on "the spirit of science," or was the goal, up to the very last day of the Third Reich, the fight against the Jews? I have argued that Nazi ideas disguised as much as reflected reality. Does the discourse of science hide an additional meaning? My argument is that the vision of modernity that sees in the Holocaust only science, race, and cold, industrial killing is too limited and is itself a construction of modernity. This image was privileged for example by a key Nazi group of the university-educated, racial technocrats in the Reich Security Main Office. But it is not that the essence of the genocide was emotionless anti-Semitism embedded in rational modernity, but instead that some of the perpetrators *presented* their actions in such a way. In reality, to be modern is precisely to mix old and new symbols, modes of thinking, and ways of behavior, to think of the potential of the future by using the traditions of the past, to use emotions while claiming rationality, to kill while upholding morality. It is this complexity we need to capture, not a superficial, cardboard dimension of an alleged modernity (using the plural, as in "German modernities," cannot salvage this notion either).

Most questionable is the wisdom of the assertion that one of Nazism's main characteristics is its emergence from the structures of modern industrial society. Given the conditions in Germany and (in most of) Europe at the time, what else is to be expected? (After all, Nazism could not have emerged from an agrarian structure promoted by eighteenth-century physiocratic doctrine.) Nazism's modern, industrial, scientific, characteristics were the symptom of their age, not its meaning. They should not be viewed as the quintessential goals of the regime. The goal was to build a racial civilization at the center of which was a Germany and later a world without Jews. This is the key issue that needs explaining, and not the means by which it came about.[27]

One important thrust of the focus on racial ideology has been to emphasize that Nazi claims to science, research, and objectivity were compatible with the most fanatical anti-Semitism. The Nazis thus legitimized their anti-Semitic hallucinations via a rhetoric of science. But of course there was nothing rational or scientific about this rhetoric. Should the historian accept (part of) the discourse of the Nazis about the scientific meaning of their anti-Semitism as the final interpretive destination? Was the rhetoric of science the deep meaning of these hallucinations, or was it merely a projection that hid as well as revealed? Anti-Semitic hallucinations were a system of meanings that represented a reality that existed only in the imagination. Where did this imagination come from?

My thoughts of ideology and culture have been inspired by a scholar who wrote about two very different topics. Before Inga Clendinnen wrote her meditation about the Holocaust, she studied the Aztecs.[28] Her work is a model for exploring the culture of racial imagination and anti-Semitism in the Third Reich.

The story of the Aztecs takes place in the period before August 1521, when the city of Tenochtitlan fell to the armies of Hernando Cortes. Her aim is to "catch attitudes and characteristic styles and emotions" among ordinary Mexican men and women to understand how they "made sense of their world. By this I do not mean anything as self-conscious as 'ideology' nor as passive as 'world view,' but rather those characteristic ways of apprehending, evaluating, enjoying, and managing the world . . . that we obscurely but comfortably label as 'culture.'"

Why is this relevant to the Holocaust? "There is one activity for which the Aztecs were notorious: the large-scale killing of humans in ritual sacrifice. The killings were not remote top-of-the pyramid affairs. . . . The people were implicated in the care and preparation of the victims, their delivery to the place of death, and then in the elaborate processing of the bodies: the dismemberment and distribution of heads and limbs, flesh and blood and flayed skins."[29] What followed is an analysis of notions of war, death, gender, victimhood, and the sacred, all linked to the ritual of human sacrifice.

When I first read this book several years ago, my thoughts drifted to the Holocaust. Consider this description of a dedication ceremony that took place after a successful Aztec battle:

Possibly twenty thousand victims died for that dedication: four patient lines stretching the full length of the processional ways and marshalled along the causeways, slowly moving towards the pyramid. Surprisingly, the mode of the disposal of the bodies remains mysterious. . . . Mexica victims were purely victims. It is a combination of violence with apparent impersonality, the bureaucratic calculation of these elaborate Mexica brutalities, together with their habituated and apparently casual incorporation into the world of the everyday, which chills.[30]

There are obvious fundamental differences between Aztec society and Nazi Germany. But what is insightful is the way Clendinnen investigates mass murder as made possible not only by "beliefs at [the] formal level [what we call ideology], but [by] sensibility: the emotional, moral and aesthetic nexus through which thought comes to be expressed in action, and so made public, visible, and accessible to our observation."[31]

Shifting the historical exploration from ideology to sensibilities is perhaps more difficult in the case of the Holocaust than in the case of the Aztecs because this event is still a signal part of contemporary history, politics, and identity. This kind of investigation will reveal things directly related to the foundation of Judeo-Christian culture today. Terms like modernity, industrial killing, state-sponsored extermination, scientific racism, resettlement, and university-educated and technocratic true believers are useful to varying degrees, but they also convey a world of pragmatism and rationalism for a topic whose core is a leap in human imagination. In terms of voice, they often reflect the way some Nazis, such as the university-educated technocrats, saw themselves and wanted others to see them. The notion of ideology, based on these terms, has thus partly had the unintended effect of neutralizing the issue of fantasies and imagination. For a historical topic whose essence was the belief in fantasies of redemption on a universal scale–"The great challenge is to exterminate eternal Judaism. . . . The Jews are guilty of everything. . . . Only then will the world find its eternal peace," a soldier wrote home from the Eastern Front in 1942–this is quite remarkable.[32]

To move beyond ideology it is imperative to center differently the power of racial ideas in the Third Reich. The historiography of the last three decades documented conclusively that Nazism's historical novelty was its attempt to create a racial biological society. This view, which emerged after years of obfuscating the meaning of National Socialism under terms such as "fascism" or "totalitarianism," is unassailable. But the interpretive hegemony of race now itself obfuscates ways of life and death in the Third Reich. It often sets race in opposition to other identities, while the issue is how identities existed in relationships of commingling and reciprocal influence. It often severs the racial regime from pre-1933 and post-1945 German history, instead of locating the period within long-term German traditions and forms of beliefs. It often suggests a cohesion and uniformity to racial thought and practice and to Nazi culture and aims, while a much better explanatory metaphor is Nazism as a work in progress. The prevalence of race in the Third Reich, then, is not in question: the question is how to interpret it with respect to Germans' beliefs and actions.

An insightful historiography has shown that race penetrated every aspect of life in Nazi Germany, even those aspects that several decades ago seemed wholly unrevealing about the period. Racial ideology informed the Nazi pursuit of happiness linked to the satisfaction of consumption and traveling pleasures.[33] Hitler's sentiment for well-being and unlimited consumption – "we resemble the Americans in that we have wants and desires," he mused – was realized through racism, war, plundering, and extermination.[34] Even Coca Cola, whose sales in Germany doubled each year between 1933–1938, was racialized. The Nazi regime publicly integrated the soft drink into Hitler's racial *Volksgemeinschaft,* or national community. It was marketed as a drink with a "German character," representing the promise of the Third Reich as a new, more affluent, and prosperous Germany. In the 1937 spectacular Nazi trade exhibition in Düsseldorf, many of the almost 7 million visitors stopped to enjoy the drink, then known by the slogan, "The Pause That Refreshes." Hermann Göring, who promoted the drink, was among those visitors.[35] In addition, in the spheres of sexual policy and mores, Dagmar Herzog has shown that "Nazism advanced an often bald and unapologetic celebration of sexual activity... even as it sought to harness those liberalizations... to a savagely racist, elitist, and homophobic agenda."[36] The German landscape was racialized under Nazism, as were German roads, the antismoking campaign, and even policies against asbestos-induced lung cancer.[37] Indeed, everything was. On one level, race seems to have been the measure of all things and the source of all beliefs in the Third Reich.

But there is another way to evaluate this evidence. Take the Heimat, or homeland, idea, for example. After unification in 1871 Germans constructed the idea of Heimat as representing the ultimate German community – real and imagined, tangible and symbolic, local and national – of people who had a particular relationship to one another, sharing a past and a future. This idea endowed the abstract national community with a sense of intimacy and hominess that had been naturally and effortlessly reserved to the locality. The Heimat movement was large and popular and included social and cultural activities conducted in civic associations, museums, and research into history, nature, and folklore.[38] The Nazis appropriated the Heimat idea, racializing and using it for their ideological purposes. It can be argued that here is another example of the hegemony of race, but this appropriation can also be interpreted very differently. The Heimat idea was a historical mentality that had articulated national and local sentiments since 1871, and by 1933 it was perceived as an essence of Germanness. Consequently, the main point about the relationship of Nazis to the Heimat idea was not that they racialized it: Heimat was used for different ideological purposes before and after the Nazis, as Heimatlers in imperial Germany infused it with nationalism, Nazis with race, East German communists with socialism, and West Germans with dreams of victimhood, lost territories, and local democratic renewal. Rather the main point is that the Nazis identified their sentiment of nationhood, localness, and political legitimacy with the Heimat idea, building the revolutionary idea of race on tradition. The racialized Heimat idea fit within the boundaries of the Heimat genre that existed before and after the Third Reich, as the Nazis articulated their Heimat in familiar, traditional rhetoric and images.[39] It is not so much race that made sense of Heimat in the Third Reich, as the Heimat idea that gave meaning to racial sentiments, making them amenable, legitimate, familiar.[40]

Viewed from this perspective, National Socialism enjoyed remarkable stability not simply because of the idea of race, but because the idea of race commingled successfully with other identities of German and European culture, in particular Christianity, nationhood, consumption, and private property. Nazism set fundamental limits for itself by being defined by the preservation of these ideas. In 1933 Germans founded the racial state, but this was only the beginning of the process of commingling race with the multitude of other identities in German society.[41] Nazism was a racial civilization that could not exist without major ideas of German and European culture, and it often fit quite comfortably with them. To be sure, there were conflicts between race and other identities. There is nothing new about such conflicts: identities coexist in tension. But the point is that they coexisted in tension but without breaking, thus creating a Nazi civilization that was bigger than the sum of its parts.

An interesting question about the Third Reich is not about conflicts of identities, but rather about the stability of the regime. The Nazi revolutionary attempt to construct a new society raises the question, what were the elements that gave stability to this revolutionary project, which was characterized by the absence of serious internal opposition and the presence of loyalty among many Germans? Coercion alone explains too little and does not give an answer to the motivations and willingness of the great many who exercised it.[42] It is also inconceivable that a body of racial ideas, which was present but not dominant before 1933, was received and internalized so quickly thereafter while successfully marginalizing other important identities. That is not how identities work. In human affairs, even the most radical transformations are maintained by previous memories, beliefs, and habits of mind. With respect to the Holocaust, the claim that the extermination of the Jews was determined by "the attempt to build a German empire along racial lines" has underplayed a whole set of identities, beliefs, and memories that shaped Nazi Germany.[43]

Let us take for example the important relations between race and religion in the Third Reich. Major histories and interpretations of the persecution and extermination of the Jews have marginalized religious elements, if they treated them at all. Explanations that emphasize industrial killing, state-sponsored extermination, the administrative process of annihilation, the crisis of liberalism, or modernity, which are all important in

various respects, represent a secular worldview of historians that, implicitly or explicitly, often sees modern times and religion as antagonists.
Religious beliefs are often irrelevant to these explanations. I do not argue
that religious elements are not considered at all in the history of the
Holocaust; of course they are. My argument is that they are ultimately
seen as marginal in a historiography that finds it difficult to integrate
religion into the mainstream narrative of the Holocaust as the inexorable
forward movement of racial ideas. Thus, reading some studies on scientific racism would make one believe that after 1933 all Germans believed
that Jews were microbes. Some studies do mention the presence of traditional, religious anti-Semitism and discuss the religious beliefs of Nazis
and Germans, but in the main, these elements are not an integral part of
the explanation of how the Nazis built their racial civilization. One also
notes that these studies often represent religion as tradition and therefore
somewhat arcane, while racial science represents modernity. But religion
is part of modernity as well and is not old-fashioned at all.

One illustration of the place of religious beliefs in explaining the Holocaust is the discussion of Nazism as a political religion, which views
National Socialism, as Michael Burleigh argued, as a "secularized religion" that provided "liturgies, ersatz theologies, vices and virtues."[44]
Nazism is thus viewed as a substitute for religion, and it is assumed that
religious beliefs as such were marginal to understanding Nazism. But
Germans' religious beliefs should be taken not as a backdrop to a presumed "real" secular ideology, but as a fundamental factor in making
Nazism amenable to many Germans who believed in God. If Germans
took their religious beliefs seriously and if they took Nazi beliefs seriously,
we should go beyond the level of ideology to find out how people made
the two worldviews interact, as well as support and at times oppose each
other. In some ways Friedländer's *The Years of Extermination* is representative of the historiography as a whole because the study focuses
on racial ideology while ignoring the role of religious beliefs and symbols (he discussed at length on the other hand the anti-Jewish policies
of Catholic and Protestant religious institutions). At the end, he argues,
"[T]here remains but one plausible interpretation": Nazism was a form
of "sacralized modernism."[45] Whether as "secularized religion" or as
"sacralized modernism," Nazism according to this view became sacred
in a Third Reich in which religious beliefs were superseded. The concepts
of political religion, secularized religion, or sacralized modernism presuppose a specific theory of modernity that assumes that modernity (and by
extension Nazism) and religion are distinct entities. Instead, the question
should be how the presence of religious beliefs, commingling with racial

beliefs, affected Germans' imagination and actions against the Jews in the Third Reich.

Scientific racism embodied a relatively novel set of images with which to imagine Jews, and it thus had to negotiate with Christian anti-Semitic images of the Jews, as well as with religious images of the Jews as the people of the Bible, the Ten Commandments, the Law, and, therefore for some, of morality. After 1933 scientific racism depicting the Jews as vermin did not simply conquer the imagination of Nazis and other Germans, no matter how diffused and loud was Nazi propaganda. This is simply not the way in which people make images of the world. There is always a commingling of old and new ideas. This process of negotiation gave meaning to Nazi anti-Semitic ideas: whatever the Nazis said about the Jews as racial enemy, they still had to imagine them also within the past religious tradition of the Jews as the people of the Hebrew Bible. Was it really possible in Germany in 1933 to imagine the Jews without the Bible? Is it credible to propose, often implicitly, that racial ideas swamped religious images and came to define Jews exclusively in the German imagination? Also when Nazis were antireligious – acting against the Catholic Church or (there were few of those) seeing Nazism as a substitute for Christianity – they still had to call forth in their imagination, if only to vanquish them, their anti-Jewish Christian images before they could move on to build the racial civilization. It could not have been otherwise. Modern, racial anti-Semitism was closely connected to the tradition of Christian anti-Judaism. The two entities were different but not separate because modern, racial anti-Semitism took shape within the context of memories, habits, and beliefs inherited by Christian anti-Judaism. We should not confuse here explicit expressions of Nazis who were antireligious with mentalities and imagination of the same Nazis whose anti-Semitism also included a jumble of Christian and racial images. Whatever Nazi ideologues and supporters thought about the Jews, they thought it within a framework of ideas about the Jews that existed before 1933. We need to acknowledge the persistence of a Christian imaginary tradition about the Jews to understand the transformation of this tradition into a racial idiom.[46]

The 1935 racial laws are a case in point. Nazis viewed racism as a variegated source of German identity. When, after the stabilization of the regime, the leadership set out to define racial categories in the September 1935 Nuremberg Laws, race commingled seamlessly with religious and historical origins – not with science – to identify who was an Aryan and who was a Jew. Germans were classified into four groups: Germans, with four Aryan grandparents; Jews, with three or more Jewish grandparents; half-Jews first degree, with two Jewish grandparents; and half-Jews second degree, with one. Aryans could be described only by the absence of Jewish blood, a negative definition. It is a mistake to see this definition (as some historians do) as absurd and a travesty of Nazi claims that biological categories unrelated to religion defined Jewishness because this view is too narrow an understanding of racial identity. Discussing the issue of race and religion in the Nuremberg Laws, Richard Evans defined the laws as "arbitrary" and making "nonsense of scientific claims about the importance of race and blood in determining Jewish or German identity."[47] His claim assumes that Nazi racism had a single, even fixed meaning, while in fact it combined scientific presumption with national and religious anti-Jewish (and other) traditions to say something, fundamentally, not about science or the German body but about identity. The power of racial ideas in Nazi Germany was precisely their ability to combine different ways of thinking that appeared contradictory, as race became a metaphor of historical origin commingling racial, religious, and national attributes. This explains why Germans accepted the Nazi worldview, and themselves as Aryans, in an incredibly short time.

In fact, Nazism did not and could not reject Christianity. Religious sensibilities in German society during the Third Reich were profound. According to the count in 1939, more than 95 percent of Germans were registered, baptized, tax-paying members of Protestant and Catholic churches.[48] (Hitler himself never left the Catholic Church.) Many did not regularly observe religious practices, but the important point was that Germans shared a sense of Christian tradition and connected it to a German national identity. The Nazis themselves were part of this Christian tradition. Religious practices and images were too present to be tossed away effortlessly. The Nazi revolutionary attempt to construct a new racial society had to consider that even the most radical transformations are maintained by links to the past. The Bolsheviks, to introduce to our discussion a historical analogy from the period, provide a perspective about the type of relationship that existed between National Socialism and Christianity. "The 1920s and 1930s," wrote Catherine Merridale, "were decades of demolition. Church buildings . . . were turned into grain stores, cowsheds, arsenals; their roofs were stripped; their stones recycled; and the most annoying were blown up. . . . A faction in the Bolshevik Party will set out to break the grip of the past . . . the anti-religious campaigns will ultimately affect every Soviet citizen . . . and change the framework of their memories forever."[49] Nazism never seriously considered adopting such policies. It is safe to assume that it would not have survived in power had it attempted them.

It is worthwhile noting how many traditional, Christian anti-Jewish motifs found their way into Nazi racism. The Nazis routinely linked the Jews and the devil. Children's literature particularly emphasized this linkage, as well as a range of commingling Christian and racial anti-Semitic ideas. This is of interest because instruction for children was based on familiar and easy-to-grasp themes that were supposed to fashion the Germans of tomorrow. A 1938 book *A German Mother* instructed, "Children, look here! The man who hangs on the cross was one of the greatest enemies of the Jews of all time. . . . He said further to the Jews: Your father is the Devil! Do you know, children, what that means? It means that the Jews descend from the Devil."[50] The Jew as portent of disease and epidemics had been a well-known idea in Christian Europe. Linked to that idea were the Nazis' fear of racial contamination and the metaphorical statement by Hitler in *Mein Kampf* that the Jew is "a pestilence, a moral pestilence, with which the public was infected . . . worse than the Black Plague."[51]

There were also more direct applications of the idea that Jews carried disease. In April 1933 Jewish scientists at the Kaiser Wilhelm Institute in Berlin were denied access to germs of typhus, cholera, and other diseases lest they poison the water supply in Germany. Shortly after the invasion of Poland, the Nazi organ *Völkischer Beobachter* reported that Jews poisoned the water supplies used by German troops. On November 20, 1939, the *New York Times* reported from Berlin that Germans planned to confine Warsaw Jews into a ghetto because, according to the Germans, "they are dangerous carriers of sickness and pestilence."[52] The Nazi depiction of Jews as physically ugly and smelly also derived from a tradition of representation. The Jewish badge was a medieval invention (the first one was introduced in 1218 featuring the Tablets of the Law), as was the use of Hebrew or pseudo-Hebrew lettering to connote Jewish evilness and accuse the Jews of crimes against Christ and Christians.[53] The reputation of Jews for having supernatural and historical powers had been a running theme in European culture; the Nazis articulated this idea anew after 1933 and with special vigor during the war when they argued that world Jewry instigated the fight in order to eliminate Germany.

In the Middle Ages, Jewish amulets with Hebrew inscriptions were greatly coveted as bringing good luck.[54] Nazis who burned the synagogue in Aachen on Kristallnacht on November 9, 1938 kept scraps of the Torah in their pockets for good luck.[55] It is not known whether they ever heard of the medieval precedent, but probably they had not. The point is not to construct a genealogy that sees Nazism as originating in medieval society; this is a terrible way to understand history. It is also not always clear whether the Nazis were aware of the historical precedents of their anti-Semitic repertoire (they certainly were aware of some and unaware of others). Rather, the point is precisely that, often unintentionally and not consciously, the Nazis used a repertoire of anti-Semitic images and symbols while giving it a new, modern meaning. Certain kinds of symbols appear again and again over long periods of history because they come to be identified with a certain object. They make up a certain archetypal symbolic manual that is available for use, although their meaning changes from one historical context to the next. Racial "science" gave anti-Semitism the legitimacy of modern rationality, making modern the anti-Jewish imagination. In this respect, the Nazi anti-Jewish imagination was not only German but also belonged to a European culture of Christianity and anti-Semitism.

In their aim to eradicate Germany of Jews and Judaism, the Nazis found some support in the German churches. The German Christian movement was an enthusiastic pro-Nazi group within the German Protestant church that during the Third Reich slowly gained control of most of the regional Protestant churches in the country, attracting between a quarter and a third of church members. The Confessing Church, a minority group within the Protestant church that attracted some 20 percent of church members, opposed what it viewed as the efforts of the German Christian movement to undermine Christian doctrine, but did not contest Hitler or the Nazi regime. The Catholic Church had the most complex struggle with Nazism over political and religious power. Most importantly for our discussion is that the three churches were united in support of the idea of the Jews as a degenerate moral and spiritual influence on German Christians that should be removed, in one way or another. None of the churches defended the Jews after 1933.

Although the Nazi regime tried to weaken the political power and moral authority of the institutional churches, especially of the Catholic Church that was linked to the pope in Rome, on another level there was a fundamental affinity between Christianity and Nazism. The single most persistent aspect of Nazism was anti-Semitism, just as Christianity provided Nazism with the richest tradition of anti-Judaism. At the same time, in the decades before 1933, German Protestant theologians and clergymen (and also some Catholics) came to appreciate the potential of racism as a vehicle to rid Christianity of everything Jewish while shaping a

German national Christianity. Racism made it possible to argue that Jesus
was not a Jew and that Christianity owed nothing to the Old Testament.
In the Third Reich, the Catholics also shared the idea of dejudaizing
German Christianity. Cardinal Faulhaber of Munich argued in his Advent
sermons in 1933 against eliminating the Old Testament as a Jewish book,
as demanded by the German Christian movement, because, he claimed,
it was in fact an anti-Jewish text proving the sinful ways of the Jewish
people.[56]

It is on this ground that Nazism and aspects of German Christianity
found a common denominator in the Third Reich: they both proposed
a project of national identity based on the physical removal of the Jews
from Germany and on the cultural removal of any (real or perceived) trace
of Judaism. For the Nazis, this identity was expressed more in modern,
racial terms, as they sought in the first years of the Reich the removal of
Jews from the German economy, culture, and politics. For some German
Christians, this identity was expressed more in religious terms, as they
sought to cleanse Christian texts and liturgy of Jewish influence. In this
case, race and Christianity were more complementary than contradictory.

Viewed from this perspective, the removal of the Jews sharpens the
focus on some related issues. Whatever they thought of the inferiority of
the Jews, the Nazis operated against them within their own civilization –
sharing with the Jews a history, culture, and religious origins – and both
the Nazis and the Jews were aware of it. Colonial empires, in contrast,
set out to conquer cultures and societies viewed as distinctly outside of
their own European civilization. The Jews were subhuman, but unless
the situation would change they still stood as the origins of Jesus and the
New Testament, and therefore of any notion of German Christianity. The
culture of colonized people in Africa was not viewed as part of or equal
to British and French identity. The Nazis persecuted the Jews as a symbol
that came from within German and European-Christian civilization: they
sought to destroy part of their own culture to reconstruct it anew. The
relation to colonial genocides is instructive. Colonizers rarely if ever saw
the colonized as part and parcel of their own history and identity, while
the Nazis and other Germans viewed the persecution and extermination
of the Jews with conviction commingled with a sense of transgression
precisely because victims and perpetrators shared a historical common
denominator.

The problem faced by many Nazis therefore was not so much to commingle race and Christianity, to return to where this discussion began,
as it was to justify the violent uprooting of their own heritage. Siegfried

Leffler, a pro-Nazi, German Christian leader and official in the Thuringian Ministry of Education, explained this problem in February 1936 in a meeting of theologians[57]:

In a Christian life, the heart always has to be disposed toward the Jew, and that's how it has to be. As a Christian, I can, I must, and I ought always to have or to find a bridge to the Jew in my heart. But as a Christian, I also have to follow the laws of my nation [Volk], which are often presented in a very cruel way, so that again I am brought into the harshest of conflicts with the Jew. Even if I know "thou shall not kill" is a commandment of God or "thou shall love the Jew" because he too is a child of the eternal father, I am able to know as well that I have to kill him, I have to shoot him, and I can only do that if I am permitted to say: Christ.

Leffler was not perturbed by his call to kill the Jews. Nor did his audience ever comment on or discuss these remarks. Apparently, these ideas did not sound very original. What disturbed him was how to reconcile his aim to create a Germany without Jews and Judaism with his acknowledgment of the historic position of Jews in Christianity. His words make clear that he had already decided that the link between Judaism, on the one hand, and German Christianity and national identity, on the other, had to be violently severed. He and his audience were beyond this moral mental threshold.

Many Germans viewed the Third Reich project not as anti-Christian, but more as a refounding of German Christianity. The churches in Germany, for example, did not criticize the anti-Jewish measures or Kristallnacht publicly, a stance that was only partly determined by political calculations. Kristallnacht did create tension between the German Catholic Church and the state. But the actions and statements of the churches, distancing from the Jews and their plight, in effect began to create a new Germany with no Jewish roots. On November 10 the National Socialist Association of Teachers decided to expel all remaining Jewish pupils from German schools, as well as to forbid giving them Christian religious education, claiming that "a glorification of the Jewish murderers' nation could no longer be tolerated in German school." Cardinal Bertram protested to Reich Education Minister Rust that everyone knows that "this assertion [that the Christian religion glorified the Jews] is false and that the contrary is true."[58] In February 1939, the Evangelical Church of Thuringia banned its own baptized Jews from its churches. The measure soon spread to Saxony, Anhalt, Mecklenburg, and Lübeck. Soon thereafter all pastors of non-Aryan ancestry were dismissed. In April 1939 the Evangelical Church Leaders' Conference signed an agreement with the Ministry of Religious Affairs formalizing the relations between the Protestant churches and the state. The Godesberg Declaration of the same month articulated the new principles: "What is the relation between Judaism and Christianity? Is Christianity derived from Judaism and has therefore become its continuation and completion, or does Christianity stand in opposition to Judaism? We answer: Christianity is in irreconcilable opposition to Judaism."[59]

In this brief discussion I have attempted to show that some Germans supported Nazism because it allowed them to remain a certain kind of Christian while becoming a new kind of German. The larger point I have tried to make has been that questioning the explanatory hegemony of racial ideology is interpretively useful in capturing the composite world of Germans' culture and identities in the Third Reich.

To capture this commingling of identities beyond the hegemonic racial paradigm, it is important to revise the current chronological boundaries of Holocaust narratives. Chronologically, the Holocaust is narrated now within the context of the war, during the years 1933–1945, and often reaching as far back as World War I, but not earlier.[60] There are good reasons for this chronology, but it also raises some issues. It is a narrative that reproduces in different form the Nazi narration of modern Germany, including the myth of World War I, the defeat of 1918, and the role of Jews. It risks reifying the identity that was most visible in public and ideological discourse – namely, race – and underplaying elements of memory, culture, and belief that were less visible or not admitted publicly and consciously by contemporaries.

An example of this sort of methodological consequence is Friedländer's history of the Holocaust. He was always attentive to the psychological and fantasy elements of Nazi anti-Semitism, and the main argument of his study is that redemptive anti-Semitism was the motivation for the extermination. But because the study focuses on racial ideology between 1933–1945, we hear nothing about the symbols and memories that constituted this fantasy, when and how they originated before 1933, and how and why they were received in German society thereafter. The book thus reflects much of current historiography in its attribution of an excessively determining role to racial ideology and in its strict periodization. His is a history of the Holocaust with pre-1933 cultural antecedents left out, which makes it impossible to explore in depth the idea of redemptive anti-Semitism. The overdetermined presence of the notions of ideology and the context of the war in the interpretation of the Holocaust obscures the importance of the presence of the past in its making.

Of course, for German and Holocaust historians, talk of continuities raises specters of a crude argument of simplistic causality, of a tale of timeless anti-Semitism inevitably leading to Auschwitz. Yet, historical understanding is made of continuities as much as of change and context. In terms of method, we should reject arguments of continuity that view causality between the starting and the end points of the continuum in favor of analysis of memory and symbolic forms that influenced the Third Reich. The mode of proceeding should not be to go from the past toward the Third Reich, choosing necessarily cultural artifacts that had long histories because doing so may result in a new teleology whereby continuities are narrated by ignoring evidence that does not fit in the script leading to the Holocaust.[61] Instead, the historian should start from the memories and symbols that fashioned the world of Germans in the Third Reich and trace their construction backward, wherever they may lead.

Doing so means viewing the association between Nazi memories and the past in the same way that scholars of nationhood view the association between new nations and their perceived roots. The discourse about French national identity in the Third Republic proclaimed that modern French people had, as their ancestors, the ancient Gauls. In reality, there was no such causal link between the two groups; the link was invented and imagined from a selected body of tales and histories about the French and pre-French pasts. To understand the meaning of this memory we do not need to start with the Gauls but rather with French society after 1871 and how it gave additional meanings to old symbols. German culture, similar to any culture, was fashioned from a repertoire of symbols and memories that were differently adapted, adopted, and changed as each generation chose certain elements within the constraints of the evolving tradition. The configuration of the Heimat idea in modern German history is one example, as it was used as a symbolic manual to articulate the relations between localness and nationhood in very different ideological regimes from Bismarck's Germany to the present.[62] Which symbols and memories came together to make the persecution and extermination of the Jews imaginable and possible?[63]

We feel that the meaning of the extermination of the Jews has to be *somehow* more than a combination of racial ideology and the circumstances of the war, and we feel correctly. It reminds me of Lincoln's view in his second inaugural address that everyone knew that the Civil War was "somehow" fought over slavery.[64] Profound historical writing is based on intuition and historical sensation. But these elements must ultimately be based on sound evidence, method, and theory.

It is precisely new studies on comparative genocides and colonialism that bring into sharp focus elements of historical specificity about the Holocaust. At first sight, this new approach, which draws on commonalities among modern genocides and the Holocaust, seems to undermine a search for the historically particular. But in fact, it is precisely the clear articulation of commonalities that reveals the historically specific. "The historically specific": my argument is not, in case this needs to be spelled out this far into the book, about some unique, ahistorical notion of the Holocaust. Rather it is about finding the historically specific within a genre of historical events. Not all revolutions are born equal – think of the differences among the French, Russian, Cuban, and Iranian revolutions – and neither are all genocides. We explain nothing either by treating the Holocaust as a unique historical event or by treating all genocides as similar to such a degree as to deny each its historical particularity. By articulating similarities among genocides, comparative genocide studies has made clear also some of the specificities of the extermination of the Jews to its time and place.

Studies on modern genocides and colonialism as we have already seen in these pages, have identified factors common to genocides: the combination of settlement of land, a millennial utopian thinking, security anxieties, and murder among the colonizers. A firm ideology, exterminationist rhetoric, and the concepts of race and space are also important. This approach, together with studies on Nazi occupation and resettlement plans in Eastern Europe, as well as the contributions of the race paradigm that highlighted the multiplicity of Nazi victims, show that the Jewish genocide was tied up with a whole set of racial ideas that have produced other genocides.[65] The Nazi genocide was a future-oriented program of German renewal in which Jews were one target among many, if symbolically the most important one. As Mazower put it, the Holocaust emerged "out of even more ambitious Nazi plans for a racial reorganization of much of eastern Europe . . . the Jews constituted only one – albeit the most urgent – of the regime's ethnic targets."[66]

It is exactly this issue of symbolic urgency that seems fundamental to interpreting the Holocaust. The enmity against and extermination of the Jews were part of a Nazi universe of racial enemies and exterminations.

But this only begs the question: what was that symbolic urgency that gave meaning to the persecution and extermination of the Jews? No amount of racial ideology and of context of war, to return to where this discussion began several chapters ago, are sufficient to capture what is essentially a historical problem of culture.

In 1939, courts ruled that race defilement did not require a conscious attempt at seduction or any physical contact. A Jewish man was convicted of race defilement for merely glancing at a young Aryan girl across the street.[67] By 1940, Jews were banned from listening to German music or performing German plays: any connection between the German spirit and a Jew contaminated the source. In the Warsaw ghetto, the historian Ringelblum recounted in his diary that Jews "were forbidden to use German marks that bore the likeness of H. [Hitler]. Apparently they're afraid Jews might give him the Evil Eye!"[68] In 1942, Jews were not allowed to keep pets anymore. The animals had to be killed even if Jewish owners found non-Jewish friends to take care of them – because the animals were now "Jewish." Eva and Victor Klemperer brought their Jewish cat to the vet on May 19, 1942 to be put to sleep.[69]

Are these human affairs best understood by racial ideology? By the context of World War II? A world of meaning is lost when these views predominate because the question is not only how ideology and context made possible the Holocaust but also what was the ground of culture, memories, and sensibilities that made them possible to begin with. How and why did these fantasies speak to key elements of life in Germany at the period, and what made them persuasive as ways to experience the world?

Afterword

We end, then, with the kind of a question that initially triggered the exploration into the historical sensations embedded in the persecution and extermination of the Jews. I set out in this book to show the need to ask that kind of question not from some metaphysical, ahistorical sense of the uniqueness of the Holocaust, but from the point of view of the historical method. I made the case for posing questions this way by thinking through some essential notions of historical reconstruction, namely, of beginnings and ends, context, contingency, and ideology. I also provided an answer that sought to direct Holocaust interpretations based on a certain understanding of culture. I am aware that I provided only a general answer. The crux of this book was not found in a comprehensive answer but rather in the journey traversed through Holocaust historiography and problems of historical method to articulate how to capture the underlying cultural elements in the Nazi obsession with the Jews. And in this respect, I hope I showed that this study only reveals more clearly in the case of the Holocaust what are some of the fundamental elements in all historical reconstruction.

The book suggests a broad approach to interpret the Holocaust that has no single mode of operation. It can be used in different ways, being more or less effective depending on the topic under investigation. Initially, I planned on finishing the book where we are right now. But in the process of research and writing, a specific argument, building on the cultural approach, has come into sharp focus. I end the book therefore by articulating one possible outcome of the argument developed in the last several chapters.

FIGURE 1. "The Jew Leaves the Ghetto." (Courtesy of Scherl / Sueddeutsche Zeitung Photo)

Two years ago I came across a 1937 poster that combined the French Revolution and Nazi anti-Semitism into a single, arresting image. Shown in the exhibition at the Berlin Reichstag on the perceived perils posed by the Jews to Germans and other Europeans, it stated: "The Jew Leaves the Ghetto: sustained by the ideals 'liberty, equality, fraternity' Judaism demanded and achieved full equal status with the citizens of its host nations" (Figure 1).[1]

I thought about the meaning of this poster from the perspective of the symbolic difference that characterized the persecution of the Jews. The menacing Jew, portrayed as an ageless figure in traditional anti-Semitic imagery, is leaving a dark, menacing, impersonal town and is hovering over Germany, which is represented in the classic Heimat image of a peaceful, small community set amidst nature.[2] The poster contrasts past against past, one notion of origins against another: the Jew, evoking an image of timeless evil origins, is propelled by the ideas of the French Revolution to destroy Germany, represented by the essential image in German culture for historical roots, for the immemorial, transcendent national community.

The poster represented a Nazi idea of historical time. Deciphering its meaning belongs, therefore, to the exploration of the construction of representations of the past. This topic has been investigated in the last generation by using the notion of memory. Holocaust memory, as we know, is a huge field of study. But as I looked at the field more closely, a striking gap appeared. There is a massive literature on post-1945 German memory and quite a large one on pre-1933 memory, but virtually nothing on the memories of Germans during the Third Reich.[3] Of course, there is no obligation to use every historical approach to study every period. But one must surely see the dissonance between the current primacy of the notion of memory in German historiography and in the historical discipline overall, and the glaring omission of the period of the Third Reich as a topic of memory study; between the use of diverse approaches to understanding Nazism – such as gender, everyday life, political, military, economic, colonialism and empire, and others – and the overlooking of memory. Explaining this dissonance away – for example, by clinging to the notion of ideology, or to written evidence culled from state documents, or to the idea that memory studies are a fleeting fad – is part of the problem, not the solution.

In their most innovative rendition, memory studies changed the way historians understand the presence of the past in the lives of people by making it into an essential empirical, analytical, and theoretical tool with which to understand social, political, cultural, and even economic phenomena that typically had been seen as determined by a very different set of factors. The question is not whether memory is a fashionable notion among historians; something can be fashionable and still be useful. It is rather, has memory contributed to our historical knowledge? And here the answer is no doubt "yes" because memory studies have brought to the fore topics and uncovered knowledge that were simply unknown a generation ago. The insights of memory with respect to the Third Reich are unexplored.[4]

This perspective that uses memory studies adds something new to our understanding of the Third Reich. The historiography defines Germans in this period in terms of their various attitudes toward racial ideology, the regime, or the war; we know an enormous amount on these topics. But what happens if we define Germans also in terms of their constructed histories and representations of the past and then ask which German representations of the past constituted the mental universe, at times explicit and at other times subterranean, that made the persecution and extermination of the Jews imaginable and possible?

Differently put, notions of empire, race, war, and space have been
central in recent historiography of the Third Reich in understanding Nazi
policies of expansion and projects of annihilation. Yet, an element is
missing from this picture: the element of time. Nazi spatial policy was
revolutionary: an empire devoted to expansion – from the Atlantic in the
west to the Pacific shores of Siberia in the east – and to the annihilation
of whole groups of people. What, then, was the revolutionary concept of
time that accompanied this revolutionary policy of space? What was the
imagination of time and of history that gave meaning and legitimacy to
this radical spatial policy and to the symbolically urgent extermination
of the Jews? Exploring the presence of the past in Nazi Germany seems
especially relevant with respect to the Holocaust, an event that, while
it was happening, was already perceived as recasting common ideas of
humanity. What was this sense of the past in the Third Reich that made
the persecution and extermination of the Jews conceivable and justifiable?
What happens if we posit that Germans were, among others things, the
sum of their representations of the Jews?

Interpreting this poster with these queries in mind means shifting our
interest from problems of strict causes and structures to those of plots,
meanings, and narrative, this essential component of every identity. In
this small representation of anti-Semitism the Nazis created a narrative
of Germany's existence in time, a historical tale of where they came
from, where they were heading, and why. But what exactly was it? The
Nazis chose as their main enemy the Jews who played a key symbolic
role in Christian, European, and German society. This choice must have
influenced their historical narrative: "as far as contemporary events are
experienced and interpreted by contemporaries," observed Jan Assmann
in relation to a different case, that of the memory of Egypt in Western culture, "history (in the sense of res gestae) is already imbued with
narrative, quite independently of its being told or written in the form of
narrative. Narrative structures are operating in the organization of action,
experience, memory, and representation."[5] What narrative structure (or
structures) inspired this poster and, more generally, the persecution and
extermination of the Jews?

I returned to the poster. It is notable how it commingles a set of
opposite, even contradictory, symbols: modernity (the French Revolution)
and ancientness (both the Heimat idea and the Jew); race (the image of
the Jew could not be disconnected from the context of the time), religion
(the Jew is represented as old and religious), and nationhood (the Heimat
idea). It speaks about the present by using images that evoke the past. Its
combination of conflicting images is precisely the point: in the hands of

the Nazis the Jew became a symbolic manual to imagining historical time from time immemorial to present-day modernity. Thinking along with this poster, therefore, points to an interpretation according to which the Jews symbolized for the Nazis historical origins that had to be extirpated for the new Germany to arise. The representation of the Jew as possessor of historical origins – of the present, past, and future, of modernity, the nation; and ultimately humanity – was a fantasy that made persecution and extermination possible by making them conceivable.

The hypothesis of Nazi ideas of time as represented in the persecution and extermination of the Jews is intriguing; it explores how the Nazis attempted to set themselves free from the symbolic historical power they assigned to the Jews and to replace them with their own civilization. Nazism was an act of creation of a new society, a racial civilization that would mold Germany, Europe, and the world based on the systematic persecution and extermination of groups of people. Precisely because it saw itself as a radical, novel historical departure, Nazism paid particular attention to the past, that protean and essential factor of life in all societies. By doing so, Nazism fit within a broader pattern of all national and revolutionary movements in the modern world that sought to build new life based on invented and constructed memories.

To push the argument further, this hypothesis posits that Nazis and other Germans constructed the image of the Jew as a new register of historical time that linked notions of origins embedded in the ideas of race, Christianity, nationhood, and history. How does the notion of race fit within this argument? I suggest viewing Nazi racial ideas from the perspective of memory of origin. Because the Nazi biological worldview was based on the idea of origins that could not be mutated, memories of the past became fundamental to endowing the movement with that legitimacy and authenticity that came with roots. Race theories did leave some room for evolution and transformation, but the basic racial traits of groups, such as Aryans and Jews, could not be fundamentally changed. The idea of race saw the genesis of human history as a crucial moment, for something happened in that moment that forever defined the positive or negative distinctiveness of racial groups. The notion of race, therefore, was *the* metaphor of origins in the Third Reich. By making race into the principal idea in Germany, the Nazis transformed the notion of historical origins into the fundamental aspect of their policies, mentalities, and memories.

From this perspective of origins, beliefs associated with Christianity also seem to have found their place in the galaxy of ideas that was the Third Reich. Because Judaism was the origin of Christianity, the latter was somehow part of the imagination of historical time that underlined the fantasy of a Germany without Jews. Siegfried Leffler's assertions, cited in the previous chapter, become understandable in this context: in the Third Reich, we remain Christian, he implied, but without having to carry the burden of Christianity's Jewish roots. Nazism's goal thus seemed not to eradicate Christianity, but to eradicate Christianity's Jewish roots by establishing a German national church. This project received support from some Germans and churches in Germany, as we have seen. In terms of national origins, the Heimat idea contributed to this imagining of historical time as shown in the poster, in which the immemorial German past embedded in the notion of Heimat starkly confronted the evil Jew who threatened it.

The cumulative result, then, was the commingling of racial, Christian, and nationhood ideas that existed in German society into imagining the Jew as a symbol of historical time that had to be removed for Nazi Germany to arise. The construction of this imagination in the prewar years of the Third Reich was not predicated on mass murder, but once the war began, this anti-Jewish imagination made it possible to conceive of a world without Jews realized by other, infinitely more violent means. It accounted among other factors for the transgressive element of Nazi anti-Semitism, which was sensed by Germans, Jews, and Europeans at the time: by excising the Jews, Nazis and other Germans excised part of their own religious and historical origins. This was transgressive but also liberating: by adopting an identity that owed nothing to the moral authority of the past, the Nazis also owed nothing to previous moral constraints in dealing with other Christian Europeans. The Nazi empire of destruction was made possible first by imagining a new Nazi empire of historical time.

Viewing the persecution and extermination of the Jews as underlined by conscious and unconscious representations of historical time puts several perennial problems in the interpretation of the Holocaust, which we have discussed in the previous chapters, in a new explanatory light. The total removal of Jews from German society immediately after January 1933 was done in the name of Nazi modernity. The adjective *jüdisch*, or Jewish, was attached to every phenomenon of the modern world objectionable to the Nazis, and then some: from communism, liberalism, and democracy to psychoanalysis, feminism, jazz music, and abstract painting. The Nazis opposed the versions of modernity proposed by communism and liberalism, but it was the Jews who represented the overall meaning of the Nazi revolution – the crushing of one modernity and the making of another – because only they represented in the minds of the Nazis and other Germans at one and the same time all, even opposing modern enemies. By representing Marxism and liberalism, democracy and Bolshevism, the Jews became a Nazi symbolic manual for an evil modernity.

Had the Nazis limited their aims to a narrow political change from Weimar democracy to dictatorship, then removing Jews from economic and cultural positions – as symbols of the origins of modernity – would have been enough. But because their aim was to found a racial civilization, a new humanity, it demanded a creation of a new historical past and therefore the destruction of ancient roots that stood as origins of Europe, Christianity, and a certain sense of morality. What was the meaning of setting on fire 1,400 synagogues on Kristallnacht if the Nazis intended to construct a racial civilization? Kristallnacht was part of the Nazi construction of the Jew as possessors of origins that threatened the Third Reich. By burning Jewish religious objects the Nazis constructed a national community that was independent of Jewish origins. In this respect, the idea of race provided the immemorial proof of Jewish crimes for a national community that set out to liberate itself from the symbolic authority of the Jews represented in the religious past. Racial ideology, as a myth of origins par excellence, provided modern, scientific "proof" of the Jews' eternal guilt. It is in this sense that Kristallnacht was not about Jews but about Judaism, and here lies the answer to Frau Marks's question, "What have we ever done to you?"

The extermination of the Jews between 1941 and 1945 was the final evolution of Nazi time as represented in the Jews. This stage was articulated in the idea of the Reich Press Office in 1944 that "*The Jewish question is the key to world history.*"[6] The total eradication of the Jews was the basis for a new page of history. It now becomes more understandable why the metaphor of creation, which we have already encountered, became crucial to imagining the extermination of the Jews. The extermination was imagined (with different meanings) by Nazis, by other Germans, and by Jews as an act of creation, in the sense of genesis, because the Jewish world was in the process of being destroyed to make space for the Nazi one. The notion of creation allowed contemporaries to make sense of the extermination as a radical rupture – a genesis has no proper origins – while also fitting within the Nazi narrative of the Jews since 1933 as registers of time. A key argument unfolds: however radical the extermination was, it also shared continuities with the German racial, religious, and national cultural imagination of the preceding years,

for the progressive removal of Jews meant the conquering of time – of the
present in 1933 through their exclusion from German society; of the past
in 1938 through the elimination of Judaism and the Hebrew Bible; and
ultimately of history, and therefore of the future, in 1941 through total
extermination.

Historical roots carry enormous symbolic power, especially in a changing modern world: the Nazis made the Jews into the symbolic lynchpin of
their existence because the Jews represented for them competing notions
of historical time. This view proposes a shift in perspective – from what
happened during the Holocaust and what Germans did or did not know
about it, and from an emphasis on Auschwitz – to how Germans came
to conceive of the idea of a Germany without Jews: how they came,
from 1933 onward, to imagine this world, internalize it, make it part of
their own vision of the present and future, at times even when they were
opposed to Nazi policies.

This hypothesis will have to be explored and verified. But I am
deeply sympathetic with the basic approach it presents to exploring the
Holocaust, an approach that emerges from this book. To articulate it in
relation to my own project as a historian, let me modify a few lines from
the passage of Huizinga cited in the Introduction: "There is in all historical
awareness a most momentous component that is most suitably characterized by the term historical sensation . . . this contact with the past . . . can
be provoked by an image from a poster . . . as an understanding that is
closely akin to the understanding of . . . the world *by* music."

Notes

Introduction: Edges of the Past

1. Paul Veyne, *L'inventaire des différences. Leçon Inaugurale au Collége de France* (Paris, 1976), p. 9.
2. There is a growing discussion about the meaning of the Holocaust as a global symbol. See Daniel Levy and Natan Sznaider, *The Holocaust and Memory in the Global Age* (Philadelphia, 2006); Duncan Bell, ed., *Memory, Trauma and World Politics* (London, 2006); Jeffrey Alexander, "On the Social Construction of Moral Universals: The 'Holocaust' from War Crime to Trauma Drama," in J. Alexander, R. Eyerman, B. Giesen, N. Smelser, and P. Sztompka, eds., *Cultural Trauma and Collective Identity* (Berkeley, 2004), pp. 196-263; and Martin Davies and Claus-Christian Szejnmann, eds., *How the Holocaust Looks Now? International Perspectives* (New York, 2007).
3. Art Spiegelman, *Maus: A Survivor's Tale*. Vol. 1 and 2 (New York, 1986, 1991). *Momik* is the first story in David Grossman, *See under Love* (1986; New York, 1989). On these and other Holocaust representations, see James Young, *At Memory's Edge: After-Images of the Holocaust in Contemporary Art and Architecture* (New Haven, 2000).
4. As in, for example, Christopher Browning, *Ordinary Men: Reserve Police Battalion 101 and the Final Solution in Poland* (New York, 1992).
5. Lawrence Langer, *Admitting the Holocaust: Collected Essays* (New York, 1995) and Saul Friedländer, *Probing the Limits of Representation: Nazism and the "Final Solution"* (Cambridge, MA, 1992).
6. *History and Memory* 1, 2 (1989): 61–76.
7. Dan Stone, *Constructing the Holocaust: A Study in Historiography* (London, 2003), p. 30.
8. Dan Diner, "The Destruction of Narrativity: The Holocaust in Historical Discourse," in Moishe Postone and Eric Santner, eds., *Catastrophe and Meaning: The Holocaust and the Twentieth Century* (Chicago, 2003), p. 67.
9. United Nations 60 General Assembly, GA 10413, Plenary 42nd meeting. http://www.un.org/News/Press/docs/2005/ga10413.doc.htm.

10. The speech is available in Wolfgang von Hippel, ed., *Freiheit, Gleichheit, Brüderlichkeit? Die Französische Revolution im deutschen Urteil von 1789 bis 1945* (Munich, 1989), pp. 344–5.

11. Cited in Eric Hobsbawm, *The Age of Revolution: Europe 1789–1848* (1962; London, 1977), p. 19. I am indebted to Sophia Rosenfeld for pointing out to me the complexity of this sentence.

12. Claudia Koonz, *The Nazi Conscience* (Cambridge., MA, 2003), p. 205

13. *Das Schulungsbrief 6* (1939): 220–1. This was a journal of the Nazi Party and the German Labor Front (Deutsche Arbeitsfront).

14. Gerhard Sauder, "Akademischer 'Frühlingssturm.' Germanisten als Redner bei der Bücherverbrennung," in Ulrich Walberer, ed., *10. Mai 1933. Bücherverbrennung in Deutschland und die Folgen* (Frankfurt a/M, 1983), p. 143.

15. A speech of July 13, 1929, in Klaus Lankheit, ed., *Hitler. Reden, Schriften, Anordnungen. Februar 1925 bis Januar 1933*. Vol. 3, no. 2 (Munich, 1994), p. 297. See also the speech of August 29, 1930, Ibid., p. 371. And see Norman Baynes, ed., *The Speeches of Adolf Hitler. April 1922–August 1939* (London, 1942), p. 210.

16. Victor Klemperer, *I will Bear Witness, 1933–1941*. Vol. 1 (New York, 1998), pp. 180, 208, 404. At the beginning of the diary Klemperer viewed Hitler as the direct offspring of Rousseau, but as the years went by he learned to appreciate the differences between them. He planned on changing his chapter on Rousseau because "the men of the French Revolution speak to an assembly of the people, which is present," while Hitler speaks in front of a silent mass (p. 404).

17. Ibid., pp. 114, 117.

18. Beatrice Hyslop, "Recent Work on the French Revolution," *American Historical Review* 47, 3 (April 1942): 488.

19. Beatrice Hyslop, "Historical Publication since 1939 on the French Revolution," *Journal of Modern History* 20, 3 (September 1948): 232.

20. For the history of this linkage in theater, see Freddie Rokem, *Performing History: Theatrical Representations of the Past in Contemporary Theater* (Iowa City, 2000). The book examines theater performances after 1945 that present the French Revolution and the Holocaust, focusing on the efforts to bring together the historical past and the theatrical present in two extreme historical events that called into question issues of witnessing.

21. François Furet, ed., *Unanswered Questions: Nazi Germany and the Genocide of the Jews* (New York, 1989).

22. François Furet, "The French Revolution Revisited," in Gary Kates, ed., *The French Revolution: Recent Debates and New Controversies* (London, 1997), p. 72.

23. See Chapter 1, note 4.

24. Claude Ribbe argued that Napoleon, not Hitler, was the first to perpetrate a final solution by gassing rebellious slaves when putting down the uprising in Haiti in the early nineteenth century. Claude Ribbe, *Le crime de Napoléon* (Paris, 2005). *Le Livre noir de la Révolution française*, edited by Renaud Escande (Paris, 2007), viewed the Revolution as a precursor to Nazism and

the Holocaust. Mona Ozouf responded to these claims in the essay, "Non, Danton n'est pas Hitler!" *Le Nouvel Observateur*, February 21, 2008.

25. The discussion among historians about the uniqueness of the Holocaust raged especially in the 1980s and 1990s, a period during which Holocaust representations assumed a growing public role. It is noteworthy that the claim that the Holocaust was unique has lost its intellectual and emotional power, at least among scholars. For an example of the old trend, see Alan Rosenbaum, ed., *Is the Holocaust Unique? Perspectives on Comparative Genocide* (Boulder, CO, 1996). About the debate in general, see Steven Aschheim, *In Times of Crisis: Essays on European Culture, Germans, and Jews* (Madison, WI, 2001), chapters 4 and 10.

26. François Furet, *Interpreting the French Revolution* (Cambridge, 1981), p. 3. The original title was *La Révolution française est terminée.*

27. Since the publication of Furet's essay there have been arguments against the pastness of the Revolution. Most recently, Vincent Peillon, *La Révolution française n'est pas terminée* (Paris, 2008).

28. Furet, ed., *Unanswered Questions*, p. viii.

29. Of course, there have been other turning points in European history since 1789. My point is not to make a ranking or construct a model. Still, other events did not create a similar sense of rupture as did the Revolution and the Holocaust. The Russian Revolution offered an alternative to liberal capitalism that was not only a new beginning but also, in the beliefs of its creators, a follow-up to the model set by the French Revolution. It was original, yet as a second act to the major play of Marxist modern history that began with the bourgeoisie in 1789 and ended with the proletariat in October 1917. World War I was a fundamental social and cultural break and did produce new, shattering human experiences, but did not cause a total reevaluation of history and morality as did the Revolution and the Holocaust. Moreover, both World War I and the Russian Revolution coexisted with the period of the French Revolution as foundational past. What is interesting in the relations of the Revolution and the Holocaust as foundational pasts is that one succeeded the other; each represented and was constructed by the memories and political hopes of its own period.

30. See Chapter 1 for further references.

31. Frank Ankersmit, *Sublime Historical Experience* (Stanford, CA, 2005), pp. 120–1. I use Ankersmit's translation.

Chapter 1: Between the French Revolution and the Holocaust

1. Henry Friedlander writes about the Fall of Rome, the French Revolution, and the Holocaust as each being "one of those historical events that represent an age" in "Towards a Methodology of Teaching about the Holocaust," *Teachers College Record* 80, 4 (May 1979): 519–42.

2. The first quote is from Alexander Herzen, *Letters from France and Italy, 1847–1851*. Ed. and trans. by Judith Zimmerman (Pittsburgh, 1995), p. 128 (Letter Nine, Paris, June 10, 1848). The second is from Alexander Herzen, *My Past and Thoughts* (Berkeley, 1973), p. 323.

3. Hippolyte Taine, *The Origins of Contemporary France*. Ed. and with introd. Edward Gargan (Chicago, 1974), p. 124.

4. On the comparison of the Revolution to Nazism see Steven Kaplan, *Farewell Revolution: Disputed Legacies* (Ithaca, NY, 1995), pp. 91–7. On feminism and the Revolution, see Lynn Hunt, "Forgetting and Remembering: The French Revolution Then and Now," *American Historical Review* 100, 4 (October 1995): 1131. For a balanced discussion of the differences between the Vendée and genocide see David Bell, *The First Total War: Napoleon's Europe and the Birth of Warfare as We Know It* (Boston, 2007), pp. 157–61.

5. Leo Tolstoy, *War and Peace*. Trans. by Rosemary Edmonds (London, 1988), pp. 21–2.

6. Since then this heroic narrative has changed, and Israeli memory of the Holocaust now focuses on Jewish victimhood. Israel's Holocaust Remembrance Day has had multiple meanings. See Tom Segev, *The Seventh Million: The Israelis and the Holocaust* (New York, 1993); Oz Almog, *The Sabra: The Creation of the New Jew* (Berkeley, 2002), chap. 2; James Young, "When a Day Remembers: A Performative History of Yom Ha-Shoah," *History and Memory* 2 (Winter 1990): 54–75.

7. David Cesarani and Paul Levine, eds., *'Bystanders' to the Holocaust: A Re-Evaluation* (London, 2002).

8. Primo Levi, *The Drowned and the Saved* (New York, 1989), pp. 37, 49, 58. Janusz Korczak expressed the idea of shades of evil behavior in the relations between Jews in the ghetto and the surrounding Polish population: "Well yes. The devil does exist. But even among devils some are more and some are less wicked." Janusz Korczack, *Ghetto Diary* (New Haven, CT, 1978), p. 17.

9. Browning, *Ordinary Men*, pp. 225–6.

10. Levi, *The Drowned and the Saved*, p. 86. And see Jonathan Petropoulos and John Roth, eds., *Gray Zones: Ambiguity and Compromise in the Holocaust and Its Aftermath* (New York, 2005).

11. Friedrich Meinecke, *The German Catastrophe: Reflections and Recollections* (Boston, 1967) and Gerhard Ritter, "The Historical Foundations of the Rise of National Socialism," in Maurice Beaumont et al., *The Third Reich: A Study Published under the Auspices of the International Council for Philosophy and Humanistic Studies with the Assistance of UNESCO* (London, 1955), pp. 381–416. And see Ritter's apologetic *Europa und die deutsche Frage. Betrachtungen über die geschichtliche Eigenart des deutschen Staatsdenkens* (Munich, 1948) and Jonathan Knudsen, "The Historicist Enlightenment," in Keith Baker and Peter Hanns Reill, eds., *What's Left of Enlightenment? A Postmodern Question* (Stanford, 2001), pp. 39–49.

12. A founding text of the *Sonderweg* view is Hans-Ulrich Wehler, *Das deutsche Kaiserreich* (Göttingen, 1973), which appeared in English as *The German Empire 1871–1918* (Leamington Spa, 1985).

13. Hannah Arendt, *Essays in Understanding: 1930–1954*. Ed. by Jerome Kohn (New York, 1994), p. 108. See also Anson Rabinbach, "The Abyss That Opened up before Us: Thinking about Auschwitz and Modernity," in Moishe

Postone and Eric Santner, eds., *Catastrophe and Meaning: The Holocaust and the Twentieth Century* (Chicago, 2003), pp. 57–8.

14. For a different view see Steven Aschheim, *Scholem, Arendt, Klemperer: Intimate Chronicles in Turbulent Times* (Bloomington, IN, 2001), p. 52.

15. Daniel Gordon, "Introduction: Postmodernism and the French Enlightenment," in Gordon, ed., *Postmodernism and the Enlightenment: New Perspectives in Eighteenth-Century French Intellectual History* (New York, 2001), pp. 1–2.

16. Patrick Williams and Laura Chrisman, eds., *Colonial Discourse and Post-Colonial Theory: A Reader* (New York, 1994).

17. Paul Betts, "The New Fascination with Fascism: The Case of Nazi Modernism," *Journal of Contemporary History* 37, 4 (October 2002): 541–58.

18. See, Peter Fritzsche, "Landscape of Desire, Landscape of Design: Crisis and Modernism in Weimar Germany," in Thomas Kniesche and Stephen Brockmann, eds., *Dancing on the Volcano: Essays on the Culture of Weimar Germany* (Columbia, SC, 1994), pp. 29–46 and "Nazi Modern," *Modernism/Modernity* 3, 1 (1996): 1–21.

19. Marshall Berman, *All That Is Solid Melts into Air: The Experience of Modernity* (New York, 1982), pp. 13–14.

20. Mark Mazower, *Dark Continent: Europe's Twentieth Century* (New York, 2000).

21. Zygmunt Bauman, *Modernity and the Holocaust* (Ithaca, 1989).

22. Jacob L. Talmon, *The Origins of Totalitarian Democracy* (London, 1952) and *The Myth of the Nation and the Vision of Revolution: The Origins of Ideological Polarisation in the Twentieth Century* (London, 1980).

23. François Furet, *The Passing of an Illusion: The Idea of Communism in the Twentieth Century*. Trans. Deborah Furet (Chicago, 1999). He writes in *Interpreting the French Revolution*: "Today the Gulag is leading to a rethinking of the Terror precisely because the two undertakings are seen as identical" (p. 12).

24. Omer Bartov, *Murder in our Midst: The Holocaust, Industrial Killing, and Representation* (New York, 1996), p. 67.

25. From another perspective, the relation between Nazism and its adversaries is illuminated when considering Maria Todorova's idea of Balkanism: "In the realm of ideas, Balkanism evolved partly as a reaction to the disappointment of the West Europeans' 'classical' expectations in the Balkans, but it was a disappointment within a paradigm that had already been set as separate from the oriental." Similarly, the Nazi ideas in the 1920s and 1930s evolved as a reaction to the disappointments from the liberal and communist political alternatives offered in Europe and North America, and as such were a reaction within the paradigm of European political and cultural thought. Maria Todorova, *Imagining the Balkans* (Oxford, 1997), p. 19.

26. Ute Frevert, "Europeanizing Germany's Twentieth Century," *History and Memory* 17 (Spring/Summer 2005): 87–116. Paul Kulke, "National Socialist Europe Ideology," in Hajo Holborn, ed., *Republic to Reich: The Making of the Nazi Revolution* (New York, 1971), pp. 343–94.

27. Bundesarchiv Lichterfelde, NS 5 VI 6237, "Freude und Arbeit" 8, August 1937.
28. Berel Lang, *Act and Idea in the Nazi Genocide* (Chicago, 1990).
29. On "Europe's crusade," see Hitler's speech in 1942 in M. Domarus, *Hitler – Reden and Proklamationen 1932–1945. Kommentiert von einem Zeitgenossen.* Vol. II (Neustadt/Aisch, 1963), p. 1920. Hitler's speech against "the most evil world enemy of all times" was delivered on January 30, 1942. See, Domarus, *Hitler – Reden and Proklamationen*, p. 1828. See the analysis of Hitler's speeches about the Jews by Christopher Sauer, "Rede als Erzeugung von Komplizentum: Hitler und die öffentliche Erwähnung der Juden-Vernichtung," in Josef Kopperschmidt, ed., *Hitler der Redner* (Munich, 2003), pp. 413–40, for this specific speech, p. 426.
30. The term "civilization break" is from Dan Diner, *Zivilisationsbruch: Denken nach Auschwitz* (Frankfurt, 1996).
31. Robert Palmer, *The World of the French Revolution* (1967; New York, 1971). The only exception was a brief discussion of the United States.
32. For example, Laurent Dubois, *A Colony of Citizens: Revolution & Slave Emancipation in the French Caribbean, 1787–1804* (Chapel Hill, 2004); David Gaspar and David Geggus, eds., *A Turbulent Time: The French Revolution and the Greater Caribbean* (Bloomington, IN, 1997); Rebecca Schloss, "The February 1831 Slave Uprising in Martinique and the Policing of White Identity," *French Historical Studies* 30, 2 (Spring 2007): 203–36; Alec Hargreaves, ed., *Memory, Empire, and Postcolonialism: Legacies of French Colonialism* (Lanham, MD, 2005).
33. Philippe Girard, "Caribbean Genocide: Racial War in Haiti, 1802–4," *Patterns of Prejudice* 39, 2 (2005): 138–61.
34. Cited in Christopher Miller, "Unfinished Business: Colonialism in sub-Saharan Africa and the Ideals of the French Revolution," in Joseph Klaits and Michael Haltzel, eds., *The Global Ramification of the French Revolution* (Cambridge, 1994), p. 112.
35. Dubois, *A Colony of Citizens*, pp. 4–5.
36. Robert Bernasconi, "When the Real Crime Began: Hannah Arendt's *The Origins of Totalitarianism* and the Dignity of the Western Philosophical Tradition," in Richard King and Dan Stone, eds., *Hannah Arendt and the Uses of History: Imperialism, Nation, Race, and Genocide* (New York, 2007), pp. 54–67.
37. Martinique Aimé Césaire, *Discourse sur le colonialisme* (Paris, 1950).
38. Michael Rothberg, *Multidirectional Memory: Remembering the Holocaust in the Age of Decolonization* (Stanford, CA, 2009) and "Between Auschwitz and Algeria: Multidirectional Memory and the Counterpublic Witness," *Critical Inquiry* 33, 1 (Fall 2006): 158–84.
39. Hannah Arendt, *The Origins of Totalitarianism* (New York, 1951).
40. Richard King and Dan Stone, "Introduction," in King and Stone, eds., *Hannah Arendt and the Uses of History*, p. 8.
41. For a full discussion and references see Chapters 4 and 7.
42. Jürgen Zimmerer, "Colonialism and the Holocaust: Toward an Archeology of Genocide," in A. Dirk Moses, ed., *Genocide and Settler Society: Frontier*

Violence and Stolen Indigenous Children in Australian History (New York, 2004), p. 67

43. Benjamin Madley, "From Africa to Auschwitz: How German South West Africa Incubated Ideas and Methods Adopted and Developed by the Nazis in Eastern Europe," *European History Quarterly* 34, 3 (2005): 429–64.

44. For a critique of this see Matthew Fitzpatrick, "The Pre-History of the Holocaust? The *Sonderweg* and *Historikerstreit* Debates and the Abject Colonial Past," *Central European History* 41 (2008): 477–503.

45. Dan Stone, "Genocide and Memory," in Donald Bloxham and A. Dirk Moses, eds., *The Oxford Handbook of Genocide* (Oxford, 2010), pp. 102–19.

46. Mona Ozouf, "Revolution," in François Furet and Mona Ozouf, eds., *A Critical Dictionary of the French Revolution* (Cambridge, MA, 1989), p. 809.

47. Cited in Peter Fritzsche, "How Nostalgia Narrates Modernity," in Alon Confino and Peter Fritzsche, eds. *The Work of Memory: New Directions in the Study of German Society and Culture* (Urbana, 2002), p. 66. See also his *Stranded in the Present: Modern Time and the Melancholy of History* (Cambridge, MA, 2004).

48. Cited in William Doyle, *The French Revolution: A Very Short Introduction* (Oxford, 2001), p. 75.

49. Cited in Fritzsche, "How Nostalgia Narrates Modernity," p. 66. On Hegel's response to the French Revolutionary Terror and its influence on Germany, see Rebecca Comay, *Mourning Sickness: Hegel and the French Revolution* (Stanford, CA, 2010).

50. Schlegel, *Athenäum*, fragment 424 (1798) is cited in Ehrhard Bahr and Thomas Saine, eds., *The Internalized Revolution: German Reactions to the French Revolution, 1789–1989* (New York, 1992), p. 3. Jean François Lyotard, *The Differend: Phrases in Dispute* (Manchester, 1988), p. 56.

51. Nicholas Berg, *Der Holocaust und die westdeutschen Historiker: Erforschung und Erinnerung* (Göttingen, 2003), p. 343.

52. Ibid., pp. 447–63.

53. Three quite different renditions are Daniel Goldhagen, *Hitler's Willing Executioners: Ordinary Germans and the Holocaust* (New York, 1996); Michael Burleigh, *The Third Reich: A New History* (New York, 2001); and Omer Bartov, *Mirrors of Destruction: War, Genocide, and Modern Identity* (Oxford, 2000).

54. For example: "No amount of erasing the traces by exhuming and cremating the murdered, bulldozing the death camps, and planting forests over mass graves would purge our moral universe of this redefinition of ethics and decency." Bartov, *Mirrors of Destruction*, p. 29.

Chapter 2: A Dominant Interpretive Framework

1. For excellent overviews see Michael Marrus, *The Holocaust in History* (New York, 1987); Ian Kershaw, *The Nazi Dictatorship: Problems and Perspectives of Interpretation*, 4th ed. (London, 2000); and Dan Stone, ed., *The*

Historiography of the Holocaust (London, 2004). A recent comprehensive study is David Bankier and Dan Michman, eds., *Holocaust Historiography in Context: Emergence, Challenges, Polemics and Achievements* (Jerusalem, 2008). The best study of Holocaust historiography is now Dan Stone, *Histories of the Holocaust* (Oxford, 2010).

2. Saul Friedländer, *The Years of Extermination: Nazi Germany and the Jews, 1939–1945* (New York, 2007).

3. The book won the Pulitzer Prize and the Friedenspreis (Peace Prize) of the Frankfurt Book Fair and garnered rave reviews. See Jeffrey Herf, "The Whole Horror," *The New Republic*, October 9, 2007; Peter Pulzer, "How the Holocaust Happened," *Times Literary Supplement*, January 2, 2008; Richard Evans, "Whose Orders?" *New York Times*, June 24, 2007; Dan Diner, "Jahre der Vernichtung," *Die Welt*, September 30, 2006; Norbert Frei, "Gesichter des Schreckens," *Neue Züricher Zeitung*, October 2, 2006; Ulrich Herbert, "Die Stimmen der Opfer," *Süddeutsche Zeitung*, September 29, 2006; and Volker Ullrich, "Gesichter des Schreckens," *Die Zeit*, September 28, 2006.

4. Friedländer, *The Years of Extermination*, pp. xvii, xix.

5. Kershaw, *The Nazi Dictatorship*, chap. 5 and Ulrich Herbert, "Extermination Policy: New Answers and Questions about the History of the 'Holocaust' in German Historiography," in Herbert, ed., *National Socialist Extermination Policies: Contemporary German Perspectives and Controversies* (New York, 2000), pp. 1–52. Short histories of the Holocaust are an excellent source to tease out the dominant interpretive ideas because they convey the general consensus without getting into the detailed debates that often obscure it. See the excellent book of Doris Bergen, *War & Genocide: A Concise History of the Holocaust* (Lanham, Md., 2003) that represents accurately the dominant interpretive framework portrayed here. Concerning agreements among Holocaust scholars, Peter Fritzsche begins his article "The Holocaust and the Knowledge of Murder" by saying, "There is a remarkable consensus about the origins of the Holocaust that was not imaginable twenty years ago." *Journal of Modern History* 80 (September 2008): 594.

6. Herbert, "Extermination Policy," p. 16.

7. The work of Omer Bartov is central here. See *The Eastern Front 1941–45: German Troops and the Barbarisation of Warfare* (London, 1985), and "Operation Barbarossa and the Origins of the Final Solution," in David Cesarani, ed., *The Final Solution: Origins and Implementation* (New York, 1996), pp. 99–136. See also Rolf-Dieter Müller and Gerd Ueberschär, eds., *Hitler's War in the East, 1941–1945: A Critical Assessment*, 3rd ed. revised and expanded (New York, 2009).

8. Kershaw, *The Nazi Dictatorship*, p. 130.

9. Dieter Pohl, *Nationalsozialistische Judenverfolgung in Ostgalizien, 1941–1944: Organisation und Durchführung eines staatlichen Massenverbrechens* (Munich, 1996); Thomas Sandkuhler, *"Endlösung" in Galizien: der Judenmord in Ostpolen und die Rettungsinitiativen von Berthold Beitz, 1941–1944* (Bonn, 1996); Christian Gerlach, *Krieg, Ernährung, Völkermord: Forschungen zur deutschen Vernichtungspolitik im Zweiten Weltkrieg* (Hamburg, 1998); and Peter Black, "Central Intent or Regional Inspirations? Recent

German Approaches to the Holocaust," *Central European History* 33, 4 (2000): 533–49.

10. Herbert, "Extermination Policy," p 18.

11. As Yehuda Bauer put it, "without a guiding ideological motivation and justification, mass murder generally and the intent to annihilate the Jewish people in particular, would have been unthinkable. Ideology is central." Yehuda Bauer, *Rethinking the Holocaust* (New Haven, CT, 2002), p. 44.

12. Michael Ruck, *Bibliographie zum Nationalsozialismus* (Darmstadt, 2000). The first edition was published in 1995.

13. Christopher Browning, "The Decision Concerning the Final Solution," in Browning, *Fateful Months* (New York, 1991), pp. 8–38. Philippe Burrin, *Hitler and the Jews* (London, 1994), pp. 23–4. See also Stone, *Constructing the Holocaust*, pp. 68–70.

14. Thus, for example, the contrast between Nazi leadership and the extensive participation of Germans in the extermination is no longer tenable. Recent research has shown Hitler's central role without minimizing the energy and actions of ordinary Germans. Mark Roseman, "Ideas, Contexts, and the Pursuit of Genocide," *Bulletin of the German Historical Institute, London* XXV, 1 (May 2003): 64–87, here pp. 64–5.

15. Intentionalism and functionalism continue to influence Holocaust interpretations. The debate serves as a point of departure to evaluate Holocaust historiography in the most recent collections and encyclopedia entries. See Michael Marrus, "Historiography," in Walter Laqueur, ed., *The Holocaust Encyclopedia* (New Haven, CT, 2001), pp. 279–85. A synthesis between functionalism and intentionalism is portrayed as the main achievement of current historiography. See Omer Bartov, "Introduction," in Bartov, ed., *The Holocaust: Origins, Implementation, Aftermath* (London, 2000), pp. 4–5, and Aviel Roshwald, "Accounting for Complicity: Recent Works on the Holocaust," *European History Quarterly* 31, 4 (2002): 582–3. The terms are still important markers of recognition. Bergen defines herself as a "modified intentionalist" in *War & Genocide*, p. 30, as well as Jeffrey Herf, *The Jewish Enemy: Nazi Propaganda during World War II and the Holocaust* (London, 2006), p. vii. Kershaw, *The Nazi Dictatorship*, chapter 5 frames the historiographical discussion around the debate between intentionalists and structuralists and concludes that "neither model offers a wholly satisfactory explanation" (p. 131). Dan Stone noted that "it would be a mistake to assume that the fierce debates between intentionalists and functionalists of two decades ago have disappeared altogether," because they are just differently situated in a current "much broader, empirically richer as well as more complex historical context." Dan Stone, "The Holocaust and Its Historiography," in Stone, ed., *The Historiography of Genocide* (New York, 2008), pp. 377–8. The terms change although the meaning remains much the same; thus, Michael Geyer termed the two interpretive camps "the rationalists" and "the idealists" in Konrad Jarausch and Michael Geyer, *Shattered Past: Reconstructing German Histories* (Princeton, 2003), pp. 120–1. There are attempts to go beyond this framework only to commend its value several

years later. Christopher Browning, "Beyond 'Intentionalism' and 'Function-alism': The Decision for the Final Solution Reconsidered," in Browning, *The Path to Genocide* (Cambridge, 1992), pp. 86–121, and Richard Bessel, "Functionalists vs. Intentionalists: The Debate Twenty Years on *or* Whatever Happened to Functionalism and Intentionalism?" *German Studies Review* 26 (2003): 15–20.

16. Friedländer, *The Years of Extermination*, p. xv.

17. Ibid., p. xix.

18. Mark Mazower, *Hitler's Empire: How the Nazis Ruled Europe* (New York, 2008), pp. 412, 414.

19. See the theme issue of *History and Theory* on historical revision (vol. 46, December 2007), esp. Gabrielle Spiegel, "Revising the Past / Revisiting the Present: How Change Happens in Historiography," pp. 1–19.

20. Lucy Dawidowicz, *The War against the Jews, 1933–1945* (New York, 1975).

21. Goldhagen, *Hitler's Willing Executioners*, pp. 9, 69, 71.

22. Martin Broszat, "Hitler and the Genesis of the 'Final Solution': An Assess-ment of David Irvine's Thesis," in H. W. Koch, ed., *Aspects of the Third Reich* (London, 1985), pp. 390–429.

23. Diner then adds an insightful sentence to his essay published in 1997: "Such an 'objective' or 'sober-minded' choice of perspective serves as an anodyne, neutralizing deep strata of consciousness in which the traditional conception of the Jews continues to live on." Diner, "Memory and Method: Variance in Holocaust Narrations," in Jonathan Frankel, ed., *The Fate of the European Jews, 1939–1945: Continuity and Contingency?* (New York, 1997), pp. 84–99, here 96. This assessment fits the case of Martin Broszat who was one of the leading historians of the functionalist school and, as we have seen, had dismissed the work of Wulf as emotional and not sufficiently objective. In 2003, six years after Diner's observation, Nicholas Berg revealed in his book *Der Holocaust und die westdeutschen Historiker* that Broszat was a member of the Nazi party, an affiliation to which Broszat had never admitted during his lifetime, although he did acknowledge having admired Hitler as a youth. Still, Broszat support of functionalism is more complex, and cannot simply be attributed to personal motives. He suffered, similar to many historians of his time, a certain delusion about the ability of empirical history to tell accurately about the past. Functionalism-structuralism had also an international context, and was subscribed to by many non-German historians.

24. Dawidowicz and Broszat, who lived through National Socialism and were professionally active in the postwar decades, are illustrative of the genera-tion of Jewish intentionalists and German functionalists. A later generation broke the dichotomy of this scheme, although not quite the essence of the interpretive framework as a whole. Thus Christopher Browning, a moder-ate functionalist, explains the Holocaust in *Ordinary Men* as a result of the context of war and its radicalizing process at the expense of ideology, but his subject matter is from the atelier of the intentionalists: who were the perpetrators and what were their motives.

25. See Furet, *Interpreting the French Revolution*; Keith Baker, *Inventing the French Revolution: Essays on French Political Culture in the Eighteenth Century* (Cambridge, 1990); Maurice Agulhon, *Marianne into Battle: Republican Imagery and Symbolism in France, 1789–1880* (Cambridge, 1981); Mona Ozouf, *Festivals and the French Revolution* (Cambridge, MA, 1988); and Lynn Hunt, *Politics, Culture, and Class in the French Revolution* (Berkeley, 1984). It symbolically displayed its historiographical authority in the publication of the Revolutionary bicentennial multivolume study: Keith Baker, *The French Revolution and the Creation of Modern Political Culture*. 3 vols. (Oxford, 1987–9).

26. Suzanne Desan, "What's after Political Culture: Recent French Revolutionary Historiography," *French Historical Studies* 23, 1 (Winter 2000): 163–96.

27. Ibid., p. 178.

28. Baker, *Inventing the French Revolution*, p. 305.

29. Timothy Tackett, "Interpreting the Terror," *French Historical Studies* 24, 4 (Fall 2001): 577.

Chapter 3: Narrative Form and Historical Sensation

1. Ian Thomson, *Primo Levi: A Life* (New York, 2002), pp. 227–35.

2. Raul Hilberg, *The Politics of Memory: The Journey of a Holocaust Historian* (Chicago, 1996), pp. 105–19, 156.

3. Dan Diner, "The Irreconciliability of an Event: Integrating the Holocaust into the Narrative of the Century," in Dan Michman, ed., *Remembering the Holocaust in Germany, 1945–2000* (New York, 2002), p. 96.

4. Saul Friedländer, "The 'Final Solution': On the Unease in Historical Interpretation," in Peter Hayes, ed., *Lesson and Legacies: The Meaning of the Holocaust in a Changing World* (Evanston, IL, 1991), p. 23.

5. The Holocaust is seen now by some scholars, such as Gabrielle Spiegel, as the intellectual and cultural force behind poststructuralism and postmodernism that doubted grand narratives and questioned the meaning of historical knowledge. Spiegel, "Revising the Past / Revisiting the Present."

6. Kershaw, *The Nazi Dictatorship*, p. 3. Emphasis in the original.

7. Christopher Browning, *The Origins of the Final Solution* (Lincoln, NE, 2004); Ian Kershaw, *Hitler: 1936–1945 Nemesis* (New York, 2000), p. xviii; and Richard Evans, *The Coming of the Third Reich* (New York, 2003), p. xix. See also the important study of Peter Longerich, *Politik der Vernichtung: eine Gesamtdarstellung der nationalsozialistischen Judenverfolgung* (Munich, 1998). For the interpretive limits of the massive accumulation of facts see Omer Bartov, "As It *Really* Was," *Yad Vashem Studies* 34 (2006): 339–53.

8. Martin Broszat, "A Plea for the Historicization of National Socialism," in Peter Baldwin, ed., *Reworking the Past: Hitler, the Holocaust and the Historians' Debate* (Boston, 1990), pp. 77–91.

9. "The paradox is that, although it has become *de rigueur* for historians to begin their studies by observing that the Holocaust denies notions of progress

and civilization, they then often write using a philosophy of history that implies the opposite." Stone, *Constructing the Holocaust*, p. 16.

10. Friedländer, "The 'Final Solution,'" p. 32. Emphasis in the original.
11. Friedländer, *The Years of Extermination*, p. xxvi.
12. Ibid., pp. xxv–xxvi.
13. Ibid., p. 182.
14. The key text in the last generation is Hayden White, *Metahistory: The Historical Imagination in Nineteenth-Century Europe* (Baltimore, 1973).
15. The point of view of contemporaries that is often unfettered by the hindsight preserved for historians adds to the literary feel of the story. The discussion of the global situation after December 1941, when America entered the war but the Axis powers enjoyed victories, ends with the following question: "Would the strategic balance tip to Hitler's side?" (p. 331), as if we do not know how things unfolded. The author rarely preempts the future with a remark about what will happen. A rare exception is on page 578 when information about Austrian SS captain Tony Burger, who was appointed first commandant of Theresienstadt in 1943, is added in parentheses "(whose main claim to fame – the deportation of the Jews of Athens – was still a year away)." Friedländer also hardly ever uses the term "we," which creates a bond between reader and author, as well as between these two and (some) people of the past.
16. Friedländer, *The Years of Extermination*, p. 29.
17. Ida Fink, *A Scrap of Time and Other Stories* (New York, 1987), p. 3.
18. Peter Gay, *Style in History* (New York, 1974), p. 156.
19. Friedländer, *The Years of Extermination*, p. 757, note 133.
20. Saul Friedländer, ed., *Probing the Limits of Representation: Nazism and the "Final Solution"* (Cambridge, MA, 1992). Hayden White expressed in the volume a compromise position that attempted to escape the extreme consequences of his relativism.
21. Friedländer, "Introduction," *The Years of Extermination*, p. 20. See also p. 8.
22. In "Just One Witness," Carlo Ginzburg tells the story of two Jewish witnesses who survived the extermination of their communities in fourteenth-century France. Ginzburg brings forth the most radical argument against White's relativism: the voice of one single witness is enough to reach a certain historical reality and therefore some historical truth. In the "Introduction," Friedländer summarizes Ginzburg's contribution. In the following paragraph, which is very short and separated by a double space, he points out without commentary that at Belzec extermination camp, where 600,000 Jews were massacred, two witnesses survived to tell the tale. Here we can see the origins of the narrative form of *The Years of Extermination*.
23. *Limits of Representation*, p. 7. Friedländer's rhetoric is to argue that for most historians a description of facts does carry its own truth, setting himself apart from this group. He makes this point in relation to the essay of Christopher Browning in the volume.
24. Ibid., p. 20. He cites Shoshana Felman.
25. Friedländer, "The 'Final Solution,'" pp. 23, 31. Emphasis in the original.

26. Allan Megill, "Narrative and the Four Tasks of History Writing," in Megill, *Historical Knowledge, Historical Error: A Contemporary Guide to Practice* (Chicago, 2007), p. 103.
27. Friedländer, *The Years of Extermination*, p. xxvi.
28. Frank Ankersmit, *Sublime Historical Experience* (Stanford, 2005), p. 115.
29. Dan Stone writes eloquently on this point in *Constructing the Holocaust*, p. 30.
30. Walter Manoschek, ed., *"Es gibt nur eines für das Judentum: Vernichtung." Das Judenbild in deutschen Soldatenbriefen 1939–1944* (Hamburg, 1995), p. 29.
31. Abraham Lewin, *A Cup of Tears: A Diary of the Warsaw Ghetto* (Oxford, 1988), pp. 232, 133, 157, 183.
32. Karel Berkhoff, *Harvest of Despair: Life and Death in Ukraine under Nazi Rule* (Cambridge, MA, 2004), p. 75.
33. Dan Diner is an exception. See *Beyond the Conceivable: Studies on Germany, Nazism, and the Holocaust* (Berkeley, 2000).
34. On Friedländer's use of the victims' voice see Amos Goldberg, "The Victim's Voice and Melodramatic Aesthetics in History," *History and Theory* 48 (October 2009): 220–37.

Chapter 4: Beginnings and Ends

1. Isaiah Berlin, "Historical Inevitability," in Berlin, *Four Essays on Liberty* (London, 1969), p. 43.
2. "Tout ce que la Révolution a fait se fût fait, je n'en doute pas, sans elle." Alexis de Tocqueville, "Etat social et politique de la France avant et depuis 1789," in *Œuvres complétes*. Vol. II: *L'ancien régime et la révolution* (Paris, 1952), pp. 65–6. The essay was originally published in English in 1836 in *London and Westminster Review* and translated by John Stuart Mill. See also Robert Gannett Jr., *Tocqueville Unveiled: The Historian and His Sources for the Old Regime and the Revolution* (Chicago, 2003).
3. Hunt, *Politics, Culture, and Class in the French Revolution*, pp. 4–10.
4. Baker, *Inventing the French Revolution*, p. 305. See also Baker, "The Idea of the Declaration of Rights," in Dale Van Kley, ed., *The French Idea of Freedom: The Old Regime and the Declaration of Rights of 1789* (Stanford, CA, 1994), pp. 154–96, and Peter Campbell, ed., *The Origins of the French Revolution* (Houndmills, 2006).
5. Berlin, "Historical Inevitability," p. 51.
6. Omer Bartov, "Germany as Victim," *New German Critique* 80 (Spring–Summer 2000): 39. This is also the gist of his *Mirrors of Destruction*.
7. Chartier, *The Cultural Origins of the French Revolution*, p. 5.
8. Furet, "The French Revolution Revisited," p. 80. See the special issue of *Tocqueville Review* XXIX, 2 (2008) on "L'histoire en questions: François Furet et les révolutions." See also Furet, *Le due Rivoluzioni. Dalla Francia del 1789 alla Russia del 1917* (Turin, 2002).
9. Furet, *Interpreting the French Revolution*, p. 3.

10. Steven Ozment, *A Mighty Fortress: A New History of the German People* (New York, 2004), p. 278.
11. See the reconstruction of the conference by Mark Roseman, *The Villa, the Lake, the Meeting: Wannsee and the Final Solution* (London, 2002). The citation is from the protocol of the conference provided in the book, p. 109.
12. Both descriptions are by Michael Marrus. Marrus, "Holocaust, Historiography of the," in Daniel Woolf, ed., *A Global Encyclopedia of Historical Writing.* Vol. 1 (New York, 1998), p. 421, and Marrus, *The Holocaust in History*, p. 1.
13. Daniel Blatman, *The Death Marches: The Final Phase of Nazi Genocide* (Cambridge, MA, 2011).
14. Michael Matsas, *The Illusion of Safety: The Story of the Greek Jews during World War II* (New York, 1997), pp. 83, 115–17. *German Foreign Office Documents on the Holocaust in Greece (1937–1944).* Compiled, translated, and annotated with an Introduction by Irith Dublon-Knebel (Tel Aviv, 2007), esp. pp. 188, 190, 208. See also Götz Aly, "Die Deportation der Juden von Rhodos nach Auschwitz," *Mittelweg* 36, 12 (2003): 79–88.
15. Rafael Lemkin, *Axis Rule in Occupied Europe* (New York, 1973), pp. 79ff. On the Holocaust as an extreme genocide, see Bauer, *Rethinking the Holocaust*, pp. 8–11. There is a growing literature on Lemkin. See Samantha Power, *"A Problem from Hell": America and the Age of Genocide* (New York, 2002), pp. 17–78, and the *Journal of Genocide Research* 7, 4 (2005), a special issue on "Raphael Lemkin: The 'Founder of the United Nation's Genocide Convention' as a Historian of Mass Violence."
16. Dirk Moses, "Empire, Colony, Genocide: Keywords and the Philosophy of History," in Moses, ed., *Empire, Colony, Genocide: Conquest, Occupation, and Subaltern Resistance in World History* (New York, 2008), pp. 3–54. The literature is big and growing. See Dirk Moses and Dan Stone, eds., *Colonialism and Genocide* (London, 2007) and Dan Stone, ed., *The Historiography of Genocide*, esp. his discussion of "Holocaust and/as Genocide," pp. 387–91. For a critical view, see Robert Gerwarth and Stephan Malinowski, "Hannah Arendt's Ghosts: Reflections on the Disputable Path from Windhoek to Auschwitz," *Central European History* 42, 2 (2009): 279–300.
17. Ernst Klee and Willi Dreßen, *"Gott mit uns": Der Deutsche Vernichtungskrieg im Osten 1939–1945* (Frankfurt, 1989), p. 13.
18. Jarausch and Geyer, *Shattered Past*, p. 132.
19. Götz Aly, "'Jewish Resettlement': Reflections on the Political Prehistory of the Holocaust," in Herbert, ed., *National Socialist Extermination Policies*, p. 58.
20. Koonz, *The Nazi Conscience*, p. 245.
21. Klemperer, *I Will Bear Witness, 1933–1941.* Vol. 1, p. 251.
22. Oskar Rosenfeld, *In the Beginning Was the Ghetto: Notebooks from Łódź* (Evanston, IL, 2002), pp. 50–1.
23. See Longerich, *Politik der Vernichtung*, chap. 4.
24. Klemperer, *I Will Bear Witness*, Vol. 1, p. 382.

25. Tackett, "Interpreting the Terror," p. 569. See also David Andress, *The Terror: The Merciless War for Freedom in Revolutionary France* (New York, 2005).

26. Baker, *Inventing the French Revolution*, p. 5.

27. Jürgen Habermas, *Eine Art Schadensabwicklung* (Frankfurt, 1987), p. 163.

28. Furet, "The French Revolution Revisited," p. 82.

29. Tocqueville, "Etat social et politique de la France avant et depuis 1789," p. 66. Cited in Alexis de Tocqueville, "The Political and Social Conditions of France," in Marvin Cox, ed., *The Place of the French Revolution in History* (Boston, 1998), p. 29.

30. Ian Ousby, *The Road to Verdun: France, Nationalism, and the First World War* (London, 2002).

31. Robert Moeller, *War Stories: The Search for a Usable Past in the Federal Republic of Germany* (Berkeley, 2001), p. 83.

32. Jürgen Zimmerer, "Colonialism and the Holocaust: Toward an Archeology of Genocide," in Dirk Moses, ed., *Genocide and Settler Society: Frontier Violence and Stolen Indigenous Children in Australian History* (New York, 2004), pp. 66–7. See Jürgen Zimmerer and Joachim Zeller, eds., *Genocide in German South-West Africa: The Colonial War (1904–1908) in Namibia and its Aftermath* (Monmouth, Wales, 2008).

33. Jürgen Zimmerer, "The Birth of the *Ostland* out of the Spirit of Colonialism: A Postcolonial Perspective on the Nazi Policy of Conquest and Extermination," *Patterns of Prejudice* 39, 2 (2005): 211, and "Colonial Genocide: The Herero and Nama War (1904–8) in German South West Africa and Its Significance," in Stone, ed., *The Historiography of Genocide*, pp. 323–43.

34. Mazower, *Dark Continent*, p. 180.

35. Isabel Hull, *Absolute Destruction: Military Culture and the Practices of War in Imperial Germany* (Ithaca, 2005), pp. 2–3.

36. Dan Stone, "Bio Power and Modern Genocide," in Moses, ed., *Empire, Colony, Genocide*, pp. 164–7.

37. Bartov, *Murder in our Midst*, p. 33.

Chapter 5: The Totality and Limits of Historical Context

1. "Always historicize!" is of course the opening words of Fredric Jameson, *The Political Unconscious: Narrative as a Socially Symbolic Act* (Ithaca, NY, 1981), p. 9. His Marxist-inflected method is very different from mine, but his idea that we always apprehend texts "through sedimented layers of previous interpretations" is not.

2. Historians do not use context in isolation, of course. In both the historiographies of the Revolution and the Holocaust the issues of context and of ideology have been intertwined. To clarify explanatory strategies, I look at the notion of context in this chapter and at ideology in a later chapter.

3. Robert Darnton, *What was Revolutionary about the French Revolution* (Waco, TX, 1990), pp. 14–16.

4. Ibid., p. 11.

5. Alphonse Aulard, *The French Revolution: A Political History*. Vol. II: *The Democratic Republic 1792–1795* (New York, 1910), pp. 277–8.

6. Furet, *Interpreting the French Revolution*, pp. 62–3. See also Jeremy Popkin, "Not over after All: The French Revolution's Third Century," *Journal of Modern History* 74, 4 (December 2002): 802.

7. Cited in Albert Mathiez, "The French Revolution," in Cox, *The Place of the French Revolution in History*, p. 82.

8. Kaplan, *Farewell Revolution: The Historians' Feud*, p. 89.

9. Popkin, "Not over after All," p. 818. Desan, "What's after Political Culture," p. 180.

10. Browning, *Ordinary Men*. Rev. ed. 1998, p. 222.

11. Ibid., p. 159.

12. Bartov, "Operation Barbarossa and the Origins of the Final Solution," pp. 119–36.

13. George Steiner, *Errata. An Examined Life* (New Haven, CT, 1997), p. 21.

14. I am reminded of Frank Ankersmit's observation that "the contemporary cult of the context has blinded us more than anything else to the notion of (historical) experience." Ankersmit, *Sublime Historical Experience*, p. 125.

15. The classic work is Browning, *Ordinary Men*.

16. Mazower, *Hitler's Empire*, p. 11.

17. For excellent overviews of the historiography, see Mark Roseman, "Beyond Conviction? Perpetrators, Ideas and Action in the Holocaust in Historiographical Perspective," in Frank Biess, Mark Roseman, and Hanna Schissler, eds., *Conflict, Catastrophe and Continuity: Essays in Modern German History* (New York, 2007), pp. 83–103; George Browder, "Perpetrator Character and Motivation: An Emerging Consensus?" *Holocaust and Genocide Studies* 17, 3 (2003): 480–97; J. Matthäus, "Historiography and the Perpetrators of the Holocaust," in Stone, ed., *The Historiography of the Holocaust*, pp. 197–215.

18. Koonz, *The Nazi Conscience*, p. 15. She notes that the mid-1990s debate between Daniel Goldhagen and Christopher Browning on the origins of the Final Solution concentrated on the war years while virtually ignoring the prewar Nazi period.

19. Furet, "The French Revolution Revisited," p. 84.

20. Alexander Rossino, *Hitler Strikes Poland: Blitzkrieg, Ideology, and Atrocity* (Lawrence, KN, 2003).

21. Michael Wildt, *Generation des Unbedingten: Das Führerkorps des Reichssicherheitshauptamt* (Hamburg, 2002).

22. Götz Aly, "'Jewish Resettlement': Reflections on the Political Prehistory of the Holocaust," in Herbert, ed., *National Socialist Extermination Policies*, p. 54.

23. "*Economic interest and crises* were far more important influences on the tempo of the liquidation of the Jews, *especially in the phases of acceleration*. The various liquidation programs in Belorussia, particularly those against non-Jewish population groups, were in large part responses to pressures related to food economics." Christian Gerlach, "German Economic Interests, Occupation Policy, and the Murder of the Jews in Belorussia," in

Herbert, ed., *National Socialist Extermination Policies*, p. 227. Emphasis in the original.

24. Christoph Dieckmann, "The War and the Killing of the Lithuanian Jews," in Herbert, ed., *National Socialist Extermination Policies*, p. 262. And see Black, "Central Intent or Regional Inspiration?" pp. 541–3.

25. Giovanni Levi, "On Microhistory," in Peter Burke, ed., *New Perspectives on Historical Writing* (University Park, PA, 1992), p. 98.

26. Bruno Latour, *Reassembling the Social* (Oxford, 2005), p. 148. He uses the expression of Rem Koolhaas. I am indebted to Rita Felski for this reference.

27. I owe the Wittgenstein quote to Levi, "On Microhistory," p. 95.

28. See Eugen Weber, "The Nineteenth-Century Fallout," in Geoffrey Best, ed., *The Permanent Revolution: The French Revolution and Its Legacy, 1789–1989* (Chicago, 1988), p. 167.

29. On Göring's speech, see Susanne Heim and Götz Aly, "Staatliche Ordnung and 'organische Lösung.' Die Rede Hermann Görings 'Über die Judenfrage' vom 6. Dezember 1938," in Wolfgang Benz, ed., *Jahrbuch für Antisemitismusforschung* 2 (1993): 378–404, here 385.

30. See the special issue of the *Journal of Contemporary History* 45 (July 2010), "Before the Holocaust: New Approaches to the Nazi Concentration Camps, 1933–1939," ed. Christian Goeschel and Nikolaus Wachsmann. Robert Gellately argues in *Backing Hitler* that "the Germans generally turned out to be proud and pleased that Hitler and his henchmen were putting away certain kinds of people who did not fit in.... On balance, the coercive practices, the repression, and persecution won far more support for the dictatorship than they lost." Robert Gellately, *Backing Hitler: Consent and Coercion in Nazi Germany* (Oxford, 2001), pp. vii, 259.

31. This is an important part of the argument of Patrice Gueniffey, *La politique de la Terreur: Essai sur la violence révolutionnaire, 1789–1794* (Paris, 2000).

Chapter 6: Contingency, the Essence of History

1. Klemperer, *I Will Bear Witness*. Vol. 1, pp. 60, 314, 382.

2. Chartier, *The Cultural Origins of the French Revolution*, p. 169.

3. I am using again the expositions of Kershaw, *The Nazi Dictatorship*, chap. 5 and Herbert, "Extermination Policy," pp. 1–52.

4. See, for example, Wildt, *Generation des Unbedingten*.

5. Herbert, "Extermination Policy," p. 27.

6. On the "cumulative radicalization" argument among functionalists such as Martin Broszat, Christopher Browning, and Hans Mommsen, see Herbert, "Extermination Policy," p. 10.

7. Furet, *Interpreting the French Revolution*, pp. 69, 70, 77.

8. Edward Ayers, *What Caused the Civil War?* (New York, 2006). And see Ayers' *In the Presence of Mine Enemies: War in the Heart of America, 1859–1863* (New York, 2003), conceived around the notion of "deep contingency."

9. Timothy Tackett, *When the King Took Flight* (Cambridge, MA, 2003), pp. 219–23. See also his *Becoming a Revolutionary: The Deputies of the*

French National Assembly and the Emergence of a Revolutionary Culture (1789–1790) (Princeton, NJ, 1996).

10. The king did send to their death the Jews of Thrace, a region annexed after the Axis conquest of Greece. These Jews were not considered Bulgarian.

11. For such a narrative of the events in the summer and autumn of 1941 that led to the decision to kill European Jews, see Ian Kershaw, *Fateful Choices: Ten Decisions That Changed the World, 1940–1941* (New York, 2007), chap. 10

12. Edward Ayers, "Narrative Form in *Origins of the New South*," in John Roper, ed., *C. Vann Woodward: A Southern Historian and His Critics* (Athens, 1997), p. 39.

13. Eugen Weber, *Peasants into Frenchmen: The Modernization of Rural France, 1870–1914* (Stanford, 1976), p. 493.

14. Koonz, *The Nazi Conscience*, chaps. 5 and 8.

15. Fritzsche, *Life and Death in the Third Reich*, p. 8.

16. See Longerich, *Politik der Vernichtung* and Wildt, *Generation des Unbedingten*.

17. Stephen Jay Gould, *Wonderful Life: The Burgess Shale and the Nature of History* (New York, 1989), p. 283.

18. "Threshold of revelation" is from Tony Kushner, *Angels in America: A Gay Fantasia on National Themes. Part II: Perestroika.* Rev. ed. (New York, 1996), p. 83.

19. Stephen Jay Gould, *Time's Arrow, Time's Cycle: Myth and Metaphor in the Discovery of Geological Time* (Cambridge, MA, 1987), pp. 2–3.

20. Gershom Scholem, *A Life in Letters* (Cambridge, MA, 2002), April 18, 1933, p. 229.

21. Wildt, *Volksgemeinschaft als Selbstermächtigung. Gewalt gegen Juden in der deutschen Provinz 1919 bis 1939* (Hamburg, 2007), pp. 164, 204.

22. For Hindenburg and Dinslaken, see Ben Barkow, Raphael Gross, and Michael Lenarz, eds., *Novemberpogrom 1938: Die Augenzeugenberichte der Wiener Library, London* (Frankfurt a/M, 2008), pp. 525, 660. For Baden-Baden, see Yad Vashem photographic archive, no. 139B01. For Regensburg, see the Web site of the Jüdische Gemeinde Regensburg, www.jg-regensburg.de. For both cases as well as Zeven see Martin Gilbert, *Kristallnacht* (New York, 2006), pp. 34–35, 89.

23. Friedländer, *The Years of Persecution*, pp. 277–8.

24. Steve Hochstadt, ed., *Sources of the Holocaust* (Houndmills, Basingstoke, 2004), p. 87.

25. Friedländer, *The Years of Persecution*, p. 31.

26. Ibid., p. 33.

27. Ibid., p. 82.

28. Hermann Graml, "The Genesis of the Final Solution," in Walter Pehle, ed., *November 1938: From 'Reichskristallnacht' to Genocide* (Providence, RI, 1991), p. 175.

29. Ibid., p. 178.

30. Friedländer, *The Years of Persecution*, p. 39.

31. Cited in Bergen, *War & Genocide*, p. 112.

32. Emmanuel Ringelblum, *Diary and Notes from the Warsaw Ghetto: September 1939-December 1942* (Jerusalem, 1999, in Hebrew), pp. 52, 87.
33. Richard Evans, *The Third Reich in War* (New York, 2008), p. 62.
34. Chaim Kaplan, *Scroll of Agony. Hebrew Diary of Ch. A. Kaplan Written in the Warsaw Ghetto* (Tel Aviv, 1966, in Hebrew), pp. 202, 367.
35. Ibid., pp. 3–4.
36. Friedländer, *The Years of Extermination*, pp. 458–9 and, for the citation, 539–40. See also Friedländer, *Kurt Gerstein: The Ambiguity of Good* (New York, 1969).
37. Victor Klemperer, *I Will Bear Witness: A Diary of the Nazi Years, 1942–1945* (New York, 2001), p. 415.

Chapter 7: Ideology, Race, and Culture

1. Johan Huizinga, *The Waning of the Middle Ages* (Garden City, NY, 1954), p. 94.
2. Popkin, "Not Over after All," p. 803.
3. Friedländer, "The 'Final Solution,'" pp. 32–3. Emphasis in the original.
4. Cited in Mazower, *Dark Continent*, p. 143.
5. Bauer, *Rethinking the Holocaust*, p. 34. See Götz Aly and Karl Heinz Roth, *The Nazi Census: Identification and Control in the Third Reich* (Philadelphia, 2004).
6. Geyer and Jarausch, *Shattered Pasts*, p. 140.
7. Franz Neumann, *Behemoth: The Structures and Practice of National Socialism 1933–1944* (New York, 1942; reprint, New York, 1963), p. 467.
8. Mazower, *Dark Continent*.
9. Bartov, "Operation Barbarossa and the Origins of the Final Solution," pp. 124, 131.
10. Bauer, *Rethinking the Holocaust*, p. 44.
11. Geoff Eley, ed., *The "Goldhagen Effect": History, Memory, Nazism – Facing the German Past* (Ann Arbor, MI, 2000), p. 23. Emphasis in the original.
12. Peter Fritzsche, *Life and Death in the Third Reich*, p. 8. For this approach to ideology see the studies on the Soviet Union by Igal Halfin, *Terror in My Soul: Communist Autobiographies on Trial* (Cambridge, MA, 2003) and Jochen Helbeck, *Revolution on My Mind: Writing a Diary under Stalin* (Cambridge, MA, 2006). See also Peter Fritzsche and Jochen Helbeck, "The New Man in Stalinist Russia and Nazi Germany," in Michael Geyer and Sheila Fitzpatrick, eds., *Beyond Totalitarianism: Stalinism and Nazism Compared* (Cambridge, 2009), pp. 302–41.
13. Koonz, *The Nazi Conscience*, p. 3; Harald Welzer, *Täter. Wie aus ganz normalen Menschen Massenmörder werden* (Frankfurt am Main, 2005); and Werner Konitzer, "Antisemitismus und Moral. Einige Überlegungen," *Mittelweg* 14, 2 (2005) 24–35. Raphael Gross is completing a study on Nazism and moral feelings such as guilt, shame, disgrace, loyalty, and honor. I am grateful to Gross for sharing his work with me. See his "Zum Fortwirken der NS-Moral: Adolf Eichmann und die deutsche Gesellschaft," in Raphael Gross and Yfaat Weiss, eds., *Jüdische Geschichte als Allgemeine Geschichte*.

Festschrift für Dan Diner zum 60. Geburtstag (Göttingen, 2006), pp. 212–31; and "Moral und Gott im NS," in Martin Tremel and Daniel Weidner, eds., *Nachleben der Religionen* (Munich, 2007), pp. 176–87.

14. Louis Althusser, "Ideology and Ideological State Apparatuses," in *Lenin and Philosophy and other Essays* (New York, 1971), pp. 121–76.

15. Benedict Anderson, *Imagined Communities: Reflections on the Origins and Spread of Nationalism* (London, 1983), p. 12.

16. To be clear, at one point I part ways with Anderson's logic. I do not think that we can disconnect the tie between the Holocaust and ideology in the same way Anderson disconnects nationhood and ideology, because ideology is part of the motivation to exterminate others while it is not a reason one feels national (one does not feel Italian because Giollitti, Mussolini, Andreotti, or Berlusconi is in power, but regardless of who is in power). Anderson, *Imagined Communities*, pp. 15–16.

17. Bloch, *The Historian's Craft* (New York, 1953), pp. 194–5.

18. See Victor Turner and Edward Bruner, eds., *The Anthropology of Experience* (Urbana, IL, 1986), pp. 5–7.

19. Geyer and Jarausch, *Shattered Past*, p. 135.

20. Cited in Turner and Bruner, eds., *The Anthropology of Experience*, p. 12.

21. See Friedländer, *Nazi Germany and the Jews*, pp. 307–8.

22. David Bankier, "Signaling the Final Solution," in Bankier and Israel Gutman, eds., *Nazi Europe and the Final Solution* (Jerusalem, 2003), pp. 15–24.

23. Koonz, *The Nazi Conscience*, pp. 31, 38, 40, 42, 100.

24. Detlev Peukert, "The Genesis of the 'Final Solution' from the Spirit of Science," in Thomas Childers and Jane Caplan, eds., *Reevaluating the Third Reich* (New York, 1994), pp. 234–52.

25. Saul Friedländer, "Ideology and Extermination: The Immediate Origins of the 'Final Solution,'" in Postone and Santner, eds., *Catastrophe and Meaning*, p. 20.

26. Herbert, "Extermination Policy," p. 37. See also Michael Marrus, "Auschwitz: New Perspectives on the Final Solution," in Frankel, ed., *The Fate of European Jews*, pp. 74–83, esp. 81–2.

27. I am building here on the important work of earlier scholars such as Léon Poliakov, *Harvest of Hate: The Nazi Program for the Destruction of the Jews of Europe* (1951; New York, 1979, rev. and expanded ed.). For the writings of George Mosse on race, anti-Semitism, and ideology, see Saul Friedländer, "Mosse's Influence on the Historiography of the Holocaust," in Stanley Payne, David Sorkin, and John Tortorice, eds., *What History Tells: George L. Mosse and the Culture of Modern Europe* (Madison, WI, 2004), pp. 134–47. See also Uriel Tal, *Religion, Politics and Ideology in the Third Reich: Selected Essays* (New York, 2004); Dan Diner, *Beyond the Conceivable: Studies on Germany, Nazism, and the Holocaust* (Berkeley, 2000); Philippe Burin, *Ressentiment et apocalypse: Essai sur l'antisémitisme Nazi* (Paris, 2004); and Friedländer, of course.

One reason for avoiding fantasies has been that for a long time telling the bare story of the Holocaust was challenging enough. Now that a detailed narrative of what happened in the Holocaust is available, historians can turn to topics that are less visible. Another reason is that because historians found the topic so emotional they sought to distance themselves from it. Jill Stephenson, arguing against a new interpretive trend "to affirm the Germans' 'collective guilt' for the Holocaust," explained recently why emotions should have no place in the historical research of the Holocaust: exploring the Third Reich via critical evidence "is particularly necessary when dealing with a historical phenomenon, Nazism, whose appeal was strongly directed at people's emotions and whose adherents [made] claim[s] – without verifiable supporting evidence.... Invoking spurious theories of 'race' and 'value' owed more either to emotions such as prejudice and hatred... than to rigorous intellectual investigation. It was utterly irrational.... Those who study this phenomenon are therefore at their strongest when they do so with a cool head and rational thought processes." There is much that can be commended in this statement. But one is struck by how the fear of Nazism's emotionalism leads Stephenson away from its essence that she identifies so clearly: irrationality and fantasies. Jill Stephenson, "Generations, Emotions and Critical Enquiry: A British View of Changing Approaches to the Study of Nazi Germany," *German History* 26, 2 (2008), pp. 272–3. In many respects I find Stephenson's main argument – about moralizing tendencies among historians who "set up camp on the moral high ground" – spot on in principle, if not in its examples and theoretical implications.

28. Inga Clendinnen, *Reading the Holocaust* (Cambridge, 1999) and *The Aztecs: An Interpretation* (Cambridge, 1991)

29. Clendinnen, *The Aztecs*, pp. 1–2.

30. Ibid., pp. 89–91.

31. Ibid., p. 5.

32. Walter Manoschek, ed., *"Es gibt nur eines für das Judentum: Vernichtung." Das Judenbild in deutschen Soldatenbriefen 1939–1944* (Hamburg, 1995), p. 59.

33. On tourism in the Third Reich see Hasso Spode, "Ein Seebad für zwanzigtausend Volksgenossen: Zur Grammatik und Geschichte des fordistischen Urlaubs," in P. J. Brenner, ed., *Reisekultur in Deutschland: Von der Weimarer Republik zum "Dritten Reich"* (Tübingen, 1997), pp. 7–47; Shelley Baranowski, *Strength through Joy: Consumerism and Mass Tourism in the Third Reich* (Cambridge, 2004); Rudy Koshar, *German Travel Cultures* (Oxford, 2000), chap. 3; and Kristin Semmens, *Seeing Hitler's Germany: Tourism in the Third Reich* (New York, 2005). The literature on consumption is huge and growing. A place to start is the special issues on consumption in twentieth-century Germany in *German History* edited by Alon Confino and Rudy Koshar (vol. 19, April 2001) and in *Le Mouvement Social* edited by Gerhard Haupt (no. 206, January–March 2004), and Paul Lerner, "An All-Consuming History? Recent Works on Consumer Culture in Modern German," *Central European History*, 42, 3 (2009): 509–43.

34. Cited in Wolfgang Schievelbusch, *The Culture of Defeat: On National Trauma, Mourning, and Recovery* (New York, 2001), p. 285.

35. Jeff Schutts, "'Die erfrischende Pause': Marketing Coca Cola in Hitler's Germany," in Pamela Swett, S. Jonathan Weisen, and Jonathan Zatlin, eds.,

Selling Modernity: Advertising in Twentieth-Century Germany (Durham, 2007), pp. 151–81.

36. Dagmar Herzog, *Sex after Fascism: Memory and Morality in Twentieth-Century Germany* (Princeton, 2005), pp. 4–5.

37. Thomas Zeller, *Driving Germany: The Landscape of the German Autobahn, 1930–1970* (New York, 2007); Thomas Lekan, *Imagining the Nation in Nature: Landscape Preservation and German Identity, 1885–1945* (Cambridge, 2004); and Robert Proctor, *The Nazi War on Cancer* (Princeton, 1999).

38. Celia Applegate, *A Nation of Provincials: The German Idea of Heimat* (Berkeley, 1990) and Alon Confino, *Germany as a Culture of Remembrance: Promises and Limits of Writing History* (Chapel Hill, 2006), pt. 1.

39. For this argument about the meaning of the Heimat idea, see Confino, *Germany as a Culture of Remembrance*, chap. 5.

40. With respect to the scholarship on consumption and travel, key studies have also sought their meaning in the Third Reich beyond the idea of race. As Shelley Baranowski argued, "while promoting an edifying tourism that would bind its participants to the Nazi racial community, [*Strength through Joy*, the Nazi leisure organization] increasingly encouraged self-fulfillment, pleasure seeking, and individual voice." Baranowski, *Strength through Joy*, p. 8. See also, for example, Schutts, "'Die erfrischende Pause,'" pp. 156, 170–4.

41. An overdetermined role of racial ideas in Nazi Germany reminds me of earlier studies of nationhood that portrayed nationalism as obliterating other identities that existed in the nation, such as local identity. This view was wrong because, while national sentiment was paramount, it could not exist without linking with an older sense of localness that did not simply support but constructed and shaped national sentiments.

42. For the coercion argument, see Richard Evans, "How Willing Were They?" *New York Review of Books* 55 (June 26, 2008); Niel Gregor, "Nazism – A Political Religion? Rethinking the Voluntarist Turn," in Gregor, ed., *Nazism, War and Genocide: Essays in Honour of Jeremy Noakes* (Exeter, 2005), pp. 1–21.

43. Fritzsche, *Life and Death in the Third Reich*, p. 241. Fritzsche considers consumption, but not religion, nationhood, or other identities in the "becoming" of Germans into Nazis during the Third Reich.

44. Michael Burleigh, *The Third Reich: A New History* (New York, 2000), pp. 5–6. See the special issue of *Journal of Contemporary History* 42, no. 5 (2007) on "Nazism, Christianity, and Political Religion," especially the thoughtful critique by Stanley Stowers, a theologian and religious historian, of how historians of National Socialism use the notion of political religion: "The Concepts of 'Religion,' 'Political Religion,' and the Study of Nazism," pp. 9–24.

45. Friedländer, *The Years of Extermination*, p. 657.

46. In many respects, this is the direction of some current research. Arguing against the view that saw the Nazi movement as inherently anti-Christian, Richard Steigmann-Gall claimed in *The Holy Reich* that a "wide swath of the party believed themselves and their movement to be Christian.... Christian

Nazis did not just 'distort' or 'infect' Christian ideas to suit their party"
because these ideas "were articulated by acknowledged theologians and
Christian intellectuals before Nazism ever came to power." In a pattern
similar to that evinced by the Heimat idea, Nazism latched itself to existing ideas to build something new. Richard Steigmann-Gall, *The Holy Reich:
Nazi Conceptions of Christianity* (Cambridge, 2003). See the debate over
the book in the special issue of the *Journal of Contemporary History*, 42, 1
(2007). The citations are from Steigmann-Gall's response, pp. 186–7.

47. Richard Evans, *The Third Reich in Power* (New York, 2005), pp. 545–6.
48. Doris Bergen, "Nazism and Christianity: Partners and Rivals," *Journal of
Contemporary History* 42, 5 (2007): 29.
49. Catherine Merridale, *Night of Stone: Death and Memory in Twentieth-
Century Russia* (New York, 2002), pp. 137, 129.
50. Marvin Perry and Frederick Schweitzer, *Antisemitic Myths: A Historical and
Contemporary Anthology* (Bloomington, IN, 2008), p. 177.
51. Victoria Newall, "The Jew as a Witch Figure," in Newall, ed., *The Witch
Figure* (London, 1973), p. 116.
52. Joshua Trachtenberg, *The Devil and the Jews: The Medieval Conception
of the Jew and its Relations to Modern Antisemitism* (New Haven, 1943),
p. 240, n. 38.
53. Ruth Mellinkoff, *Outcasts: Signs of Otherness in Northern European Art of
Late Middle Ages*. Vol. 1 (Berkeley, 1993), pp. 103–4, 106.
54. Newall, "The Jew as a Witch Figure," p. 109.
55. Ben Barkow, Raphael Gross, and Michael Lenarz, eds., *Novemberpogrom
1938: Die Augenzeugenberichte der Wiener Library, London* (Frankfurt
a/M, 2008), p. 351.
56. See the insightful book of Susannah Heschel, *The Aryan Jesus: Christian
Theologians and the Bible in Nazi Germany* (Princeton, NJ, 2008), here
pp. 1–2.
57. Cited in Heschel, *The Aryan Jesus*, pp. 9–10.
58. Friedländer, *The Years of Persecution*, pp. 296–8.
59. Ibid., pp. 326–7.
60. For World War I as the origin of the Holocaust, see Bartov, *Mirrors of
Destruction*, chap. 1.
61. This is the method used by Helmut Walser Smith in *The Continuities of
German History: Nation, Religion, and Race across the Long Nineteenth
Century* (Cambridge, 2008). It is Smith's merit to have argued perceptively
that it is time to understand the Holocaust again beyond the limits of the
years 1933–45 and those immediately preceding it. But the result of his
method is that continuities, as Dieter Langewiesche observed thoughtfully,
are "constructed at the expense of strict narrowing of perspective" that
overlooks alternative narratives. In addition, while Smith traces continuities
as far back as 1519, his analysis hardly covers the Third Reich itself. It is thus
not clear how the continuities actually affected Nazism and the Holocaust.
See Dieter Langewiesche, "Wie Helmut Walser Smith Kontinuitätslinien in
der deutschen Geschichte erzeugt und was dabei verloren ging," *Sehepunkte*,
9, no. 1 (2009) in a special forum devoted to the book.

62. For a similar approach see Rudy Koshar, *From Monuments to Traces: Artifacts of German Memory 1870–1990* (Berkeley, 2000).

63. For an excellent cultural history of the emergence and character of the ghetto phenomenon in the Third Reich, which goes beyond an administrative and organizational history, see Dan Michman, *The Emergence of Jewish Ghettos during the Holocaust* (Cambridge, 2011).

64. Allen Guelzo, *Lincoln's Emancipation Proclamation* (New York, 2004).

65. Götz Aly, *Final Solution: Nazi Population Policy and the Murder of the European Jews* (London, 1999). On Nazism's other victims and their link to the Holocaust, see Henry Friedländer, *The Origins of Nazi Genocide: From Euthanasia to the Final Solution* (Chapel Hill, 1995).

66. Mazower, *Hitler's Empire*, p. 414.

67. Patricia Szobar, "Telling Sexual Stories in the Nazi Courts of Law: Race Defilement in Germany, 1933 to 1945," *Journal of the History of Sexuality* 11 (January/April 2002): 160.

68. Emmanuel Ringelblum, *Notes from the Warsaw Ghetto*. Ed. and trans. by Jacob Sloan (New York, 1974), p. 289.

69. Fritzsche, *Life and Death in the Third Reich*, p. 239.

Afterword

1. United States Holocaust Memorial Museum Photo Archive, W/S #94446.

2. On Heimat iconography see my *The Nation as a Local Metaphor*, chap. 7 and *Germany as a Culture of Remembrance*, chaps 4–5.

3. I do not mean personal memories, which extend back to one's lifetime, but constructed social memories in the broader sense of cultural inheritance.

4. For an argument about the diminishing status of memory studies see Gavriel Rosenfeld, "A Looming Crash or a Soft Landing? Forecasting the Future of the Memory 'Industry,'" *Journal of Modern History* 81 (March 2009): 122–58. For the contribution of memory studies to historical analysis and method, see my essay "History and Memory," in Axel Schneider and Daniel Woolf, eds., *The Oxford History of Historical Writing*. Vol. 5 (Oxford, 2011), pp. 36–51.

5. Jan Assmann, *Moses the Egyptian: The Memory of Egypt in Western Monotheism* (Cambridge, MA, 1997), p. 15.

6. Herf, *The Jewish Enemy*, p. 240. Emphasis in the original.

Index